Research in Networked Learning

Series Editors
Vivien Hodgson
David McConnell

More information about this series at http://www.springer.com/series/11810

Thomas Ryberg • Christine Sinclair
Sian Bayne • Maarten de Laat
Editors

Research, Boundaries, and Policy in Networked Learning

 Springer

Editors
Thomas Ryberg
Aalborg University
Aalborg, Denmark

Christine Sinclair
Edinburgh University
Edinburgh, UK

Sian Bayne
Edinburgh University
Edinburgh, UK

Maarten de Laat
Open University of the Netherlands
Heerlen, The Netherlands

Research in Networked Learning
ISBN 978-3-319-31128-9   ISBN 978-3-319-31130-2   (eBook)
DOI 10.1007/978-3-319-31130-2

Library of Congress Control Number: 2016940091

Printed on acid-free paper

This Springer imprint is published by Springer Nature
The registered company is Springer International Publishing AG Switzerland

*Dedicated to the memory of Sheena Banks,
a significant figure in the establishment of
the Networked Learning Conference in 1998,
and in its development since, and whose
contribution to the field will be missed*

Contents

Part III   Researching Networked Learning

Chapter 1
The Relationships Between Policy, Boundaries and Research in Networked Learning

Thomas Ryberg and Christine Sinclair

The biennial Networked Learning Conference is an established locus for work on practice, research and epistemology in the field of networked learning. That work continues between the conferences through the researchers' own networks, 'hot seat' debates, and through publications, especially the books that include a selection of reworked and peer-reviewed papers from the conference. The 2014 Networked Learning Conference which was held in Edinburgh was characterised by animated dialogue on emergent influences affecting networked teaching and learning building on work established in earlier conferences, such as the inclusion of sociomaterial perspectives and recognition of informal networked learning. The chapters here each bring a particular perspective to the themes of Policy, Boundaries and Research in Networked Learning which we have chosen as the focus of the book. The selection of the papers has been a combined editorial and collaborative process based on our own initial review of the conference papers and notes from the conference, as well as an informal survey where we asked conference participants to recommend three papers they found particularly interesting. The papers for the Networked Learning Conference are all peer-reviewed, and as they have turned into chapters for this book, each has been re-reviewed by the editors and

T. Ryberg (✉)
Department of Communication and Psychology, Aalborg University, Aalborg, Denmark
e-mail: ryberg@hum.aau.dk

C. Sinclair
Institute for Education, Community and Society, University of Edinburgh, Edinburgh, UK
e-mail: csincla5@exseed.ed.ac.uk

© Springer International Publishing Switzerland 2016   1
T. Ryberg et al. (eds.), *Research, Boundaries, and Policy in Networked Learning*, Research in Networked Learning, DOI 10.1007/978-3-319-31130-2_1

other authors. The result is a genuinely collegial distillation of themes from a stimulating conference; a snapshot of a time when national and international policies and boundaries have been changing.

Policy issues seemed more dominant in this conference than in previous ones though they had always been present, along with questions of power and agency. Indeed, the current emphasis on policy and politics was anticipated in the previous conference held in Maastricht 2012. As Hodgson, De Laat, McConnell, and Ryberg (2014a) wrote in the introduction to the book resulting from that event:

> implementing pedagogical changes and institutional learning environments is always a political process first and only secondly pedagogical (Hodgson et al., 2014a: 7).

Our authors are alerting us to some of the less visible effects of policy and also to the impacts on boundaries. In turn, what happens at the boundaries of practice will inevitably feed back into policy. Again, boundary work has always been prevalent in networked learning discussions: it seems, however, that the time has come to re-cognise the implications and scrutinise what may be obscured through complexity and busy-ness. And while exchange of research is what networked learning conferences are all about, this time there is a sense that it is appropriate to pay attention to how the nature of research is itself changing and needs to change to respond critically to an increasingly neoliberal agenda in educational institutions.

As the contexts change, so do opportunities and methodologies for research and networked learning. We return to discuss this further in our concluding remarks after our discussion of the three central themes that each have their own section: Policy, Boundaries and Research in Networked Learning.

Part 1: Policy in Networked Learning

This part consists of three chapters that all concern different aspects of policy and politics within networked learning. As Jones argues this is an area that has been addressed previously, though not extensively, within networked learning. He notes that while policy is not always explicitly highlighted in definitions of networked learning (such as McConnell, Hodgson, and Dirckinck-Holmfeld (2012)) notions of critical pedagogy and ethical considerations have always been central. However, what stands out as a strong message from the three chapters here is that policy and politics deserve more attention and recognition within the field. We will briefly summarise the three chapters by Sarah Hayes, Ben Williamson and Chris Jones and then draw out some wider themes we think part: are particularly interesting across the contributions.

Sarah Hayes takes a transdisciplinary look at 'rational' (or common sense) policy discourse about use of technology. She examines a corpus of UK policy texts through the lenses of critical discourse analysis and critical social theory. The chapter demonstrates how policy statements frequently remove or obscure human agency from the notion of 'the (effective) use of technology', privileging a narrative of economic gain over higher education labour. Hayes calls for academics to restore the visibility of human labour by writing specifically about how they themselves work with technology.

Williamson's chapter is perhaps the place where the three broad themes of the title of this book are most strongly linked, through a process of policy network analysis bringing together the notion of the boundary broker organisation and the theoretical construct of the sociotechnical imaginary. Boundary brokers work as intermediaries across public, private and third sector organisations and individuals—helping to create a decentralised politics based on networks. Sociotechnical imaginaries are shared visions of future life made possible through technology. Williamson illustrates through contemporary examples how boundary brokers are using sociotechnical imaginaries to envision the governance of education systems through data analytics and database pedagogies, and the concomitant governing of individuals to participate in personalised lifelong learning. These networked technologies can accelerate changes in spatial and temporal aspects of educational governance and signal a move away from more bureaucratic forms of government.

Chris Jones calls for researchers in networked learning to engage with the broader political landscape. The issues at stake can be illustrated through the rise of Massive Open Online Courses (MOOCs) where, Jones argues, utopian aims have been superseded by more neoliberal ones as austerity policies began to affect higher education. Jones draws attention to rhetorical moves—especially the technological determinism argument—that create an impetus for forms of education that are regarded as necessarily dominated by a neoliberal perspective. This necessity is an illusion fostered through newer forms of long-standing positions that ignore or drown out alternative arguments and values in higher education. Jones demonstrates that we need to be alert to moves towards neoliberal and technological determinism in order to mount a resistance.

Discussion

The chapters all concern how political actors and policy networks conjure or mobilise 'sociotechnical imaginaries' to use the term Williamson introduces in his chapter (referring to Jasanoff (2015)). A socio-technical imaginary is a shared vision of a future life made possible through particular technologies or as Williamson puts it:

> a collectively held, institutionally stabilized, and publicly performed vision of a desirable future […] Sociotechnical imaginaries are the result of relations between technology and society, are also temporally situated and culturally particular, and simultaneously descriptive of attainable futures and prescriptive of the kinds of futures that ought to be attained. (Chap. 3).

Although not all three chapters employ the particular term they all in our view concern different socio-technical imaginaries. Ben Williamson discusses data-base pedagogies and learning analytics as contemporary imaginaries; Sarah Hayes scrutinises UK policy text to analyse how 'technology', 'technology enhanced learning', or 'effective use of technology' are used as broad labels of assumed good in future classroom practices; Chris Jones tackles the concept of MOOCs and looks critically at how such an imaginary (or perhaps a constellation of imaginaries) has shifted its form over the years at it has been co-opted from a pedagogical network to being adopted and circulated in commercial and administrative-managerial networks instead. Common to the social imaginaries are that they linger between an accomplishable now and a close-enough future. They live somewhere between present reality and a dawning brave new world.

The examples drawn out in the chapters are already-existing technologies, services or ideas, but they draw their persuasiveness not out of their current status but out of their imagined potential, in the things to come. As the authors point out, education has always been on the brink of major breakthroughs: all the way back to Sidney Pressey's early 'teaching machine' developed in the 1920s that Williamson is referring to, and to the recently predicted disruptive avalanche of the MOOC Jones refers to. Most researchers within educational technology, and networked learning in particular, probably recognise there is a recurrent narrative of imminent and/or necessary change with the advent of 'new' technologies. In general new technologies are often imagined to bring about immense changes to society in the near future (Jones, 2015). While many researchers and practitioners are probably somewhat resistant and sceptical about many of the claims made by pundits and techno-optimists it could be, as suggested by Selwyn (2014), that the educational technology community has a blind spot for the politics of educational technology. As said, policy, and more widely critical theory and ethics, have been ongoing issues of debate within networked learning. In fact the early 'networked learning manifesto' (Beaty, Hodgson, Mann, & McConnell, 2002) was specifically written to inform policy and to realise an alternative future for educational technology. A future emphasising diversity, inclusion, democratic dialogue and learners' participation in knowledge creation over transmission of knowledge. While these blind spots might be less pronounced within the area of networked learning the chapters certainly provoke us to collectively revisit our thinking of the politics of educational technology.

What the chapters in our view help us see is the extent to which these narratives are not exclusively put in circulation from within the educational technology community, but how they are formed by wider policy networks and how cross-sectoral organizational networks spanning public, private and third sector actors increasingly are driving learning agendas. This is the specific object of Williamson's inquiry where he explores the role of cross-sector boundary brokers in the education political landscape and trace how policy making and governance is performed in mobile networks rather than exclusively in the traditional, hierarchical bureaucracies of the ministries. However, this is equally visible in Jones' critical discussion of MOOCs, where he cites a report from the think tank "Institute for Public Policy Research" written by authors employed by Pearson (which is an example of such a cross-sectoral policy network). Here Jones traces how an original intention of opening up education, born and bred within a public university and envisioned to act with the free, public, university as the backbone was co-opted and superseded by a network of private universities and spin-off companies who transformed also the very pedagogical idea of the MOOC; from a view emphasising learning as connections towards a more traditional instructionalist model copying what several open universities had done for decades, but managing to rebrand it as both a pedagogical and educational 'disruptive innovation'.

This is what is often referred to as the difference between cMOOCs and xMOOCs, although, as Jones points out, this distinction is too crude and overlooks that also the Edx and Coursera MOOCs come in great variety and certainly also with pedagogical innovation (see also Conole (2013)). What overshadows this, however, and should provoke reflection within academia is the speed, veracity and reach with which sociotechnical imaginaries associated with the MOOC have spread within both the administrative-managerial networks within Higher Education, as well as the general public. While it has been propelled from within the academic edtech circuit, there are certainly also other forces in play, and as all the authors suggest there is a strong pressure from several sides to open up education—not to the public—but to more actors such as multinational companies.

This provokes us to reflect on our practices within academia. Do we, as a community, too uncritically embrace technologies or designs without proper reflection? Do we perhaps too uncritically follow the funding streams, shrug our shoulders at hyped concepts and believe we can do as we have always done—just appropriating new words for the same? In case of the latter, do we need to think about whether we just appropriate a new vocabulary, or whether concepts as MOOCs, Web 2.0, 21st century skills, and social media appropriate us and enroll us in particular sociotechnical imaginaries that we have little control over? Should we snowboard down on top of the avalanche or should we be working on caving in the snow? Should we as a research community contribute to applications and reproduce the linguistic constructs of 'effective uses of technology' and nominalisations that Hayes unfolds and critique in her chapter? Do we need, as Jones suggests, to pay greater attention to formal or 'high' politics within Networked Learning? To help us answer these questions the most recent books in the Networked Learning Research series by Jandric and Boras (2015) and Jones (2015) are welcome contributions and can hopefully assist in leveraging the awareness of policy and politics in Networked Learning.

Another theme emerging from the three chapters on policy in networked learning is the gradual disappearance of humans in technology enhanced learning—and not in a critical, considered way to do with actor-network theory or critical posthumanist approaches. Rather, humans seem to disappear or become backgrounded in different ways in the three chapters. In Hayes' chapter she eloquently shows how this erasure is accomplished through linguistic nominalisation where it becomes hazy as to who the acting subjects are. In contrast, constructs such as 'the strategy will aim to' gloss over the actual human work that needs to be done to realise such strategies. As Hayes puts it: "The discourse promises much but is in fact deceptively spacious, because both staff and students are missing from it." While such nominalisations perhaps often occur within legalese, Hayes suggests that these acts of rendering human work invisible are particularly problematic within areas where there are already hidden workloads acting as silent barriers to the implementation of technology in higher education. Hayes highlights a particular citation in her chapter: "The use of technology to create digital archives to improve documentation of practice and to support curricular developments as well as more effective use of technology" (Chap. 2). As Hayes comments herself this seems to generate a curious circular outcome where 'the use of technology' becomes a means to ensure 'more effective uses of technology'. This might, however, not be so far-fetched if we direct our attention to the database pedagogies discussed by Williamson. In fact this seems to be the very rationale of algorithmic governance e.g. that traces and activities of humans are aggregated, ordered and analysed by machines and then used to improve the algorithms and machines which can then provide a better service or perhaps help humans to understand better their own learning or skill development. For example this is imagined in the following way by Beluga Learning (as cited in Williamsons chapter):

> The data is allowing the software to make a real-time prediction about the learner and changes the environment, … the pedagogy and the social experience. … This process occurs continually and in realtime, so that with every new piece of data collected on the student, their profile changes and the analytical software re-searches the population to compare once more. … The content and environment then adapt continually to meet the needs of the learner. (Beluga Learning 5–6) (Chap. 3)

Thus the software is imagined as making (better?) sense of the learner's learning and surroundings to foresee and adapt in real-time to the learner's needs. Much is said about the role of the algorithms, less is said about the learner's or human agency. More importantly, however, what is also rendered invisible is the human labour lying behind the algorithms. Similarly to the erasure of human agency in the policy texts it seems that 'data', 'software', 'algorithms' act almost autonomously (and inherently rational) rather than being designed by particular people (or companies) with particular professional skills, worldviews, pedagogical understandings, and commercial or political agendas. Rather than foregrounding political or commercial actors this erasure surgically removes intent and agendas and place accountability with assumed (rational) machines who seem to autonomously learn through mere (objective) observation and collection of human behaviour.

In the final chapter by Jones, human erasure is seen in a more indirect way. Namely in the sense that some versions or imaginaries of MOOCs are viewed as a solution to what Wiley (2003) termed the 'bottleneck' problem i.e. that 'the teacher' is a bottleneck which some educational technologists view as replaceable with reusable educational resources and intelligent tutoring systems. Obviously, a model of massive courses with few teachers and with automatic or peer-graded assessments seems a new way of solving the bottleneck problem and delivering education to a massive audience.

While in many ways the idea of replacing teachers with technology seems a way of eradicating human agency in learning, we should not forget that some saw (and see) this as a move to empower other people—namely the disadvantaged learner or the learners who cannot attend an 'ordinary' education (Jones, 2015). Access for the disadvantaged learner and to those with no access to educational provision has been a prominent discourse within the MOOC circuit; although the reality of these ideals has been questioned (Jones, 2015).

What perhaps comes out of these chapters is the need for an increased focus on disentangling discourses and varying perspectives. As mentioned Selwyn (2014) argues that the edtech community seems inattentive to the politics of educational technology. Further, he illustrates how—in principle—irreconcilable perspectives such as anti-institutionalism and neo-liberalism, live happily together around imaginaries such as those associated with MOOCs, the notion of 'open', or social media. While they might have vastly different pedagogical ideals and seek different outcomes they perhaps too easily meet and hold hands to sing edtech's praise. Obviously, as Jones notes, MOOCs can be pedagogically innovative as can learning analytics. What we perhaps need is a heightened, critical sensibility that seeks to render visible possible different agendas enmeshed in these terms; and which agendas we as researchers wish to pursue to avoid uncritically promoting ideas and agendas we are in fact wary of.

Part 2: Boundaries in Networked Learning

As we saw in Part 1, Williamson's boundary brokers are operating in a way that suggests that learners have choice and autonomy while at the same time positioning them as subjects managed by unseen forces. Those learners have their own boundary work to do and how they make sense of them will also be affected by how they are positioned and where they can seize opportunities to make choices. The three chapters in our part specifically devoted to boundaries share a common focus on the meaning-making activities in which learners are engaged and the tasks they are expected to do, which may seem less meaningful unless carefully designed and supported. As Goodyear, Carvalho and Dohn point out, tasks and actual activities need to be distinguished, with activity being emergent rather than designed. Activity might be influenced by boundaries that are social or material—or, more likely, both. Boundaries can impose limits on where and how the activities can take place or demand that the learners find ways of transitioning across physical or virtual spaces. Again, we summarise the chapters before drawing out their wider themes and implications for the complex relationships among learners, learning networks and activities.

Gourlay and Oliver pick up on some of the tendencies to decontextualize and obscure specific educational practices identified in our first set of chapters. In their critique of models framing the popular notion of 'digital literacies', they argue that, although the models have been derived from empirical research, their loss of specificity risks turning students into 'standardised components' in digital contexts rather than as meaning-makers in situated learning. Combining ideas from New Literacy Studies and a sociomaterial perspective and their own case studies, they show the value of taking context into account in thinking about digital literacies. This means paying attention to the unit of analysis for research in this area, which they suggest could be the 'digital literacy event' rather than the individual learner.

Goodyear, Carvalho and Dohn ask the valuable question 'What can be designed and what cannot?' in networked learning. The authors focus on the architecture of networked learning to identify design features that can be reused, particularly emphasising the material. They stress that while tasks can be designed, actual activities are not—they are emergent from within the complex assemblage that includes things, tasks and people. Revisiting the notion of affordance from a relational-material perspective, they argue that a focus on the affordances of singular things will be inadequate for a networked learning setting. Affordance, then, in networked-learning terms retains its practical significance but marries that with an acknowledgement of the complexity of actual use and practice where 'meaning' is important for the situation, human and non-human entities.

The theme of the chapter by Timmis and Williams is how students make meaning when they have to work across boundaries, for instance between work and the classroom. Timmis and Williams use Bakhtin's notion of the chronotope (the interdependence of time and space), framing student experience through 'chronotopic movements' across different forms of practice. Clinical placements and university classrooms operate under different space-time configurations, and networked learning environments can be used to create a hybrid space to allow students continuity in both. New configurations of time and space both emerge from and may be supported by forms of networked learning; but networked learning itself adds to the complexity of the chronotopes and sometimes the result is discontinuity and disruption.

Discussion

So what are the boundaries implied by our heading for this part. In all cases the authors see boundaries as necessary but permeable, expandable or crossable, and in need of recognition and response. The emphasis is different in each, but there are many crossovers. Our sequence of chapters highlights:

- boundaries imposed by context, which may go unrecognized
- boundaries within the architecture of learning networks that allow practicable framing of design for activity
- shifting boundaries of space and time which open up newer forms of practice

Gourlay and Oliver show that boundaries formed by contexts are important to overcome the notion of the 'free-floating' idealized agent learner. The tendency for researchers to create taxonomies of technologies or of student skills leads to decontextualised accounts of digital literacies—and ultimately lets in the unseen neoliberal forces anticipated in the previous part of this book. 'Free-floating' is an expression also confronted by Goodyear, Carvalho and Dohn: activity is no more free-floating than the learner, but emerges as a response to tasks and is shaped by context. That context is in turn shaped and expanded, providing a challenge for designers seeking reusable ideas for settings for activity. Timmis and Williams provide examples of the kinds of contexts that students on professional programmes find themselves in: a mix of the classroom and the work-based placement, each with its own shaping aspects. Their analysis shows that the impact on activity not only includes the social and the material but also space:time configurations, with networks providing opportunities but also entailing constraints. All the authors of these three chapters are optimistic though—working around boundaries offers opportunities for developments in networked learning.

The papers in this trio therefore draw our attention to the dangers of focusing on technological considerations or attributes of learners without reference to wider social and material contexts and the effects of networks. Their concerns about what happens at the boundaries provide further support for Sarah Hayes' case made in Part 1 for drawing attention to invisible human labour. By adopting pedagogical models that position learners and/or their activity as 'free floating', researchers or policymakers are likely to lose sight of what actually happens in practice, the duration of required tasks for students and their teachers, and how that work intersects with what happens in overlapping practices such as those identified by Timmis and Williams. Failure to take these aspects of networked learning into account results in a need for learners to improvise or find workarounds as they find themselves unable to do the tasks as they have been set, but still engage in the activities that they see as essential.

Interestingly, to illustrate such improvisations, each of the three chapters uses an example that focuses on the ability to print materials. The need arises at a point when learners want to apply or display their learning, and include: overcoming a barrier to accessing a printer, using print to overcome lack of access to the Internet, using a bike to overcome failure of email to send material to a print shop. Whether the workarounds have to be instigated by the learner or the design team, they are all evidence of attempts to cross unanticipated boundaries and are all examples of problems with access. Thus these examples indicate not only the need for newer technology-based practices to intersect with those from a pre-digital era, but also the discrepancy between intended and actual practice. This was also a feature highlighted in papers from the 2012 Networked Learning conference by Hodgson et al. (2014b).

The discrepancy between intended and actual practice is exacerbated when attention is drawn away from meaning-making and meaningful activity. If learners find their tasks (with or without the use of technology) to be without meaning, the future seems bleak. Gourlay and Oliver lament the loss of emphasis on learner understanding from current ways of talking about digital literacies. They feel this can be restored through a combined recognition of situated meaning-making, as offered by new literacy studies, and a sociomaterial perspective that allows theorisation about the connected nature of learners, texts and devices. Also welcoming the sociomaterial, Goodyear, Carvalho and Dohn emphasise the meaning of situations—and point to the role of significance both for humans and things. This clears the way for reprieving the notion of 'affordance' but now used in a relational-materialist discourse that connects activity and tasks as well as tools, software and other artefacts. Support for meaning-making is arguably most needed at boundaries themselves: Timmis and Williams offer Bakhtin's concept of the chronotope to help learners to make meaning of their transitions between workplace and educational boundaries. Learners (and teachers) do not notice the extent to which we conventionalise and operationalise our space:time configurations until they are disrupted through crossing a boundary into a different type of practice.

While the three chapters share perspectives on the value of the sociomaterial, the need for improvisation and the importance of meaning-making, they may suggest different stances on, for example, the value of taxonomies in networked learning, or the role of space and/or time in the conceptualisation of complex assemblages. Gourlay and Oliver seek to reject essentialising taxonomies of the digital or the human, while Goodyear, Carvalho and Dohn ask: 'What can be designed, and what cannot? Are these designable things all of one kind, or is a taxonomy needed?' The latter do suggest the potential of taxonomies or at least patterns of design that bring together the digital and the human. There are echoes of the chronotopic movements identified by Timmis and Williams in the question Gourlay and Oliver asked students about 'associations between spaces, tasks and times' but it's probably fair to say that time and space for the first two chapters in this part are more associated with emergence than with transition.

The differences in emphasis and potential contradictions across these papers relate to some extent to different theoretical influences and where the authors perceive barriers associated with boundaries to arise. What they have in common is stronger, and has some practical implications for people involved in networked learning who want to ensure their learners are engaged in meaningful work.

Part 2 draws our attention to the need to take account of everything relevant in our networked learning environment and not to allow a limited perspective or ideology to determine what we can say about teaching and learning. While boundaries can be helpful for sense-making, they are constantly changing especially as people have to make creative or improvised decisions to ensure that activity remains meaningful. In an environment where other people's practices—along with technologies, artefacts, tasks and intended learning outcomes—change in response to shifting dynamics, we need ways to theorise the boundary work so that we can see how politics and policy can limit or expand our work in networked learning. Because the theorising and pedagogies are themselves subject to hidden or unanticipated forces around and across boundaries, they are also likely to need to change, a topic which is considered in our final part.

Part 3: Research in Networked Learning

This part encompasses three papers that address in various ways research in networked learning and reflections on how to do networked learning research. Further they again touch upon policy and boundaries though to a lesser extent than the previous chapters. The common core of the three chapters is a concern with research in networked learning, albeit at different levels of scale.

In their model of mobile and field learning, Gallagher and Ihanainen emphasise the need for a pedagogy that takes account of time, space and social presence and their simultaneous relationships. The ephemeral nature of learning in open environments does not deter them from attempting to do this, though it does point to the need for reflective practice. The multifaceted 'pedagogy of simultaneity' model the authors present provides a framework for considering continuums of pedagogical field activities. However, it also presents a way in which researchers can collect data together with colleagues or students. They conclude that meaning emerges from the establishment of trust especially at the point where students select their focus in the field, discussion and sharing of knowledge, and the construction of collages resulting from formal and informal learning practices.

Along with the other authors in this volume, Dohn stresses the importance of context, as might be expected from her practice-grounded approach. She highlights the notion of 'primary contexts' that 'anchor' our understanding and are important to who we are. She employs two metaphors to explore context: the container (from an individualist-cognitive perspective) and the rope (from a sociocultural one). The learning context as container is pre-established and bounded; the rope is formed of discontinuous elements but presents as a unity. Dohn uses these concepts to critique current uses of motivation and engagement in networked learning and to offer some new questions.

How we research networked learning is itself opened to scrutiny in Jandric's chapter. Petar Jandric's exploration of the dialectical relationship of academic disciplines and research methodologies surfaces the problems that this relationship causes for networked learning. The nature of networked learning leads to the use of postdisciplinary methods; yet, Jandric argues, these are still 'haunted' by disciplinary perspectives. Jandric considers the emancipatory potential of various forms of postdisciplinarity: multidisciplinarity, interdisciplinarity, transdisciplinarity and anti-disciplinarity to seek the best options for critical emancipatory research, favouring the final two.

Discussion

The first two chapters are in different ways concerned with studying and understanding contexts, and more so learners' engagement with context. In Gallagher and Ihanainen they explore the mutability and complexity of context when engaging with 'mobile' pedagogical field activities—an idea that also relates well to Timmis and Williams' reflections on chronotopic movements across different forms of practice. Whilst field activities are well-known pedagogical practices, the inclusion of mobiles and mobility adds new layers to the data collection process including both multimodal data (audio, video), but equally geo-spatial data, as well as classic field notes, maps etc. However, what is more important is how learners may engage with the messy, cacaphonic field of opportunities they are presented with when entering real-life contexts outside the classroom. Here Gallagher and Ihanainen present three variables, or perhaps continuums, as part of their pedagogy of simultaneity. The continuums represent tensions between serendipity vs intentionality, informal vs formal, initiative vs seduction and all concern the ways in which the students engage with the context at hand; are they seduced by its offers and serendipitously experience in a very informal way what it has to offer; or are they intentionally taking initiative and engaging more strategically with the setting to satisfy perhaps more formal requirements. What the continuums highlight is that engagement with learning context is highly complex and multifaceted.

This resonates very well with the chapter by Dohn who introduces two distinct understandings of contexts—that of the rope and the container. These stem from a socio-cultural and an individual-cognitivist perspective respectively. Dohn contrasts and discusses these two perspectives as ends of a continuum of motivation and engagement. The socio-cultural view emphasises how motivation is socially negotiated, whereas the individualist-cognitive perspective sees motivation as a highly individual process of pursuing conscious, self-determined goals. However, the latter often ignores the 'learning context' and understands this as merely a container that learners as self-contained entities move in and out of. Unlike the container metaphor the rope metaphor suggests that contexts are not just something we are 'in'; rather they are practices we are deeply enmeshed or entangled with. Other threads (or fibres) are part of the rope and even if our own engagement might only be for a shorter period of time the rope (or practice) will sustain. It also suggests that contexts are not solitary containers for isolated individuals, but rather something we co-create. Further, the social aspects are part of why we are motivated to engage in a particular practice i.e. that motivation is not (only) an individual trait, but something that emerges as part of the social practice. This is a perspective we also see explored in Gourlay and Oliver's notion of literacy, which emphasises socio-material practice and context over an individualised and de-contextualised idea of 'digital literacies'. However, while Dohn in principle agrees with the socio-cultural perspective on context, her point is that sometimes contexts may be mere containers to the learners. Those are contexts we do not enthusiastically or fully engage with, but yet we enter, learn and leave. This, she argues, is related to whether something appears to the learner as part of their primary context. Primary contexts are those which carry a significant meaning to the person in question, those they are involved with as persons and they consider important in relation to who they are. These are contexts which are related to our development of identity and contexts that may more likely appear to learners as ropes or 'becoming ropes' rather than containers.

While Dohn highlights the different metaphors and their underlying (and conflicting) theoretical outset her real purpose is to develop a practice-grounded approach that can include both perspectives. Thus, she argues that even though motivation may often be a negotiated social enterprise, we also see examples of highly self-chosen enterprises, such as a kid picking up bird-watching on her own with no apparent cue or support from the environment. Likewise, she argues that while some contexts might be ropes, others will forever remain containers to the individual learner. This also eschews 'motivation' from being imagined as a designable issue where particular pedagogical levers and sliders can be manipulated and set to become an optimally motivating experience to become an empirical issue where we can ask questions such as 'which of the learning activities students cared about and why'. Dohn phrases it in this way:

> The overall point is that we need to accept a continuum of possible states and processes, anchored in the individual, as 'motivational' or 'engaging'. This continuum will range from the very self-directed to the fully socially constituted. Accepting this amounts to taking the claim seriously that it is always an empirical question what 'sets us going' and how. (Chap. 9)

Bringing Gallagher and Ihanainen and Dohn together we are confronted with a more complex understanding of how people might engage with particular learning contexts — mobile or not, formal or informal. It reminds us of the often discussed notion of indirect design within networked learning which is the notion that learning can be designed for but never directly designed (Carvalho & Goodyear, 2014; Jones, 2015). This is also, as written in previous part, what is explored in the chapter by Goodyear, Carvalho and Dohn when they ask what can be designed and what is emergent. The notion of indirect design suggests that there is no direct relationship between the designer's or teacher's intentions (the tasks they set), and then what will happen in practice or the learning that might emerge from this (the learners actual activities) — as Goodyear, Carvalho and Dohn phrase it:

> Unless learning is very closely supervised and directed (which it rarely is), there will usually be some slippage between task and activity, for good and bad reasons. (Chap. 6).

What they all stress is that designing for learning and motivation cannot be thought of as a process of setting up a space and an elaborate plan for tasks, which can then unproblematically be executed with a particular outcome. Designing as Goodyear, Carvalho and Dohn argue, is crucial but it is important that the designer has a good understanding of what can be designed and what is emergent. The continuums presented by Gallagher and Ihanainen as part of their pedagogy of simultaneity, as well as the metaphors of ropes and containers are conceptual tools which can help designers of networked learning reflect on the tensions between the designable and the emergent. This reflects and extends also what was discussed in the previous book in the conference series:

> The messy and unpredictable nature of networked learning highlights the tension between the expected and unexpected, and squarely emphasises 'teaching or facilitation' as a practice. While productive networked learning certainly hinges on a carefully crafted and reflexive design, we should equally view it as considerate and careful reflection-in-action. (Hodgson et al. 2014a: 24)

Another important issue brought up by Gallagher and Ihanainen and Dohn (which also ties in well with the chapters discussed in the previous part) is that of the materiality and place-ness of networked learning. While traditionally, as noted by Goodyear, Carvalho and Dohn, networked learning has been thought of as online courses with individuals sitting in their homes, connected through their desktop computers to other learners in virtual conference rooms it is also clear that networked learning is becoming increasingly more diverse than that. The pervasiveness of internet access (in some parts of the world) and the dramatic increase in ownership of mobile technologies (laptops, tablets and smartphones) are changing the places of where and how networked learning is happening. From virtual learning environments being mainly used by 'distance education' to becoming a standard component for all higher education students. From ICT and learning being an esoteric activity in labs to becoming a pervasive part of campus and lecture hall activities (whether consciously or not on behalf of the teacher). From working primarily from home to people being on the move and engaging in online activities while being on the train or in cafes, and students alternating between distributed work and meeting on campus. Mobile field activities, informal learning communities are other examples. These concerns are reflected in a recent book titled *Place-based Spaces for Networked Learning* (Carvalho, Goodyear, & De Laat, 2016) and in the Networked Learning Conferences over the past years there has been an increasing interest in sociomateriality and socio-material practices. These intersections between place, space, time and activities are reflected in all of the chapters in part 2 as part of discussing the boundaries of networked learning. This obviously also speaks to how we should understand research in networked learning and what are the boundaries of networked learning as a field compared to Technology Enhanced Learning, Computer Supported Collaborative Learning or other fields of enquiry? Can networked learning encompass also learning networks that are not primarily technologically mediated? Can we imagine any contemporary form of learning that does not—in one way or another—include the use of technology? It seems a challenge in the years to come to better understand the boundaries of research in networked learning.

These boundaries are what Jandric is challenging us to revisit. In his chapter he acknowledges the emancipatory and critical roots and ideals of networked learning, but he also challenges the networked learning community in suggesting that it might still be struggling with breaking the chains of the traditional disciplinary perspectives rather than embracing fully a post-disciplinary perspective. The latter, he argues, is a prerequisite for true emancipation.

> Disciplinarity, multidisciplinarity, and interdisciplinarity are imbued within the existing social and technoscientific orders. In spite of significant epistemological and practical achievements, therefore, these methodological approaches are structurally unable to provide radical social change. (Chap. 10)

Further, Jandric poignantly criticises the tendency for research being politically steered towards more short-sighted goals of immediate applicability, while also pointing out that research and teaching are riddled with questions of class and privilege. In relation to this Jandric argues how there are increasing gaps between those researchers and institutions who are allowed to focus on research and the growing mass of non-tenured, loosely affiliated teaching assistants, post docs and/or adjuncts who are becoming part of what has been termed the 'precariat' (class of people who have job conditions with little predictability, stability and security (Standing, 2014)). There are some interesting tensions raised in the chapter by Jandric, which are some that could be explored in the years to come. We would comment that in times of scarcity, austerity and insecurity one could perhaps expect that many researchers would be less inclined to pursue the more 'risky' transdisciplinary modes of research; particularly when pursuing tenure or at least more stable working conditions. There might seem to be more refuge and comfort in the soothing arms of 'traditional' research and it might seem an easier path in terms of publishing papers. Further, one could also speculate whether insecurity might lessen the inclination to fight for social change and social justice and becoming an advocate for radical pedagogies or pursuing a feminist agenda. This brings us back to part 1 and the discussions of policy and politics in networked learning. The area of Networked Learning is not only affected by educational politics, but equally by wider political decisions and currents. As Jandric and others in this book suggest this should encourage us to reflect, think deeper and perhaps also act in a more politically sensitive way to make sure that the field of networked learning remains an area of research grounded in emancipatory perspectives and critical thinking — an area that remains open and oriented towards transdisciplinarity and social change, as suggested by Jandric.

Concluding Reflections

Following from our summaries and discussions on the three parts of the book we shall reflect on how these resonate with and extend our current understandings of networked learning. In doing so we found it valuable to return to the concluding chapter of the book following the 2010 conference in Aalborg: the relational model of networked learning presented in that chapter is worth revisiting in the light of the chapters in this book. This integrated a number of dimensions that are central to a holistic perspective on networked learning to understand how digital technologies can be designed and enacted to support networked learning (Hodgson, McConnell, & Dirckinck-Holmfeld, 2012: 295).

In reflecting on the shifts emphasised in the 2014 conference, it seems helpful to add additional concepts and an extra bullet to this relational model:

- A pedagogical approach (values, principles, *politics*, emancipatory perspectives)
- Organisation and *policy* at different scales and levels (group, institution, the collective)
- The learner, the teacher, and *the designer* (their individual choices)
- *Different contexts and places (formal/informal, home, mobility, primary/secondary)*

In the list above we have emphasised the additions and will discuss these in more depth.

Politics and Policy

As we have discussed across the three parts, policy and politics grow increasingly important to networked learning. We have suggested that politics could be added to the first of the bullet points concerning pedagogical approaches, values and principles, as these are often political or at least reflect a particular position on learning.

As explored in the previous parts many terms within educational technology are spacious and specious in the sense that they can take on different meanings, and it might be unclear what is meant by e.g. effective or productive: Cost-efficient, scalable, democratic or high-quality? This is true for many terms and concepts within educational technology such as: MOOCs, Web 2.0, 21st century skills, and Technology Enhanced Learning (Bayne, 2015). They are deceptively spacious and work as linguistic 'boundary objects' (Star & Griesemer, 1989) i.e. terms that facilitate understanding and action across differing disciplines and actors whom however might individually conceive and read the boundary object differently. This might be part of the reason why, as Selwyn (2014) shows, quite different disciplines and ideological perspectives can rally under the same flag within educational technology. Perhaps we see only our own ideals reflected in the terms and then come to see technology X as a means to accomplish those. Thus, MOOCs, Web 2.0 or Learning Analytics become boundary terms that are commonly used, but pursued with widely different pedagogical agendas. This could be, for example, delivering educational resources and instructional support for flexible, self-paced learning (broadcast view) versus enabling new relations and patterns of collaboration between facilitators, learners and robotic agents (discussion view). Likewise, these commonly used terms might gloss over widely different political agendas, as Jones shows with his analysis of how MOOCs have changed substantially from a university driven idea of education as public good to a 'disruptive innovation' to 'fix education' with the help of private companies and strategic partnerships. We can also sense how different agendas might be underlying ideas of 21st century skills and digital literacies — from being situated accomplishments dependent equally on the environment to being understood as compartmentalised, individual skill-trees that can be 'nurtured and grown' to become an enlightened citizen and/or productive, valuable asset to society. With this we are not suggesting that networked learning designs should necessarily be political and aim for social change and emancipation. However, we argue that networked learning as a field should cherish and expand its critical roots and heighten its critical sensibilities in relation to disentangling and critiquing different underlying agendas within educational technology.

We are also suggesting adding policy to the second bullet point (organisation and *policy* at different levels of scale). While policy and politics are related and high politics seep into policies and practice as many of the authors show they also function at different levels of scale. Policies can be quite mundane, yet still affect learners, as illustrated by Gourlay and Oliver showing how not having access to a staff printer can render a task more cumbersome. In a similar vein in one of our home institutions students cannot leave material on a shelf in a seminar room because the department has only invested in the cheapest 'cleaning package' which prescribes that all shelves must be emptied every day. This, however, means that it becomes difficult for students to store models, post-its, paper, pens and other stuff they use as part of working on campus. Policies thus often gloss over or remove the actual work that needs to go into realising 'effective uses of technology'; nor are they concerned with how they might collide with existing micro-policies, established practices and the nitty-gritty work of making educational technologies function in practice. As with learning, policies are not something directly transmitted from the management to the individual employees, from state to citizen, and while we often speak of 'implementing' policies, doing so creates complex organisational dances. This for example was what John Hannon (2014) explored in analysing how a particular use and vision emerged for the local adoption of a LMS i.e. how the LMS was assembled and coming to being through organisational power games and negotiations. Likewise, Nyvang and Bygholm (2012) show how 'the implementation' of a learning system is a cacophony of multiple voices and perspectives. Perhaps as Gourlay and Oliver suggest in relation to understanding students' digital literacies we need to inspect more carefully processes of how 'deceptively spacious policies' are implemented in practice and which voices eventually come to dominate the pedagogies and practices (what we could possibly term 'organisational sense mining'). Maybe it is important to strengthen the focus on institutional and organisational aspects and understanding pedagogy, course management systems and other learning technologies as socio-technical systems that encompass issues of power, changes in division of labour and responsibilities; issues often explored in information systems research and social informatics and connected to networked learning by Creanor and Walker (2012). Thus, we should perhaps be more attentive to that designing for learning encompasses more than pedagogy and could be viewed as organisational change process where ideas from participatory or cooperative design could be relevant as suggested by Gleerup, Heilesen, Helms, and Mogensen (2014).

The Role of the Designer

We added the notion of the designer for a couple of reasons. Carvalho, Goodyear and Dohn, as well as many others, are arguing for understanding teaching as the art (or science) of designing for learning, and the area of 'learning design' is a major field of research within TEL-research and within networked learning. However, we would equally like to stress the fact that the teachers and the designers may not always be the same persons. Courses may be designed by others than the teacher or—as often with online courses—be a collaborative enterprise where multiple persons with different backgrounds are part of co-designing courses instructional designers, learning technologists, tutors, and teachers may be part of designing and running courses. However, there might also be disconnects e.g. as Jandric explores in his examples of the precariat of adjunct professors that step in and teach courses in which content and sequencing have been decided by others. Thus, they have less agency and little control over the means of production. Jandric explores these potentially emerging gaps between the haves and have-nots within academia—between the precariat and the 'tenured faculty' or a 'teaching aristocracy' and a 'pauperised teaching labour force'. This could potentially be aggravated by political agendas of seeing the main benefits of online learning as a means to reduce the number of teachers (the bottleneck problem) and thus the costs. At least the fast development of Universities' interest in 'teaching at scale' warrants critical inquiry into issues of ownership and rights in the relations between 'the designer' and the 'teacher'.

Different Contexts and Places

The changing nature of networked learning as noted by several of the authors is challenging us to think more carefully about the placeness and materiality of networked learning. This is reflected in a review of the networked learning book following the 2012 conference (Hodgson, De Laat, McConnell, & Ryberg, 2014b) by Peter Goodyear (2015). In the review Goodyear advises the networked learning community to:

> So my second, future-oriented, point is that networked learning researchers should be taking a few more gambles about the likely nature of the tools and artefacts that will be bound up in networked learning in the next decade or so. There has been too much (premature) fuss about the 'the internet of things', but we do need some strategies to ensure our research methods and problems aren't locked to technologies that were new in the 1980s. (Goodyear, 2015: 271–272)

This is specifically addressed in the chapter by Carvalho, Goodyear and Dohn, but is a theme across many of the chapters particularly in part 2. Carvalho, Goodyear and Dohn also argue that the domain of networked learning has become more diverse than primarily being concerned with off-campus, online programmes. Mobility and the pervasiveness of mobile devices and web-access reshape the boundaries of networked learning and networked learning research urging the development of concepts such as place-based networked learning, chronotopic movements, a pedagogy of simultaneity, materiality and artefacts to name a few. Likewise, the significance of context has been highlighted by a regular contributor to the Networked Learning Conference, Nina Bonderup Dohn, who proposed in the 2012 conference (and has reiterated in this volume) a change to the frequently-cited definition of networked learning offered by Goodyear, Banks, Hodgson, and McConnell (2004). Dohn's addition is highlighted in the statement below:

> Networked learning is learning in which information and communications technology (ICT) is used to promote connections: between one learner and other learners; between learners and tutors; between a learning community and its learning resources; **between the diverse contexts in which the learners participate**. (Dohn, 2014: 30 emphasis added)

We could feel tempted to rephrase this into 'between the diverse contexts and places in which the learners act'. While mentioning both context and places could seem a bit double they are nevertheless distinct concepts, although their difference and similarity would warrant much deeper theoretical discussion. Even though contexts as presented by Dohn can be places, they are not necessarily physical (or virtual) places; they could equally be certain conditions or situations people are in. Therefore adding places also suggests a careful consideration of the material aspects of those places and to interrogate or question distinctions such as virtual and physical.

The perceived need to augment a longstanding way of looking at networked learning is thus reflected throughout the chapters of this book. This is not a call to reject what has gone before—far from it—but to build on it and value the reflexivity that is prevalent in this community.

Acknowledgements   The conference held in Edinburgh 2014 was the ninth networked learning conference and we would like to call attention to the tremendous work of Vivien Hodgson and David McConnell in sustaining and developing the conference over the years. Since the first Networked Learning Conference in 1998 Vivien and David have been co-chairs of the conference and have, together with many others, been vital in sustaining and expanding a network of researchers and research environments that have endured and grown over the years. The 2014 conference was the first conference in which Maarten De Laat and Thomas Ryberg took the role as co-chairs to run the conference together with Sian Bayne, Christine Sinclair, Hamish McLeod and Jen Ross as the local organisers. We would all like to thank both Vivien and David for helping throughout the process by providing advice and sharing their experiences, but more so for their continued work to develop the conference and the research area of Networked Learning (together with many other people too numerous to mention in full). Their work has crystallised into the biennial conference, the present book series on research in networked learning, of which they serve as series editors and also a host of various research networks and projects on networked learning in and outside the EU. While the two first books in the series were reworked papers from the conference (Dirckinck Holmfeld, Hodgson, & McConnell, 2012; Hodgson et al., 2014b), as is the present book, there are now two other strong titles in the book series (Jandric & Boras, 2015; Jones, 2015) and hopefully many more to come. We would also mention the role of Chris Jones, who has served as a permanent member of the scientific committee for the conference and has been invaluable in the process of planning the 2014 conference, as well as Alice Jesmont who has been the conference secretary since 2006, and involved in the planning of the 2016 conference in Lancaster.

References

Bayne, S. (2015). What's the matter with "technology-enhanced learning"? *Learning, Media and Technology, 40*(1), 5–20. http://doi.org/10.1080/17439884.2014.915851.

Beaty, L., Hodgson, V., Mann, S., & McConnell, D. (2002). *Towards E-quality in networked E-learning in higher education*. ESRC research seminar series. Retrieved from http://csalt.lancs.ac.uk/esrc/manifesto.pdf.

Carvalho, L., & Goodyear, P. (2014). *The architecture of productive learning networks*. New York, NY: Routledge.

Carvalho, L., Goodyear, P., & de Laat, M. (2016). *Place-based spaces for networked learning*. New York, NY: Routledge.

Conole, G. (2013). MOOCs as disruptive technologies: Strategies for enhancing the learner experience and quality of MOOCs. *Revista de Educación a Distancia, 39*, 1–17.

Creanor, L., & Walker, S. (2012). Learning technology in context: A case for the sociotechnical interaction framework as an analytical lens for networked learning research. In L. Dirckinck-Holmfeld, V. Hodgson, & D. McConnell (Eds.), *Exploring the theory, pedagogy and practice of networked learning* (pp. 173–187). New York, NY: Springer. Retrieved from http://link.springer.com/chapter/10.1007/978-1-4614-0496-5_10.

Dirckinck Holmfeld, L., Hodgson, V., & McConnell, D. (Eds.). (2012). *Exploring the theory, pedagogy and practice of networked learning*. New York, NY: Springer.

Dohn, N. B. (2014). Implications for networked learning of the "practice" side of social practice theories: A tacit-knowledge perspective. In V. Hodgson, M. de Laat, D. McConnell, & T. Ryberg (Eds.), *The design, experience and practice of networked learning* (pp. 29–49). New York, NY: Springer International Publishing. Retrieved from http://link.springer.com/chapter/10.1007/978-3-319-01940-6_2.

Gleerup, J., Heilesen, S., Helms, N. H., & Mogensen, K. (2014). Designing for learning in coupled contexts. In V. Hodgson, M. de Laat, D. McConnell, & T. Ryberg (Eds.), *The design, experience and practice of networked learning* (pp. 51–65). New York, NY: Springer International Publishing. Retrieved from http://link.springer.com/chapter/10.1007/978-3-319-01940-6_3.

Goodyear, P. (2015). Review of: Hodgson, et al. (2014) The design, experience and practice of networked. *Technology, Knowledge and Learning, 20*(2), 269–273. http://doi.org/10.1007/s10758-014-9243-3.

Goodyear, P., Banks, S., Hodgson, V., & McConnell, D. (2004). *Advances in research on networked learning*. Dordrecht: Klüwer Academic Publishers.

Hannon, J. (2014). Making the Right Connections: Implementing the Objects of Practice into a Network for Learning. In V. Hodgson, M. de Laat, D. McConnell, & T. Ryberg (Eds.), The Design, Experience and Practice of Networked Learning (pp. 67–85). Springer International Publishing. Retrieved from http://link.springer.com/chapter/10.1007/978-3-319-01940-6_4.

Hodgson, V., de Laat, M., McConnell, D., & Ryberg, T. (2014a). Researching design, experience and practice of networked learning: An overview. In V. Hodgson, M. de Laat, D. McConnell, & T. Ryberg (Eds.), *The design, experience and practice of networked learning* (pp. 1–26). New York, NY: Springer International Publishing. Retrieved from http://link.springer.com/chapter/10.1007/978-3-319-01940-6_1.

Hodgson, V., de Laat, M., McConnell, D., & Ryberg, T. (Eds.). (2014b). *The design, experience and practice of networked learning*. New York, NY: Springer.

Hodgson, V., McConnell, D., & Dirckink-Holmfeld, L. (2012). The theory, practice and pedagogy of networked learning. In L. Dirckink-Holmfeld, V. Hodgson, & D. McConnell (Eds.), *Exploring the theory, pedagogy and practice of networked learning* (pp. 291–305). New York, NY: Springer. Retrieved from http://link.springer.com/chapter/10.1007/978-1-4614-0496-5_17.

Jandric, P., & Boras, D. (Eds.). (2015). *Critical learning in digital networks*. New York, NY: Springer Science + Business Media.

Jasanoff, S. (2015). Future imperfect: Science, technology, and the imaginations of modernity. In S. Jasanoff & S. H. Kim (Eds.), *Dreamscapes of modernity: Sociotechnical imaginaries and the fabrication of power* (pp. 1–47). Chicago, IL: University of Chicago Press.

Jones, C. (2015). *An educational paradigm for the age of digital networks networked learning*. New York, NY: Springer.

McConnell, D., Hodgson, V., & Dirckinck-Holmfeld, L. (2012). Networked learning: A brief history and new trends. In L. Dirckinck Holmfeld, V. Hodgson, & D. McConnell (Eds.), *Exploring the theory, pedagogy and practice of networked learning* (pp. 3–24). New York, NY: Springer.

Nyvang, T., & Bygholm, A. (2012). Implementation of an infrastructure for networked learning. In L. Dirckinck-Holmfeld, V. Hodgson, & D. McConnell (Eds.), *Exploring the theory, pedagogy and practice of networked learning* (pp. 141–154). New York, NY: Springer. Retrieved from http://link.springer.com/chapter/10.1007/978-1-4614-0496-5_8.

Selwyn, N. (2014). *Distrusting educational technology: Critical questions for changing times*. New York, NY; London: Routledge; Taylor & Francis Group.

Standing, G. (2014). *A precariat charter: From denizens to citizens*. London; New York, NY: Bloomsbury.

Star, S. L., & Griesemer, J. R. (1989). Institutional ecology, "translations" and boundary objects: Amateurs and professionals in Berkely's Museum of Vertebrate Zoology, 1907-39. *Social Studies of Science, 19*(3), 387–420.

Wiley, D. A. (2003). *The coming collision between automated instruction and social constructivism*. Columbus, OH: The Ohio State University. Retrieved from https://kb.osu.edu/dspace/bitstream/handle/1811/26/Wiley_OLN.pdf?sequence=4.

Part I
Policy in Networked Learning

Chapter 2
Learning from a Deceptively Spacious Policy Discourse

Sarah Hayes

Introduction

Networked learning, *e-learning* and *Technology Enhanced Learning* (TEL) are all terms that might further a critical theoretical debate about how people make connections with technology, and with each other, for learning in higher education (HE). Yet in policy documents such terms have mostly served as static markers, within a rational discourse about improved performance, that maintains a particular, dominant, economically-based world view of educational technology. By a *rational* discourse, I refer to a 'common sense' (Gramsci, 1971), but also 'de-humanising' form of writing of policy, that effectively separates people and their labour from the assumed achievements of technology, in a higher education context. This discourse is deceptively spacious, because it offers much promise for enhancement of people's performance via technology. Yet, in a curious way, that I will explain later through Critical Discourse Analysis (CDA, hereafter) it also removes any human presence from the very territory where we might learn more about our networked practices with technology. Given that 'academic workload' is a 'silent barrier' to the implementation of TEL strategies (Gregory & Lodge, 2015), this analysis further exposes, through empirical examples, that the academic labour of both staff and students also appears to be unacknowledged.

In this chapter I will firstly explain *networked learning* as one way to understand educational technology as relational in people's lives. This approach is distinctly different politically and organisationally from either bureaucratic hierarchies or the anarchy of the market (Thompson, 1991). As such it offers an alternative to a more commonly found deterministic approach in higher education policy that repeatedly frames technology as providing a form of 'exchange value' (Marx, 1867) for learning. I then proceed to discuss policy continuities in the UK that have helped to

S. Hayes (✉)
Centre for Learning, Innovation and Professional Practice, Aston University,
Birmingham, UK
e-mail: s.hayes@aston.ac.uk

© Springer International Publishing Switzerland 2016
T. Ryberg et al. (eds.), *Research, Boundaries, and Policy in Networked Learning*, Research in Networked Learning, DOI 10.1007/978-3-319-31130-2_2

maintain one dominant view despite regular changes in terminology. CDA provides us with a form of resistance to such universal logic. We can notice instead how simplistic arguments about value for students and staff in policy discourse, separate technology from its human social and political implications. In a trans-disciplinary approach I therefore link critical social theory about technology, language and learning with examples from a corpus-based Critical Discourse Analysis (CDA) of UK policy texts for educational technology between 1997 and 2012. Perceptions of 'value' are essentially a function of language (Graham, 2001: 764) and language is a systematic resource for exchanging meaning in context (Halliday, 1994). Unfortunately, as language is enacted as discourse, it can spread powerful viewpoints, which appear to be legitimate, yet may also limit human practice.

I draw later on theory from Weber, Ritzer and Marx to explain how examples drawn from my corpus display a *rationality*, based only on a predicted exchange value from educational technology. This reduces human choices, ultimately leading to an *irrationality* that becomes self-defeating, if it is to support university aspirations in a global knowledge-based economy (Jessop, 2008). This is a logic therefore that distorts the idea of networked learning communities (Greener & Perriton, 2005: 67). I suggest instead that we acknowledge a *technology-language-learning* nexus, as a broader basis for networked learning. In this model technology, language and learning are relational and mutually constitutive networked elements in the lives of those who are learning. Global neoliberal capitalist values have strongly territorialised the contemporary university (Hayes & Jandrić, 2014), utilising existing naïve, utopian arguments about what technology achieves. At the same time, the very spaces in which we might critically debate these 'promises' have diminished. The chapter reveals how humans are easily 'evicted', even from discourse about their own learning (Hayes, 2015). It is time then to re-occupy this important territory. We can use the very political discourse that disguised our material and verbal practices, in new explicit ways, to begin to restore our human visibility.

Networked Learning as a Way to Understand Educational Technology

Networked Learning, applied to the use of digital technologies in higher education, is understood 'to promote connections: between one learner and other learners, between learners and tutors; between a learning community and its learning resources' (Goodyear, Hodgson, & McConnell, 2004: 1). As just one choice of terminology we might use to discuss educational technology, it is considered to be 'relational' between all of these things (Jones, 2012: 3). In a networked learning approach, technology is not simply a neutral object that in modern life dictates the pace of human development, nor is it just a subject that we write about, expecting to be able to use it for automatic economic gain through increased performance.

Instead, technology is 'a dialectical process of material and linguistic negotiation between competing social forces' across networks (Hayes & Jandrić, 2014: 194).

In contrast to this broad understanding of networked learning, in policy for educational technology, in recent decades, we still find a rarely critiqued, rational underlying assumption that implementing new technologies, in themselves, determines learning. A single argument that technology might be applied to learning, to guarantee something additional and useful in return, suggests there is a presupposed exchange value (Marx, 1867). Though hardly a new argument, this deterministic approach is framed and re-framed across governments, and within both hierarchical and broader neoliberal (Campbell & Pedersen, 2001; Harvey, 2005) policies for higher education. In recent decades neoliberalism has dominated Western and increasingly global economic life (Campbell & Pedersen, 2001; Harvey, 2005), but it is the practical implementation of this complex economic and political ideology, through discourse and other elements including technology, that is the focus of my analysis in this chapter.

Policy Continuities That Support a Dominant Discourse

Greener and Perriton (2005) draw attention to a meeting of political economy with e-learning. Distinguishing between hierarchical 'Keynesian' forms of educational delivery and a 'Schumpeterian' entrepreneurial market-driven model, they draw analogies with economic models suggesting utopian rhetoric can mask other societal issues in networked learning (Greener & Perriton, 2005: 69). I refer to extremes of policy for educational provision as either hierarchical or neoliberal, though neither economic theory will be discussed in detail here, as the focus is on a critical approach to how these play out in the discourse. I demonstrate later through CDA how UK 'policy continuities' (Ball, 1999) continue to affect how people identify the role of technology economically in learning.

Some would argue that recent global economic crisis transcends the limitations of conventional economic thinking anyway. The consequent need for a radical rethinking means no longer a continuation of 'existing assumptions under a different name' (Hall, Massey, & Rustin, 2013). It is from this point of departure that I discuss how a rational vocabulary in policy texts, that tends to reflect consumer culture and self-interest (Massey, 2013), has moulded narrow conceptions of educational technology for too long. This is a discourse that positions technology (by any name), as the main driver of social change, and ultimately as the driver of how people learn. What this viewpoint often omits however are the complex political, social and economic factors that bring technologies into being and that serve to support a particular power and culture. Of more concern still is a trend towards omitting people altogether. This is an argument I pick up later through Ritzer (1998). If a simple and basic logic: that 'use of technology' might be applied to guarantee improved learning, is what underpins government policy and university strategies, then any changes in the terminology we use every few years will make very little difference.

In 2002 Chris Jones raised the question: 'is there a policy for networked learning?' This same question might have been asked repeatedly since then about e-learning or Technology Enhanced Learning, and similar conclusions could be drawn:

> Choices about how to use new technologies need to be infused with a more sharply critical edge. One that begins by asking what social interests are driving the agenda that hides behind the technology and that begins to map out alternative visions of technological possibilities more centred in the needs of education and learning (Jones, 2002)

In over a decade since, much has happened to further ideas for open education, as new technological platforms and human social networks have developed. Yet, in another sense, little has changed to provide us with a coherent and fertile theoretical space for educational technology policy development. There has, for example, been a new name provided for our practice every few years that is said to have 'subsumed' the previous one:

> E-learning is starting to subsume and replace a number of previously used terms such as communications and information technologies (C&IT or ICT), information and learning technologies (ILT), networked learning, telelearning or telematics and instructional technology (Edgehill Strategy, 2005)

> The concept of e-learning is thus becoming subsumed into a wider discussion of how learning can be enhanced by more effective and far-reaching uses of digital technologies (JISC, 2009)

> The move from 'e-learning' to 'enhancing learning through the use of technology' is now well embedded and recognised (JISC, 2012)

One might argue that in simply changing the terminology it is rather like papering over the cracks in a sub standard property. To do a thorough job we would consider the structure and base (Marx, 1867), and work from there to change the whole space to become more habitable to accommodate a diversity of theory and practice. In a fertile discursive environment there is room for all of these terms to be explored, defined and developed, rather than to assume one concept must 'subsume' the others. We can then critically acknowledge the complexities of discourse, as a social practice that connects technology, language and learning. From here we might seek a more critical, theoretical and 'fertile trans-disciplinary ground' (Parchoma & Keefer, 2012). There is though a tendency in government policy language to tidy and order ways of building knowledge into linear processes, detached chunks of learning and neat parcels of practice. The real human labour actions can get pushed aside in a quest to tell people positive-sounding outcomes from certain approaches towards technologies. People may not believe these 'operational' concepts, but they can be justified in 'getting the job done' (Marcuse, 1964). I propose then a closer examination of some constraints in policy language that can hinder development of a 'sharply critical edge' (Jones, 2002) to debates about educational technology.

A Trans-disciplinary Methodology in Corpus-Based CDA

In a trans-disciplinary approach I link critical social theory about technology, language and learning with a corpus-based Critical Discourse Analysis (CDA) of UK policy texts for educational technology between 1997 and 2012. A 'corpus' is the models of good e-learning practice Develop the effective use of technology to enable and support work-based learning Explore and support t rity of the data held to support service delivery. Effective use of technology can help deliver more secure and more joined-up public services nd staff development, helping institutions make effective use of technology for teaching and learning, research, administration, marketing an e resources that were identified confirm that the effective use of technology to enhance assessment for learning as well as the assessment o earners in a cohesive way, making efficient and effective use of technology to support academic, social and pastoral activity. Using open so IISC has had an important role in promoting the effective use of technology in the area of staff development and the role ICT has affecting sta resources to provide a valuable insight into the effective use of technology in curriculum design and delivery processes. An unrivalled sourc

Fig. 2.1 An example of how lines of text in the corpus are searched

name given to a collection, or bank of texts gathered for analysis. Understanding a corpus of words as 'net-like' (Hoey, 1991) and reflective of the 'concerns of the society which produces the texts' (Hunston, 2002: 13) is helpful in order to visualise a fluid interplay of the elements of technology and learning, within the language of policy. In a quantitative analysis of patterns of discourse, I examined through corpus linguistics (Baker, 2006; Scott, 1997), 2.5 million words of UK policy.

'Use' was one of the top word count frequencies, appearing 8131 times in the whole corpus. I chose to focus on these 8131 instances of 'use' to examine more closely the way that 'technology' and other words cluster around 'use'. 'Technology' appeared 6079 times, 'the use of' 1770 times and 'use of technology' 350 times. Below in Fig. 2.1 a few lines of text show a small section of a pattern that was often repeated, with 'effective use of' actually appearing 185 times.

The 'effective use of technology' in Fig. 2.1 is repeatedly followed by the assumption of a positive learning or assessment outcome through phrases like 'to enable and support', 'help deliver', and 'to enhance'. This was a common pattern replicated around 'use of technology' or 'the use of technology', where an exchange value for improving learning would then follow. The inference is that each gain for learning is universal and the same for everyone. However examining lines of text is really just a first step towards looking more closely at how meaning is determined by readers.

Much has been written on detailed forms of linguistic analysis. Persistent, dominant discourses in education policy have already been extensively critiqued through Critical Discourse Analysis (Fairclough, 2007; Mautner, 2005; Mulderrig, 2011), though less so, in terms of educational technology policy. Studies have revealed how ideology can communicate one particular meaning in the service of power (Foucault, 1984) and marginalise others. Gramsci's ideas on hegemony (1971) show humans internalise values from powerful prevailing social discourses. CDA can reveal how students, teachers, technologists and technology are positioned in a relationship of production and consumption by 'anonymous forces' (Ross, 2004: 456). To further investigate findings in my 'use' corpus, I undertook a more qualitative CDA to examine 'Transitivity' (Halliday, 1994), which I explain below, with regard to Halliday's Systemic Functional Linguistics (SFL). There is not scope here to describe this form of analysis in detail, but it considers the grammatical processes taking place in statements to locate the Participants (whom), the verbal Processes (what happened) and the Circumstances (how, where, when). As a generic example, taking the statement: 'a student is learning at university' the constituent grammatical elements can be located, and named in this way:

In Table 2.1 a reader can be quite clear about whom, the Participant (a student) is undertaking the Process (is learning) and in what Circumstance (at university).

Table 2.1 A generic example to show how grammatical elements are located

A student	is learning	at university
Participant (a noun)	Process (a verb)	Circumstances (an adverb)

Table 2.2 A second generic example to show how the grammatical elements located are different

Universities	are	places of learning (for students)
Participant (a noun)	Process (a verb)	Participant (a noun)

Table 2.3 Halliday's process types

Process type	Meaning—some examples	Participants
Material	creating, changing, doing (to), and acting	Actor, Goal, Scope
Mental	feeling, thinking, sensing	Senser, Phenomenon
Verbal	saying, commanding, asking, offering	Sayer, Receiver, Verbiage, Target
Existential	existing or happening	Existent
Relational	having attributes, identity, and symbolizing	Carrier /Attribute Token/Value
Behavioural	behaving, smiling, yawning, laughing	Behaver/Behaviour

Each of these elements is labelled with their grammatical names to show if they are a noun, verb or an adverb. A key point is that this is not the only way such a statement might be written. Similar words may appear in a slightly different order of grammatical elements to reveal quite a different meaning, and conceal who exactly is involved. Taking another statement: 'universities are places of learning', when this is labelled in Table 2.2, the elements are not so apparent:

The Participants (universities) and (places of learning) are both names of things (nouns). They are connected in a relationship (are), which is the process (verb). To reveal any presence of a human subject, further information is required because this has not been supplied. By adding 'for students', currently in brackets, this restores a human presence. To break down the structure of educational technology discourse, to better understand the meaning through a transitivity analysis, some new terminology needs to be introduced.

In Table 2.3 below six broad categories of Process type (Halliday, 1994: 109–143) are identified along with examples of their meanings and their related Participants.

So returning once more to the first example from Table 2.1, when labelled in a transitivity analysis using Halliday's categories from Table 2.3, it would look like this:

In Table 2.4, it is the Process 'is learning' that defines what kind of process type is taking place. In this case it is a Mental process, to do with thinking, therefore 'a student', as the participant, is labelled as 'Senser'. If the statement had said 'a student is talking' the labels would have been Sayer for 'a student' and the process type would have been Verbal.

Table 2.4 A mental process type

A student	is learning	at university
Senser	Process: Mental	Circumstances

Table 2.5 A verbal process about 'the effective use of technology' conceals other labour actions

The resources that were identified	confirm that	the effective use of technology	to enhance
Sayer	Process: Verbal	Receiver	Process: Material
assessment for learning as well as the assessment of learning	can improve		
Goal	Process: Material		
the effectiveness of teaching approaches	and	enhance	the student learning experience
Goal		Process: Material	Goal

Discussion and Analysis

To demonstrate how this aids discussion in the educational technology community, I will now provide a series of examples from policy statements in my corpus and comment on ways these conceal human labour, attributing processes instead to statements about resources, technology, assessment or policy.

In Table 2.5 above, *nominalisation* occurs. Nominalisation can be noticed where nouns stand in for verbal processes (Jørgensen & Phillips , 2002: 83). A common effect is a reduction in human agency. It becomes hard to detect who a proposition refers to, or who has declared it to be so. In Table 2.5 'the resources that were identified' take the place of the labour actions of a person, as they 'confirm' the rest of the statement. 'The resources that were identified' is labelled as Sayer because a Verbal process follows this in: 'confirm that'. It is: 'the effective use of technology' that the wording suggests is: 'to enhance' assessment and: 'can improve' 'the effectiveness of teaching approaches'. There are two instances of the Material process: 'to enhance'. After the first of these, 'assessment for learning as well as the assessment of learning' is the Goal. After the second 'enhance' the final Goal is 'the student learning experience'. The preceding 'the' earmarks students as if they all experience assessment in the same way, not in diverse contexts as individuals. It also places students at the very end of a long statement that begins with 'the resources' determining what follows. So we cannot identify any of the decision makers, teaching or support staff in this statement that, at the end, claims to enhance 'the student learning experience'. In summary, liberal sounding policy when broken down in this way can help reveal the hidden agendas of economic improvement, but these quickly become detached from the social and political choices—and indeed the human beings, who made these.

Table 2.6 Material processes suggest 'innovative use of technology' can 'enhance', and 'improve' 'the student experience'

Innovative use of technology	can enhance	learning	and improve	the student experience
Actor	Process: Material	Goal	Process: Material	Goal

Table 2.7 Material processes suggest 'the use of technology' can 'increase', 'support' and 'foster' learning

The use of technology	can increase	accessibility and flexibility of learning		
Actor	Process: Material	Goal		
and	support	resources,	address	equality and diversity issues,
	Process: Material	Goal	Process: Verbal	Verbiage
and	foster	lifelong learning		
	Process: Material	Goal		

In Table 2.6 above, once more, it is a textual construction: 'innovative use of technology' and not a human being, that through Material processes: 'can enhance' 'learning', 'and improve' 'the student experience'. As in Table 2.5, 'the student experience' appears again at the end, students are treated as if they share a common identity and are acted upon by technology.

In Table 2.7 'the use of technology' appears to take responsibility for an extraordinary number of labour actions that we would usually attribute to people. We are to understand through a Material process that it 'can increase' 'accessibility and flexibility of learning' and 'support' 'resources'. In a Verbal process it 'can address' 'equality and diversity issues' and in another Material process, it can 'foster' 'lifelong learning'.

In Table 2.8 some similar claims about what 'the use of technology' achieves on our behalf are illustrated, but this time there is a curious circular outcome where, 'the use of technology' undertakes a series of Material processes 'to create' and 'to improve' areas that would normally involve the labour of university staff, but then these actions seem ultimately 'to support' 'more effective use of technology'. It should be emphasised that examples discussed here all originate from different strategies and not the same document, revealing interesting repetition across many writers of policy. There seems to be a shared impression of guaranteed positive results from 'the use of technology', regardless of the context.

In Table 2.9 though it is a document, 'The Strategy', labelled Sayer, which 'proposes'. Once more, nominalisation prevents the establishment of human agency. 'The Strategy' surely cannot determine these things for us, can it? Looking carefully at the Receiver (or goal) that the Strategy proposes to enhance, it is all encompassing, suggesting positive change to 'the learning opportunities for all learners'. This

Table 2.8 Material processes suggest 'the use of technology' can 'create' and 'improve' as well as 'support' an even more 'effective use of technology'

The use of technology	to create	digital archives
Actor	Proc: Material	Goal
to improve	documentation of practice	and
Proc: Material	Goal	
to support	curricular developments	as well as more effective use of technology
Proc: Material	Goal	Circ

Table 2.9 'The Strategy' undertakes this verbal process

The Strategy	proposes	to enhance	the learning opportunities of all learners
Sayer	Process: Verbal	Process: Material	Receiver
through the appropriate use of elearning			
Circumstances			

cannot be the case for *all*, and indeed how would we know, but there is also a context, which defines this expectation within what is described as 'the appropriate use of elearning'. Whilst sounding common sense, readers have no further information to know the confines of 'the appropriate use'. This is a phrase that appears often in my corpus, but remains ambiguous. It may hold fast instrumental economic values, or perhaps we might understand 'appropriate use of elearning' as a critical space we might re-occupy, in order to bring a more diverse account from the educational community. To do so, people would need to reconsider the tendency in policy discourse to place 'the' before 'appropriate use' and instead promote more explicit accounts of *who* it is that really proposes something, rather than hide behind a strategy. If we do not, we simply reinforce a deterministic approach that allows one universal blueprint for educational technology to persist.

In the final example above in Table 2.10, a Relational Identifying process is shown. 'The key aims of the TEL Strategy' are labelled as the Value. Through the Relational process 'are' this is identified by the Token, 'to ensure that technology is used appropriately, effectively and efficiently'. The Token refers to the participant in the clause that embodies the other concept, or represents it. The other concept may be something more general and is labelled as Value. A Relational/identifying process is also reversible and as such is rather like placing an equals sign between two concepts. It might look like this:

'The key aims of the TEL Strategy' = 'to ensure that technology is used appropriately, effectively and efficiently'

In a sense this statement could be said to be complete if it stopped here. The main agenda has been stated. Yet the text continues on, and slowly reveals the many labour actions (Material processes) that are overshadowed by this first part of the Relational clause. The full term of Technology Enhanced Learning is not mentioned. Instead a

Table 2.10 a relational process about technology conceals other labour actions

The key aims of the TEL Strategy	are		to ensure that technology is used
Value	Process: Relational/Identifying		Token
appropriately, effectively and efficiently	to support		student learning and development;
	Process: Material		Goal
support	staff in the delivery of the curriculum;	prepare	students
Process: Material	Goal	Process: Material	Goal
to function	in a technologically-rich and changing world;		enhance
Proc: Material	Goale		Proc: Material
existing provision;	exploit		new market opportunities.
Goal	Proc: Material		Goal

TEL Strategy condenses this meaning. However, the key aims are clearly linked to a belief by policy makers that this is what a Strategy for TEL represents. The strategy should 'ensure' it, but who decides what this use of technology looks like and feels like in the multiplicity of practice? Reading further along, there are human labour actions that are intended to 'support' and 'prepare' students and staff, but ultimately the agenda is to exploit 'new market opportunities'. Whilst universities need to remain viable what is deemed 'appropriate use of technology' for student and staff learning should not be confined within 'new market opportunities'.

Rationalisation and Performativity Enact the Student Experience

Considering the examples above, a deceptively spacious language promises much. Yet in Table 2.5, in terms of flexibility and tailoring for individual students (Greener & Perriton, 2005: 72), we find reference to 'the student experience' appears right at the end of a long paragraph. Student subjective diversity is contained in a singular, universal representation: 'the student experience', as shown in examples below, whether discussing e-learning, or Technology Enhanced Learning (TEL):

> Raise the profile of examples of TEL for enhancement of **the student experience**
> (University of Westminster TEL Strategy 2008–2011)

> Provide a valid mechanism for the recognition of excellence in the use and implementation of e-learning to enhance **the student experience**
> (University of Huddersfield E-Learning Strategy 2008–2013)

Choices made in language, to express ideas about technology in education, frequently remain unquestioned because they are framed in a simplified notion of 'common sense' (Gramsci, 1971) Confronting these structures draws attention to the fact that the language of competitive economic markets is not the only way to discuss educational technology, it has simply been the dominant voice, and this can be changed by a networked learning community. To strengthen and re-build a structural base for networked learning, it is necessary firstly, for the 'hidden humans', to confront a dominant rationalisation in policy discourse which focuses *only* on economically useful knowledge. Secondly, we can learn from an application of theory to these examples, to notice where the very principles of modernity that social theorists have warned us about, are enacted before our eyes.

Weber discussed the dehumanising effect of bureaucratic decision-making (Weber, 1930), based on a rationality that transcends other forms of human action, in an impersonal application of the systemic principles of modernity: 'Rational domination suppresses individual freedom and spontaneity, and threatens to enclose society within an iron cage' (Edgar and Sedgwick, 2007: 224). In Tables 2.5 and 2.6, and also in the two university strategies above diverse learning experiences of individual students is rationally contained within: 'the student experience'. Nominalisation freezes and encloses the 'becoming' of all students. This phrase hides the human challenges, risks, commitment and resistance involved in learning (Dall'Alba, 2009: 43). Taking forward the ideas of Weber, Ritzer has since described a continuation and even acceleration of this process, termed the 'McDonaldisation' of society (Ritzer, 1998: 42). Citing the fast food restaurant as an example, it represents the components of rationalisation such as efficiency, predicatabilty, quantification and control, via the substitution of non-human for human technology (Ritzer, 1998: 46). Yet, despite economies achieved, ultimately a form of irrationality emerges from such rationalisation (Ritzer, 1998: 54). We can confront this in linguistic examples, where as shown in Table 2.8, we encountered a curious circular outcome: 'the use of technology' is ultimately expected 'to support' 'more effective use of technology'. In this process though, the human creation of digital archives, the people who work to improve documentation, and indeed those who support curricular developments, are enclosed within a linguistic cage. In Table 2.10 staff and student labour is trapped between the 'key aims of the TEL strategy' and an exploitation of 'new market opportunities'. Would Weber, I wonder, be surprised at such visible enactments of his theory, even now?

The division of society from technology, and a severing of human labour from tools, does though become a major obstacle for future advancement. In the context of higher education, extreme rationality within policy discourse starts to create a restricted context of practice where lecturers and students eventually become less able to innovate. Given that the aspirations of a globalised society, which requires individuals to adopt values such as entrepreneurism and innovation, this form of discourse is ultimately self defeating. A political emphasis on economic gain, as 'performativity', has encouraged professionals to compete to 'realise their potential', but this approach also marginalises less instrumental routes to knowledge in higher education. Barnett discusses 'supercomplexity' and the problem of universities losing their way, as enormous amounts of data on performance are generated, but much of the language of 'excellence' has little real *content* (Barnett, 2000: 2).

Small wonder perhaps, when as in Table 2.5, it is 'the resources that were identified' that confirm (on our behalf) all of the other factors, and the human content has been emptied from this discourse.

In UK policy (despite changes in government) educational technology has continually been a significant part of narratives of, for example: modernisation, standards, effectiveness, enhancement of the public sector to improve UK competitiveness in the global economy. Value has been focused though on *only* the aspects of education (and educational technology) believed to support these aspirations, missing out others. This links with points from Ritzer that this form of rationalising eventually moves humans towards irrationality, serving to limit and compromise their actions (Ritzer, 1998: 55). Policy that is aiming for actively engaged, high performing staff who utilise technology to innovate, omits those who might actually make it happen. Theses texts sever our conscious human activities from the performance of technology, in a discourse that seeks only economic gain.

Economically Useful Knowledge Omits Human Material Practices

If economically-based values are attributed to technology in language to extract a maximum quantitative return, this colonises other more developmental discourses about technological learning and human material practices that rely on debate. Furthermore, this creates a detachment from policy, where lecturers and students can fail to recognise themselves in it, and thus they fail to engage with it. If there are apparently only positive outcomes from a use of technology, as a means to an end, then it would seem there is little left *for* people to write about, or debate. Yet debate is crucial if educational technology is to be engaged with research agendas in academic subjects and not become detached from people, as only a simple external fix to improve learning. To contribute to a more networked approach, where humans are at the centre of debates about learning, I draw on a constant from Marxist theory. This is the solid point of reference, through political economy, where real people and their social relations and productive labour in specific historic periods are the focus. I acknowledge a constant need to 'examine the relationship between the capitalist mode of production and the specific problem' (Greener & Perriton, 2005: 69) to uncover underlying power dynamics.

The examples from my corpus take as their point of departure a single argument, that technology as an external solution might be applied to learning, to guarantee additional performance. An 'exchange value' gained may be the promise of a competitive edge or additional skills, as a form of 'capital' (Marx, 1867). However, to choose other routes, where 'economically useful knowledge' (Jessop, 2008: 4) is not the primary concern, is almost not considered a choice at all (Dahlberg, 2004). Whether technology can improve efficiency is not called into question in this study. Instead the more pressing problem is raised that this economical feature alone should not be considered representative of the diverse possibilities for human learning, via connections with technology and other people, across multiple networks of human and non-human actors (Latour, 1992). There is a danger that a base structure of economic policy supports a compressed version of how students might experience *technology*, *language* and *learning*. Deceptively spacious language marginalises dialectical realities and material connections (Sørensen, 2009: 193). In short, the political discourse seems to disjoin and displace people, from their material practices of learning with technology. New technological practice now takes place in universities, but to assume a direct link with learning misses out the question of how technology actually yields an increase in knowledge, as a process of inquiry and critique. Understanding enhancement too, only in terms of additional value, is restrictive, if technologies can extend us (McLuhan, 2005) to overcome endless limitations. We might consider that 'everything is technology' (Braudel, 1985), when all around us, it shapes our history, knowledge and individual lives. We in turn shape it, in multiple ways (Wajcman, 2002). 'Things' of all types form repositories of, and for, our learning, construct our social worlds (Sezneva, 2007) and contain 'traces' of us (Lash, 2002). Given these broader understandings, human pedagogical interactions with technologies across space and time are far from simply enhanced, or easily categorised as: 'the student experience', irrespective of the claims of government policies. Closely linked to both technology and learning, is the language people use to describe their interactions with knowledge. How people talk and write about technology, more specifically, educational technology reveals the values they apply to it (Fairclough, 2007; Feenberg, 2003). Yet, for understanding language, humans have developed terms that distinguish different aspects. Discourse is the 'in use' element of language and, as such, is a broad concept, because it co-evolves with all other elements it touches in society. For technology, there are less adequate terms for its heterogeneous and temporal qualities and our own levels of understanding. It presents a problem for learning though, if in policy language, the cultural and political elements of technological knowledge cease to exist, and technology means only constant improvement.

The Technology-Language-Learning Nexus

CDA has sometimes been criticised for putting forward only negative representations of texts and ideologies (Breeze, 2013). However such analysis is not only an empowering approach to reveal ways that language may restrict conceptual space, it also provides a discursive opportunity for new possibilities to learn and move on from a deceptive space. If educational technology has been 'enframed' (Heidegger, 1977) in rational policy texts, through a hegemony of 'common sense' (Gramsci, 1971) then, through CDA, we might demonstrate these restrictions. This can lead to a point where it is hard to move forward beyond having identified what seems to be 'going on'. We have exposed an ideology, now what can be done? Here I suggest that thinking of educational technology as a *technology–language-learning* nexus can contribute to a more diverse participatory culture.

Connections between technology, language and learning are dialectical (Fairclough, 2007) and mutually constitutive (Wajcman, 2002) in shaping how learners experience new media across personal networks, in relationships of power and ideology, but also of possibility. A technology-language-learning nexus is a broader critical base to theoretically differentiate educational technology and resist simplistic, linear determinism in language. If perceptions of technology for learning have become distorted through 'the logics of profit and domination' (Matthewman, 2011: 38; Jessop, 2008; Sennett, 2006), more critical pedagogies (Freire, 1969) provides 'counterlogics' (McLaren, 1994) to linear approaches. For this to work though, humans need to make a conscious choice to be present in a higher education policy discourse that has currently replaced them with technologies or strategies. Rather like the situation described by Ritzer, where non-human technology replaces humans in a fast food context, rational policy language places all of the emphasis on the acts of non human resources. This has implications for academic identity, recognition and credit, and 'hidden' academic workloads (Gregory & Lodge, 2015). Human labour is taken for granted and not even credited in statements about learning and teaching. A critical awareness of belonging in a *technology–language–learning* nexus can help people avoid such alienation from closed relationships in policy discourse and offers conceptual space in an individual context for a broader personal perception of educational technology.

Territory and University Responsibility

Global capitalism has strongly territorialised the contemporary university (Hayes & Jandrić, 2014). Yet, there are also oppositional cultures in tension and therefore this 'territory' is always subject to dispute. Some discuss an 'anthropology of policy', where policy documents are not simply external forces, or confined to texts, but rather they are 'productive, performative and continually contested' domains of meaning (Shore, Wright, & Però, 2011: 1). Yet if academics and students ignore the wider political and social context of information and communication technologies, then the discourse of only positive gain, from external instruments, remains dominant. A cautionary note, as Hayes and Jandrić (2014) point out, is that even if academics fail to question this logic, 'information and communication technologies will never ignore academics' (Hayes & Jandrić, 2014). Recalling the ideas of Barnett, we can place this observation, and my analysis, in the wider context of examining the role and values of contemporary universities. Changes in modern capitalism have altered our very ideas of what the values of the University are. Barnett however, provides us with the notion of 'supercomplexity', which refers to multiple frames of understanding, of action and of self-identity (Barnett, 2000: 77). Barnett suggests a triple role for the university where firstly, it actually generates supercomplexity in part, secondly this disturbs the whole person, and therefore finally, the university has a responsibility to help us cope with this situation and make reflexive interventions in the world (Barnett, 2000: 79). Yet Gregory and

Lodge (2015) argue that the lack of functional university policy to address excessive academic workloads now raise questions of risk to institutions and long term sustainability. Cultural change is needed to provide university-wide transparency and well-communicated expectations (Gregory & Lodge, 2015: 11). Academia therefore plays an important role in either reproducing or challenging power relationships through policy. Barnett suggests that whilst supercomplexity deprives us of a 'value anchorage', the values of rational critical dialogue that helped to generate supercomplexity can also help to keep it in its place (Barnett, 2000: 83). This provides us with a new space of possibility where we might even use the very political discourse that disguises our material practices, in new ways to begin to restore our human visibility.

A dominant ideology need not remain 'fixed'. To avoid closure through terminology and keep plural routes for networked human relationships open involves conscious decisions in how we each speak and write about technology, in language about learning. The choices people make and what they write holds the key to re-establishing their place to acknowledge their labour within the policy discourse used to discuss technology. Ideologies that are general and abstract maintain a dominant discourse therefore I suggest people might actively choose to write more specific representations about their material encounters into higher education policy. Below I provide an example of how the statement in Table 2.8 might be rewritten, urging others also to further this research by seeking concrete textual imaginaries of alternative discourses, where people are explicitly present:

> The people who have written this university strategy to support students in their learning and staff in their teaching are listed below with their contact details. As a group we present some aims within this document for ongoing discussions about support of our students in their learning and our colleagues in allocating time to their development of the curriculum. We each hope that you will find the recommendations we have shared to be relevant in a changing world that provides us all with opportunities to support our collaborative and individual engagement with technologies for learning.

This is one suggested approach to begin to write humans back into the script of higher education policy. It is simply irrational for us not to be there.

Conclusion

In conclusion, whilst *Networked Learning*, *e-learning* and *Technology Enhanced Learning* are all terms that might further critical theoretical debate about how people make connections with technology, and with each other, for learning in higher education, they often act as static markers within discourse. Yet curiously, these terms are also often attributed, in common sense policy statements, with enacting human labour processes to improve or enhance learning. When academic workload is already a 'silent barrier' to the implementation of TEL strategies (Gregory & Lodge, 2015), such logic seems to be institutionally self-defeating. Dehumanising forms of written policy effectively separate people and their labour from the assumed achievements of technology, in a higher education context where a lack of functional university policy further contributes to 'hidden workloads' (Gregory & Lodge, 2015: 10). The discourse promises much but is in fact deceptively spacious, because both staff and students are missing from it. Repeated, simplified statements may reinforce a message that this domain of meaning is inevitable, but we need to reoccupy this territory.

> If part of the 'work of policy' is to classify and organise people and ideas in new ways, then it becomes easy to understand why policies can become such powerful vehicles for social change. Policies can serve as instruments for consolidating the legitimacy of an existing social order or they can provide the rationale for 'regime change' and the subversion of an established order (Shore et al., 2011: 3).

In examining the anthropology of policy, texts can provide windows on political processes to observe how actors, agents and technologies interact in regimes of power. Policy is an organising principle, aligning these relations in particular ways that can appear to be permanent. Yet if staff and students do intervene to actively re-write a human presence back into TEL policy, this offers a powerful route for subversion.

Whilst networked learning, like the other terminologies has also been the victim of ambiguities in policy, discussed often in terms of efficiency and technical issues, less as a political choice (Jones, 2002), networks are relational. They are distinctly different politically and organisationally from either bureaucratic hierarchies or the anarchy of the market (Thompson, 1991). As such, networked learning offers an alternative to a more commonly found deterministic approach in higher education policy that repeatedly frames technology as providing a form of 'exchange value' (Marx, 1867). If the last decade of policy continuities has too easily dispensed with the tentacles of history, in a tireless series of 'makeovers' to improve and transform terminology to meet economic demands, now is a good time to transcend the limitations of conventional thinking. Radical rethinking means addressing the language we use as a network of relations, to avoid a continuation of 'existing assumptions under a different name' (Hall et al., 2013). One idea need not subsume another. Instead each may support the other, within a critical awareness of a technology-language-learning nexus. This informs a broader theoretical underpinning for educational technology, as part of a cooperative and trans-disciplinary endeavour, in our networked learning community.

References

Baker, P. (2006). *Using corpora in discourse analysis*. London: Continuum.
Ball, S. J. (1999). Educational Reform and the Struggle for the Soul of the Teacher!. Faculty of Education, Hong Kong Institute of Educational Research, Chinese University of Hong Kong.
Barnett, R. (2000). *Realising the University in an age of supercomplexity*. Oxford: SRHE and Open University Press.
Braudel, F. (1985). *Civilisation and capitalism 15th–18th century: The structures of everyday life: The limits of the possible* (Vol. 1). London: William Collins.
Breeze, R. (2013). Critical discourse analysis and its critics. *Pragmatics, 21*(4), 493.

Campbell, J. L., & Pedersen, O. K. (Eds.). (2001). *The rise of neoliberalism and institutional analysis*. Princeton, NJ: Princeton University Press.

Dahlberg, L. (2004). Internet research tracings: Towards non-reductionist methodology. *Journal of Computer Mediated Communication, 7*(1). Retrieved September 24, 2013, from http://jcmc.indiana.edu/vol7/missue1/dahlberg.html.

Dall'Alba, G. (2009). Learning professional ways of being: Ambiguities of becoming. *Educational Philosophy and Theory, 41*(1), 34–45.

Edgar, A , & Sedgwick, P. (Eds.). (2007). Cultural theory: The key concepts. Routledge.

Edgehill e-Learning Strategy (2005). Quoted in Hayes, S. (2015). Counting on use of technology to enhance learning. In Critical Learning in Digital Networks (pp. 15–36). Springer International Publishing.

Fairclough, N. (2007). Global capitalism and change in higher education: Dialectics of language and practice, technology, ideology. In BAAL conference, Edinburgh.

Feenberg, A. (2003). *What is philosophy of technology?* Retrieved September 24, 2013, from http://www.sfu.ca/~andrewf/komaba.htm.

Foucault, M. (1984). *Power/knowledge*. New York, NY: Pantheon.

Freire, P. (1969). *Pedagogy of the oppressed*. New York, NY: Continuum.

Goodyear, P., Hodgson, V., & McConnell, D. (2004). Research on networked learning: An overview. In P. Goodyear, S. Banks, V. Hodgson, & D. McConnell (Eds.), *Advances in research on networked learning*. Dordrecht: Kluwer Academic Publishers.

Graham, P. (2001). Space: Irrealis objects in technology policy and their role in a new political economy. *Discourse and Society, 12*(6), 761–788.

Gramsci, A. (1971). *Selections from the prison notebooks*. London: Lawrence & Wishart.

Greener, I., & Perriton, L. (2005). The political economy of networked learning communities in higher education. *Studies in Higher Education, 30*(1), 67–79.

Gregory, M.S.J. & Lodge, J. M. (2015). Academic workload: the silent barrier to the implementation of technology-enhanced learning strategies in higher education, Distance Education.

Hall, S., Massey, D., & Rustin, M. (2013). After neoliberalism: Analysing the present. *Soundings, 53*(53), 8–22.

Halliday, M. A. K. (1994). *An introduction to functional grammar* (2nd ed.). London: Arnold.

Harvey, D. (2005). *A brief history of neoliberalism*. Oxford: Oxford University Press.

Hayes, S. (2015). *Evicted by words: Seeking to reoccupy educational technology policy texts*. Retrieved September 21, 2015, from http://ipa2015.sciencesconf.org/resource/page/id/76.

Hayes, S., & Jandrić, P. (2014). Who is really in charge of contemporary education? People and technologies in, against and beyond the neoliberal university. *Open Review of Educational Research, 1*(1), 193–210.

Heidegger, M. (1977). *The question concerning technology and other essays*. New York, London: Garland Publishing.

Hoey, M. (1991). *Pattern of lexis in text*. Oxford: Oxford University Press.

Hunston, S. (2002). *Corpora in applied linguistics*. Cambridge: Cambridge University Press.

Jessop, B. (2008). *The knowledge based economy*. Article prepared for Naked Punch. Retrieved October 3, 2013, from http://www.nakedpunch.com/.

Joint Information Systems Committee. (2009). *Effective practice in a digital age*. Retrieved October 1, 2013, from http://www.jisc.ac.uk/publications/programmerelated/2009/effective-practicedigitalage.aspx.

Joint Information Systems Committee (JISC). (2012). *JISC strategy 2010–2012*. Retrieved October 1, 2013, from http://www.jisc.ac.uk/aboutus/strategy/strategy1012/context.aspx.

Jones, C. (2002). Is there a policy for networked learning? In Proceedings of the Networked Learning 2002 Conference, 26–28 March 2002, Sheffield, UK.

Jones, C. (2012). Networked learning, stepping beyond the Net Generation and Digital Natives. In *Exploring the theory, pedagogy and practice of networked learning* (pp. 27–41). New York, NY: Springer.

Jørgensen, M. W., & Phillips, L. J. (2002). Discourse analysis as theory and method. Sage.

Lash, S. (2002). *Critique of information*. London: Sage.

Latour, B. (1992). Where are the missing masses? The sociology of a few mundane artifacts. In *Shaping technology/building society: Studies in sociotechnical change* (pp. 225–258). Cambridge, MA: The MIT Press.

Marcuse, H. (1964). *One-dimensional man: Studies in the Ideology of Advanced Industrial Society*. London: Routledge.

Marx, K. (1867). Capitalism and the modern labour process. Capital, volume 1. In R. C. Scharff & V. Dusek (Eds.), *(2003). Philosophy of technology: The technological condition: An anthology*. Oxford: Blackwell.

Massey, D. (2013). Vocabularies of the economy. *Soundings, 54*(54), 9–22. Retrieved October 1, 2013, from http://www.lwbooks.co.uk/journals/soundings/contents.html.

Matthewman, S. (2011). *Technology and social theory*. New York, NY: Palgrave.

Mautner, G. (2005). The entrepreneurial university: A discursive profile of a higher education buzzword. *Critical Discourse Studies, 2*(2), 95–120.

McLaren, P. (1994). *Life in schools*. New York, NY: Longman.

McLuhan, M. (2005). *Understanding media: Lectures and interviews*. Cambridge, MA: MIT Press.

Mulderrig, J. (2011). The grammar of governance. *Critical Discourse Studies, 8*(1), 45–68.

Parchoma, G., & Keefer, J. M. (2012). Transdisciplinary research in technology enhanced/networked learning practices. In V. Hodgson, C. Jones, M. de Laat, D. McConnell, T. Ryberg, & P. Sloep (Eds.), *Proceedings of the 8th International Conference on Networked Learning*. Maastricht: Lancaster University.

Ritzer, G. (1998). The Weberian theory of rationalization and the McDonaldization of contemporary society. In *Illuminating social life: Classical and contemporary theory revisited* (pp. 37–61). London: Sage.

Ross, P. (2004). Globalization and the closing of the universe of discourse: The contemporary relevance of Marcuse's Marxism. *The European Legacy: Toward New Paradigms, 9*(4), 455–467.

Scott, M. (1997). PC analysis of key words—And key key words. *System, 25*(2), 233–245.

Sennett, R. (2006). *The culture of the new capitalism*. Yale, CT: Yale University Press.

Sezneva, O. (2007). We have never been German: The economy of digging in Russian Kaliningrad. In C. Calhoun & R. Sennett (Eds.), *Practicing culture* (pp. 13–34). Abingdon: Routledge.

Shore, C., Wright, S., & Però, D. (Eds.). (2011). *Policy worlds: Anthropology and the analysis of contemporary power* (Vol. 14). Oxford: Berghahn Books.

Sørensen, E. (2009). *The materiality of learning: Technology and knowledge in educational practice*. New York, NY: Cambridge University Press.

Thompson, G. (Ed.). (1991). *Markets, hierarchies and networks: The coordination of social life*. London: Sage.

Wajcman, J. (2002). Addressing technological change: The challenge to social theory. *Current Sociology, 5*(3), 347–363.

Weber, M. (1930). *The protestant ethic and the spirit of capitalism*. London: George Allen & Unwin.

Chapter 3
Boundary Brokers: Mobile Policy Networks, Database Pedagogies, and Algorithmic Governance in Education

Ben Williamson

Spaces and Subjects of Governance

Contemporary educational governance in the United Kingdom is increasingly taking place through cross-sector 'policy networks' and 'policy mobilities' rather than solely through the central bureaucratic organs of the state. Though education policy remains the responsibility of government departments, it is being influenced by other non-political organizations and actors. The main aim of this chapter is to examine these developments as exemplifying a shift in the 'governable spaces' of contemporary education policy. It offers a novel twist on 'networked learning' in that it queries the cross-sectoral organizational networks increasingly driving learning agendas. In particular it offers a critical examination of how one specific network is proposing to mine and analyse digital data from learners' online networked activities in order to predict and pre-empt their future progress and outcomes. In this sense, the emerging forms of data-based networked learning examined in this chapter, and the organizations helping to position these technologies as a policy agenda, represent a form of 'future-tense' governance of education, where the emphasis is on governing, shaping and sculpting learners' future lives and their lifelong learning trajectories. In particular, the focus is on a 'policy network' of 'boundary organizations.' Boundary organizations are conceptualized as 'intermediaries' that work to bridge borders between different professional, disciplinary or sectoral systems, for example, the scientific system and the political system (Guston, 2001; Grek, 2014). My own emphasis is on boundary organizations that operate cross-sectorally, and that combine resources and ideas from across political, social scientific and digital R&D fields in order to construct compelling visions about the future of educational governance.

B. Williamson (✉)
School of Education, University of Stirling, Stirling, UK
e-mail: ben.williamson@stir.ac.uk

© Springer International Publishing Switzerland 2016
T. Ryberg et al. (eds.), *Research, Boundaries, and Policy in Networked Learning*, Research in Networked Learning, DOI 10.1007/978-3-319-31130-2_3

It is important to state at the outset that 'governance' and 'governing' are two separate though closely interrelated concepts. The term 'governance,' taken from public policy and political studies, signifies a shift in political practices from centralized state government to a wider system of public, private and third sector actors working interdependently and interactively in networks (Cairney, 2012). The concept of governing, however, refers to all the everyday techniques and practices which seek to act upon the thoughts, feelings and actions of individual subjects, whether in the 'governable spaces' of the home, the school, the workplace, the hospital, the leisure centre or the shopping mall (Rose, 1999), or, more latterly, in the network spaces of the world wide web. While governance and governing are separate issues, they are also closely related in that the shift to governance brings new policy actors into circulation, with new repertoires of ideas, techniques and practices for governing subjects. As Hultqvist (2001: 146) explains, 'government in today's context is enacted in a decentralized way,' emanating not from the 'central point' of the state but through 'a network in which both political and non-political players are involved—the media, the government, various market players, volunteer organizations, and so on.' One result of networked forms of cross-sectoral governance in education is the production of a new understanding of the learner, 'a more or less coherent image' of the learner as an individual subject who has been 'made manageable within the range of assumed qualities and dimensions of political thought' (Hultqvist, 2001: 146). Contemporary accounts of governing counter the notion that individuals are socialized through ideological oppression and constraint, and instead emphasize how individuals in 'advanced liberal democracies' are increasingly incited to see themselves as freely choosing, responsible and 'enterprising selves':

> The enterprising self will make an enterprise of its life, seek to maximize its own human capital, project itself a future, and seek to shape itself in order to become that which it wishes to be. The enterprising self is thus both an active self and a calculating self, a self that calculates *about* itself and that acts *upon* itself to better itself. (Rose, 1996: 154)

The task of governing then becomes about acting upon the action of such enterprising selves, by steering, shaping and nudging their decisions and choices about the pathways of their own lives. This is accomplished not simply via state apparatuses, but through the involvement of all kinds of non-political players and experts such as those boundary organizations examined in this chapter.

Cross-sector educational governance, then, is not just a structural effect of changing operations of the state, but actively links up and reimagines the learner according to associated changes in political thought; in this case, a shift in emphasis from the fixed central space of government to decentralized networks of governance, and a related shift from seeing the learner as the socialized subject of the central state to an active, self-calculating and enterprising self acted upon 'at a distance' through a more distributed cross-sectoral network of authorities and experts. The education system is treated in the same way as the individual learning subject. These developments are part of a broader set of epistemological and ontological shifts in social scientific thought that have sought to emphasize space, movement, contingency, liquidity and different 'mobilities' rather than social structures, stasis and order (Urry, 2007). In this sense, the present chapter contributes to more spatialized forms of education policy analysis that emphasize concepts like 'policy mobilities', 'travelling policies', 'network governance', 'joined-up policies' and 'policies in motion' (Rizvi & Lingard, 2010; Ball, 2012), specifically by mapping out and exploring one concrete example of the shifting relationships, flows of ideas, and dynamic networks through which policy solutions are increasingly sought for educational problems.

Policy Network Analysis

The analysis presented in this chapter focuses on one particular cross-sector policy network as an example of a new space of governance within which new ways of imagining the future of education are being produced. The policy network consists of the organizations Nesta (the National Endowment for Science, Technology and the Arts), the Innovation Unit (a social enterprise working on innovation in public services), and the RSA (Royal Society of Arts, Manufacturing and Commerce), as well as others including the social innovator Nominet Trust and the think tanks Demos and the Education Foundation. These organizations constitute a network through inter-organizational connections, social relations, and a flow of staff and ideas and discourses between them, and share a commitment to ideas about digital innovation in both the administration of the education system and the pedagogic apparatus of the classroom.

In terms of the method of 'policy network analysis' (Ball & Junemann, 2012), I map out and trace some of the social relations and shared ideas flowing between these organizations. Specifically, I have selected a sample of texts from these organizations that focus on ideas around the role of online networks and data-based technologies in education, and trace how these ideas cohere into something like a stable 'sociotechnical imaginary' of the future of educational governance and pedagogic practice. A sociotechnical imaginary, as Jasanoff (2015) has defined it, is a collectively held, institutionally stabilized, and publicly performed vision of a desirable future, one that is animated by shared understandings of forms of social life and social order and made attainable through the design of technological projects. Sociotechnical imaginaries are the result of relations between technology and society, are also temporally situated and culturally particular, and simultaneously descriptive of attainable futures and prescriptive of the kinds of futures that ought to be attained. As an influential part of contemporary politics, these imaginaries have the power to shape technological design, channel public expenditures and contribute to the formation and operationalization of policy ideas. Sociotechnical imaginaries help to shape the ways in which societies and their populations are organized, and the role of technologies in governing them. As a policy network, the organizations named above are increasingly generating, sharing and circulating an imaginary of the networked and data-driven future of education, and seeking to mobilize policy support to operationalize it through the application of specific technologies. They are, in short, setting into motion a particular imagination of the future with the intention to circulate, stabilize and settle it down within the administrative and pedagogic apparatus of education, one with significant potential implications for how certain technological techniques and applications might be mobilized to govern learners' actions.

Understood as the institutional generators of a contemporary sociotechnical imaginary of the future of education, the members of the policy network examined below are neither solely governmental nor commercial actors, but straddle sectors and broker projects and connections between them as 'boundary organizations' (Guston, 2001; Grek, 2014), or, perhaps better, 'boundary brokers.' Conceptualized as boundary brokers, these intermediary organizations seek to synthesize approaches from across the borders of the state and non-state, as well as across the boundaries of media work, policy intervention, intellectual production, and innovative digital R&D. For all of them, educational change is a key objective. My focus in this chapter is on their creation, circulation and stabilization of an imaginary of education, one in which governance is to be distributed to diverse forms of cross-sectoral expertise and within which 'database pedagogies' are to be mobilized. The database pedagogies they promote for use in schools include new learning analytics and adaptive software applications which enable learners to be monitored in 'real-time' through the data they produce while performing pedagogic tasks. These data can then be calculated, visualized and used to enable learners to understand their progress and development, and to base their subsequent decisions upon such calculations. The imaginary to be operationalized through such database pedagogies carries a new image of the learner as a calculating self into the material infrastructure, discourses and pedagogic practices of schooling. Through database pedagogies such as learning analytics, learners are encouraged to see and understand themselves through their streams of data, and to monitor themselves according to calculations and visualizations of their progress in order to them calculate about themselves and act to improve themselves.

The chapter is concerned, then, with how boundary brokers are making education thinkable, practicable and governable in terms of network architectures and the algorithmic logic of databases, and with the kinds of individual subjects that are implicated in and acted upon by these new spaces and pedagogies of governing. The term 'governing through pedagogy' (Pykett, 2012) captures the ways in which pedagogy is now seeping into many aspects of everyday life, driven by public, private and cross-sector actors alike, and its role in continually sculpting, moulding and educating individuals—not just as passively socialized subjects, but as individuals subtly steered and enabled to calculate between different pedagogic pathways. The analytics examined below are now a crucial technical and calculative apparatus in the shaping of learners' pedagogic possibilities. In attempting to operationalize their imaginary of data-driven education, boundary brokering organizations are therefore seeking to shape the pedagogic identities of 'lifelong learners' who are enabled to learn throughout the lifecourse according to a calculative logic. Thus while much of the data presented in the paper pertains to policies and practices related to schooling for children, these are part of a wider shift to connect and link up learning throughout the lifecourse, a task for which sophisticated and joined-up network and database technologies are required.

To reiterate at this point, the policy network of boundary brokers examined in this chapter is circulating a sociotechnical imaginary associated with database pedagogies as part of its approach to creating a new 'governable space' in education, a space in which governing is increasingly to be done by collecting and compiling individual learner data in order to calculate and predict their future needs and to generate prescriptions for future pedagogy. This is governing being done not through intervening in the national space of the education system but performed 'up-close' within the pedagogic space of the classroom itself, all imbued with the aspiration to re-sculpt and re-educate the mind and body of the learner as a self-calculating individual. To be clear, two interrelated shifts in the governable spaces of education are to be examined: that of changing the space of educational governance from central government to cross-sector policy networks; and in relation to that, changing the space of governing practice from the national education system to the mind and body of the individual subject, facilitated through new database-driven technologies. In addition to these imagined sociospatial reconfigurations of educational governance, developments around data in education also point to a temporal reconfiguration, with data on learners increasingly collected in real-time and mobilized for 'future-tense' purposes of prediction and pre-emption.

The central argument is that techniques and discourses of 'governing by numbers' (Grek, 2009), where numerical data are used to manage and govern the education system, are being augmented with a sociotechnical imaginary of 'governing by algorithm.' While governing by numbers seeks to collect and analyze learners' performance data in order to cast a grid of statistical calculation and comparability over national education systems, governing by algorithm involves the deployment of advanced software technologies to 'know' and on that basis to forecast, predict and automate appropriate pedagogies to instruct the individual learner. Within this emerging imaginary, the learner is positioned as a 'calculable person' (Rose, 1999) rendered both as the subject of calculation by others (mediated by machine algorithms), and also a self-calculating individual endowed with the capacity to understand his or her own pedagogic identity in terms of numbers and associated data visualizations. Ultimately, emerging forms of governance and governing being promoted through the sociotechnical imaginary of boundary broker organizations are concerned with reconfiguring the future capacities, conduct, thoughts and actions of the learner.

Policy Networks and Policy Mobilities

The governance of education is increasingly understood as taking place through cross-sectoral networks of public, private and third sector interdependencies that criss-cross sectoral boundaries and traverse national and transnational borderlines.

'Networked governance,' as this style of governing is termed, is sociospatially decentralized and characterized by fluidity, looseness, complexity and instability rather than the central state mandate of hard regulative policy (Ball & Junemann, 2012). Educational 'policy networks' are a specific form of this type of governance as 'social mechanisms that can work across social, governmental and geographical boundaries' and 'build bridges that bring together a diverse range of actors, including governments, businesses and civil society' (McGann & Sabatini, 2011: 67). Made up primarily of experts from think tanks, policy institutes, multilateral agencies, media consultancies, and experts in public relations, policy networks 'perform the role of conveying ideas between different areas of the production, distribution, or circulation of ideas' in order to 'influence the decision-making process' (Lawn & Grek, 2012: 75). In a recent account of 'policy mobilities' in the context of the global movement of education policy ideas, Ball (2012: 11) refers to 'how policies move through, and are adapted by, networks of social relations' that involve diverse participants with a variety of interests, commitments, purposes and influence. Policy networks are both part of a shift to a more mobile and decentred space of educational governance—a network of participants—and also contribute to the production and movement of policy ideas.

Sometimes termed 'soft governance' that works through the establishment and nurturing of networks and partnerships of different kinds of actors (Lawn & Grek, 2012), new networked forms of governance in education are increasingly being pursued by cross-sector organizations such as Nesta, the Innovation Unit, and the RSA. However, the participation of these boundary brokers in new soft spaces of educational governance is also ushering in new governing practices. Their participation in reimagining and 'reinventing public education' involves 'moving from a bureaucratic/professional knowledge about education, a part of the public sector, to individualized, personalized and integrated knowledge about a society' (Grek & Ozga, 2010: 272). The shift to individualization and personalization is bringing about the emergence of new forms of governing expertise, and a new kind of governing expert whose claim to authority rests on the capacity to know, assess and act upon the individual—through the collection, collation and calculation of data—rather than to seek to reform the more cumbersome bureaucratic systems of the public sector.

The imaginary among boundary brokers of governing through individuals' data trails represents a significant shift in thinking about the 'governable spaces' of education. A reterritorialization of governance is imagined here, from the nationally governable space of the state to the governable body of the individual. This requires sophisticated computer technologies capable of gathering data about each individual in the population. Consequently, documents produced by boundary brokering organizations all talk of computational forms as models for reinventing educational governance. In particular, the figure of the 'network' itself is routinely deployed by these boundary organizations as a model for new kinds of political and social order, not least in education. Former cofounder of Demos and current Nesta chief executive Mulgan (2005), for example, writes of the 'co-evolution' of computational technologies with decentralized 'matrix models' of 'e.governance' that involve civil society organizations participating in all public services facilitated by software. Writing for Demos, Leadbeater (2011), who has worked in a variety of roles across Nesta and the Innovation Unit too, endorses the potential for 'government by algorithm,' an approach involving systems to mine and analyze 'big data' and algorithmic methods to create 'more effective and intelligent public systems' (Leadbeater, 2011: 18). Likewise, recently writing together in a Nesta publication, Mulgan and Leadbeater (2013) both advocate 'systems innovation,' based on the idea of networks of interconnected innovations, which specifies the form of the network as a model for reforming, adapting and creating better systems. Building on ideas about cybernetic governance, the publication is illustrated with 'systems maps' and 'diagrams' of the various feedback loops and feed-forward mechanisms, causal links and levers which underpin network dynamics. The authors embrace the notion of using 'big data' sources to track and trace individuals as they go about their daily lives online. These data include transactional data, such as that generated through online shopping, using transport, and making entertainment choices; and personal and behavioural data shared on blogs and social networks like Facebook and Twitter. Owing to the data-mineable capacities of digital networks, these boundary brokers argue, it is now possible to generate insights about the population at large.

Even more recently, Nesta has partnered with the UK Government Cabinet Office to explore the idea of 'a new operating system for government,' based on the notion of 'government as a platform' articulated by web entrepreneur Tim O'Reilly. The idea of government as a platform assumes that successful technology innovations can be used as models for the redesign of government services; for example, making government data open and accessible as a platform for the creation of 'civic apps.' Through developing this approach, Nesta and the Cabinet Office aim to anticipate how emerging technologies such as 'data science, predictive analytics, artificial intelligence, sensors, applied programming interfaces, autonomous machines, and platforms' might in the next 5 years become 'ingrained into how government thinks of itself,' 'redefine the role of government, and even create a different relationship between state and public' (Maltby, 2015). Education is one particular domain of governance in which Nesta is seeking to apply such models, by actively endorsing the distribution of expertise among diverse actors and particularly by mobilizing technological platforms to accomplish it. The Innovation Unit has likewise advocated the involvement of more 'brokers' in the management and organization of education, particularly those that operate more like high-tech networked organizations than hierarchical bureaucracies; Nesta is a named example (Horne, 2008).

Boundary brokers such as Nesta and the Innovation Unit seek both to straddle sectoral boundaries between public, private and civil society sector, and to bridge borders between political and the technological systems of thinking. Specifically, they mobilize ideas about the collection of big data for the purposes of generating insights about individuals for policy development. However, as political scientists Margetts and Sutcliffe (2013: 139) point out, big data analysis not only offers scope for understanding human behaviour, social structure, and citizens' civic engagement; it can 'also be used for algorithmic and probabilistic policymaking' and 'for more coercive modes of governance', whether by introducing conditionality into public policy and services or simply exerting "nudges." This is what Ruppert (2012: 117–118) calls 'database government,' a 'science-in-the-making' which has shifted the focus of government from the 'qualitative' governance of the social to the 'quantitative' governance of the 'informational.' The arguments of Mulgan, Leadbeater, and the approaches that the organizations to which they are attached appear to endorse, represent a form of 'digital-era governance,' which Margetts and Dunleavy (2013: 6) describe as 'the adaptation of the public sector to completely embrace and imbed electronic delivery at the heart of the government business model.' Digital-era governance, they argue, is a response to technological developments such as analysing big data from transactional processes, peer production, network effects, and to new popular ideas of 'crowdsourcing,' 'cognitive surplus,' 'wikinomics,' and the 'Internet of Things.' Significantly, digital-era governance is enabled by the coupling of network-based communications technologies with database-led information processing technologies. On the one hand, networks allow for forms of governance through communication with individuals—governance with a voice maybe. On the other hand, database technologies allow for forms of governance through gathering information about individuals—governance with a brain. Combining these technologies of networks and databases, digital styles of governance, then, are to be managed by an 'intelligent centre' but facilitated through 'decentralized delivery.'

Evidence for how such an 'intelligent centre/decentralized delivery' model figures in boundary brokers' emerging imaginaries of educational governance can be found in documents published by both the RSA and the Innovation Unit. In a report prepared for the RSA, Ormerod (2010: 10) argues that networks should be considered as an 'intellectual framework' and a 'mindset' for understanding how societies and economies function, and thus to inform how policies are devised and planned. Ormerod's essay refers to networks in terms of 'social networks' and 'social learning'—learning through observation and interaction with others—and to networks in general as the 'patterns of connections between individuals,' as well as to large-scale 'networked systems' such as crowds, stock markets, and 'scale free networks' such as the World Wide Web (Ormerod, 2010: 14–15, 29–30). Just as the network has become prevalent as a metaphor for individual and collective life, economics and politics, it has also been mobilized by the RSA as a diagram for reimagining public education.

Further evidence of the prevalence of the idea of networks among boundary brokers comes from the Innovation Unit. Sharing the RSA's networks mindset and Nesta's emphasis on networked systems innovation, the Innovation Unit endorses the idea of an 'innovation ecosystem' for education. In such an educational ecosystem school is imagined as a 'base camp for enquiry' that is supported beyond school by the internet, mobile technologies, and a 'vastly increased number of education providers,' many accessed virtually. This vision is based on a model of a network of 'extended learning relationships' including teachers, tutors, experts, mentors, coaches, peers, and families as well as industry, local businesses, cultural institutions, community organizations, and the internet (Innovation Unit, 2012: 11). In this innovation ecosystem, education is reimagined through the imagery of the use of social networking sites to encourage peer-to-peer learning and collaborative research; online chat, instant messaging and email to help to strengthen the student-teacher relationship; digital portfolios as a continuous performative record of assessment; and the use of Twitter hashtags to collate research sources (Hampson, Patten, & Shanks, 2012). The Innovation Unit imaginary articulated in these examples characterizes the pedagogic identities of networked learners who participate in a connected ecosystem of learning at home, at school and online—for a prospective future in which the internet itself is presupposed as a new learning institution. Finally, the Innovation Unit suggests the use of database-driven performance technologies which can collect data in order to 'know' learners, sort and aggregate them on the basis of personal and behavioural data, and respond with an algorithmically generated 'playlist' of appropriately personalized pedagogy (Hampson et al., 2012). Discursively framed by the RSA, Nesta and the Innovation Unit in this way, the network and the database appear 'easily and routinely to criss-cross the distinction between the technical and the social' (Barry, 2001: 14).

Networks and databases are thus the dominant spatial forms informing the reimagining of governance among boundary brokers such as Nesta, the RSA and the Innovation Unit. However, neither networks nor databases are neutral devices, but are entangled in normative imaginings of the future. In relation to the former, networks have been described as a 'typically modern fantasy' that criss-crosses the technical and the social to provide 'a diagram on the basis of which reality might be refashioned and reimagined: they are models of the political future' (Barry, 2001: 14, 87). This not to suggest that networks can be seen only in one way. There are, for example, explicitly 'democratic' ways of thinking about networks, as well as highly individualistic notions of 'network individualism.' But the notion of networks as a 'new social operating system' that stands 'in contrast to the longstanding operating system formed around large hierarchical bureaucracies' (Rainie & Wellman, 2012: 6) is certainly the dominant imaginary of networks circulating among boundary brokers. Reinforcing points raised earlier about the ways contemporary techniques of governing work through enabling rather than constraining individuals' capacities for action, Rainie and Wellman (2012: 9) argue that:

> The *networked operating system* gives people new ways to solve problems and meet social needs. It offers more freedom to individuals than people experienced in the last because now they have more room to maneuver and more capacity to act on their own.

It is this image of networks as an intrinsically *enabling* rather than ideologically *constraining* social operating system that informs Nesta's imaginary of a new operating model for government, the RSA's networks mindset, and the Innovation Unit's 'educational ecosystem.' Through these sociotechnical network imaginaries education is being reimagined as a new governable space, one to be administered by decentralized policy networks consisting of cross-sectoral combinations of public, private and cross-sector actors, with the aim of governing through the collection, compilation and calculation of informational data on the networked individual learner. These techniques of algorithmic governance are also sinking down into the apparatus of schooling itself, and into new tactics of governing through database pedagogies.

Database Pedagogies and Mobile Bodies

In recent years there has been an explosion of interest in database-led technologies of 'big data,' 'data mining,' and 'data analytics,' all of which have been taken up enthusiastically by boundary brokering organizations such as Nesta (e.g. Coyle, 2009; Davies, 2013). Database-driven technologies are today significant since 'the sociotechnical instantiation of many aspects of the contemporary world depend on database architectures and database management techniques' and the technical processes of 'ordering, sorting, counting, and calculating' that they involve (Mackenzie, 2012: 335, 338). However, interweaving individuals more and more densely into new database architectures is creating vast and new forms of social, personal and behavioural data that may not only reflect everyday existence but actively constitute and reshape social practices as they occur (Beer & Burrows, 2013). The 'database way of thinking' about governing seeks to intervene, through 'personalized packages of public services,' in 'both who people are and who they are possibly becoming' (Ruppert, 2012: 128, 130).

A specific development related to these database-led technologies in the field of education has been the growth of 'learning analytics' and 'adaptive learning' software. Built on machine learning techniques and algorithms, learning analytics platforms identify individual learners through their digital data traces, rendered visible as numbers and data visualizations, in order to assess, evaluate, and detect patterns, and then anticipate or predict their future educational progress. Nesta has advocated adaptive learning technologies which mobilize a combination of student data, algorithmic learning analytics and feedback mechanisms to adapt and personalize learning:

> Adaptive learning technologies use student data to adapt the way information is delivered to a student on an individual level. This data can range from online test scores to session time (how long users spend on a single exercise) to records of where a user has clicked or touched while figuring out a problem. Based on this feedback, the programme will understand which content to point the user at next—planning a personalized learning journey. (Nesta, 2013a)

An accompanying Nesta document claims these adaptive technologies provide 'the means to shift away from a one-to-many model of teaching, so that every child has a 'digital tutor' that is responsive to their interests, their prior-conceptions and achievement'; and the potential for 'intelligent online platforms that can use data gathered from learners to become smart enough to predict, and then appropriately assist and assess, that learner's progression to mastering the concept being taught' (Nesta, 2013b). Nesta has also specifically supported and promoted Beluga Learning, a learning system based on the application of data-based learning analytics, adaptive software and artificial intelligence technologies. The Chief Executive of Beluga has also spoken at a major Nesta event launching a 'decoding learning' report. The Beluga system makes use of two types of learner data. It collects 'intelligent data' such as curriculum data, semantic data and linked data that is often collected by educational institutions. It also collects 'off-put data' from students' own social media programmes and conducts 'smart analysis' on both of these sources of data in order to create a profile of each individual user which can be compared and matched with an entire population of user profiles:

> The data is allowing the software to make a real-time prediction about the learner and changes the environment, ... the pedagogy and the social experience. ... This process occurs continually and in realtime, so that with every new piece of data collected on the student, their profile changes and the analytical software re-searches the population to compare once more. ... The content and environment then adapt continually to meet the needs of the learner. (Beluga Learning, 2013: 5–6)

Beluga Learning utilizes advances in artificial intelligence, combined with learning analytics and adaptive learning, to develop a 'smart system' that is able to 'behave with an intelligence' and supplement or even circumvent the role and expertise of the teacher.

At this stage, it is important to reiterate that the data-based pedagogies of learning analytics platforms are being mobilized as part of boundary brokers' sociotechnical imaginary of a highly networked and data-driven future of education. In circulating such an imaginary, however, these brokers are seeking to operationalize such educational data analytics platforms in practice. For that reason, it is essential to appreciate something of the social and technical development of learning analytics techniques and applications. Learning analytics and adaptive learning technologies have a relatively long history. The dream of automated 'teaching machines' capable of providing feedback to the learner goes back to the 1920s with Sidney Pressey's 'machine for intelligence testing' (Watters, 2014). However, with the rising availability of digital data from the learning process, and technical possibilities of educational data mining, the field of learning analytics is coalescing at the present time into a stabilized multidisciplinary set of techniques and applications (Siemens, 2013) largely managed through the emerging expertise of 'educational data scientists' (Pea, 2014). Buckingham-Shum (2013) has described learning analytics as a 'digital nervous system' for education, an artificial 'brain or collective intelligence' that can measure and interpret a learner's activity, provide real-time feedback and adapt the learner's future behaviour accordingly. Particularly with the possibilities associated with educational big data, Mayer-Schönberger and Cukier (2014) imagine that learning analytics will 'reshape learning' through 'datafying the learning process' in three significant ways: through real-time feedback; individualization and personalization of the educational experience; and probabilistic predictions to optimize what students learn. The applications of learning analytics include tailored course offerings, predictive modelling, learner profiling, and the design of 'online intelligent learning systems' and 'intelligent software tutors.' The aim of some learning analytics developments is to create semi-automated pedagogic systems, or what might be termed database pedagogies. Although the specific data analytics techniques and adaptive learning software applications are new, then, they are continuous in some ways with a longer historical line of thinking about the automation of the pedagogic process, and run parallel with current attempts to mobilize new kinds of data analytics applications as a governing technique.

Database-led learning analytics and adaptive software systems such as those promoted by Nesta exemplify what Kitchin and Dodge (2011: 85) have termed 'automated management.' This term captures how new software systems can be coded to collect and process information about people and things in ways that are increasingly automated (technologically enacted), automatic (the technology performs without prompting or direction) and autonomous (making judgements and enacting outcomes algorithmically without human intervention). Automated management is a form of governance that uses surveillance data to target and reshape behaviour:

> Unlike traditional forms of surveillance that seek to self-discipline, new forms of surveillance seek to produce objectified individuals where the vast amount of [data] harvested about them is used to classify, sort, and differentially treat them, and actively shapes their behaviour. … Software … makes possible a fundamental shift in how information is gathered, by whom, for what purposes, and how it is applied to anticipate individuals' future lives. (Kitchin & Dodge 2011: 86)

As Urry (2007: 15) argues, through such data-based techniques, 'human beings are being reconfigured as bits of scattered information' and as 'mobile bodies' leaving digital traces of themselves in space. In everyday life automated management raises the issue of the 'technological challenges to human agency offered by the decision-making powers of established and emergent software algorithms' and the extent to which 'algorithmic power' may be 'becoming a part of how we live, a part of our being, a part of how we do things, the way we are treated, the things we encounter, our way of life' (Beer, 2009: 987). Continuous with the longer historical project of governing through the collection of statistics on the population, the codes and algorithms of databases work by collecting, compiling and calculating data about people, and creating profiles and classifications in order to sort and sift them for a variety of (sometimes political) purposes (Ruppert & Savage, 2012). This constructs algorithmically a digital shadow-profile, data double, or a data-based doppelganger, that can precede individuals wherever they go (shopping, travelling, working, learning) and may be used to modify how each person is treated.

This discussion illuminates how digital data are increasingly being positioned as vast resources for the governing of both individuals and wider publics. Consequently, the sociotechnical imaginary of boundary brokers can be conceived as one in which digital data are to be utilized as a governing resource for classifying, sorting and ordering learners, and for anticipating and activating their future behaviour. A key issue emerging from these developments of automated, automatic and autonomous database technologies concerns the assumptions about the learner that are programmed into the system. For Facer (2012: 715), educational databases 'reconstruct' the learner as a 'cybernetic system' made up of inputs and outputs rather than an 'embodied person.' As Ruppert (2012: 125) has argued in relation to government education databases:

> database devices are based on the logic that the subject is made up of unique combinations of distributed transactional metrics that reveal who they are and their capacities, problems and needs. An individual is not simply a child or youth, but rather a combination of needs and services.

Consequently, children can be 'discovered and made up by these technologies' as a 'potential future person yet to come' (Amoore cited in Ruppert, 2012: 131). Learning analytics is perhaps the ideal pedagogic technology for 'knowing capitalism' (Thrift, 2005) which mobilizes powerful data collecting and calculating technologies to know and act upon individuals and populations. In education this is a process which requires knowledge and information about learners to be 'collated, monitored and interpreted by service providers, and even used as the basis for forecasting future needs' (Grek & Ozga, 2010: 285). The process involves defining 'personalized packages' of pedagogies for learners that are 'formulated from distributed data about them and targeted to meet their needs but not seen by them' (Ruppert, 2012: 128). There is undoubtedly 'algorithmic power' at work in such devices, 'not of someone directly having power over someone else,' but the programmed power of 'the software making choices and connections in complex and unpredictable ways in order to shape the everyday experiences of the user' (Beer, 2009: 997). This is not technology working wholly autonomously and deterministically, but a matter of the calculations and algorithms designed by analytics experts, such as educational data scientists, being projected from afar and enacted, through specific software applications, directly inside the pedagogic apparatus of the classroom. Organizations like Pearson Education and Knewton are key organizations where educational data science is now being practised, and where learning software is being designed for application in practice (Williamson, 2016). The semi-automation of the classroom promised by learning analytics is one in which the calculative expertise housed by such organizations is now becoming co-constitutive of pedagogic practice, and intervening in how learners are known, understood and acted upon as mobile bodies of data rather than embodied persons.

Shaped recursively through such feedback loops, the subject presupposed by database pedagogy is, as Cheney-Lippold (2012) has argued in relation to databases generally, an 'algorithmic identity,' an effect of computational processes which infer categories of identity on the basis of the collection and analysis of personal information and behavioural data. The individual is to be known, understood and acted upon through its algorithmic identity, as the mobile body produced through calculation of its data. The kind of imaginary associated with learning analytics that is projected by boundary brokers is one in which an algorithmic identity, or a data double, might therefore be generated through the pedagogic apparatus of the classroom. An algorithmic pedagogic identity associated with database pedagogies is inferred from its pedagogic transactions and interactions, its generation of data, and its amenability to intervention through data-based analytics technologies. These technologies work recursively and dynamically to identify individuals based on patterns and regularities; on that basis to make predictions and recommendations for learners; and through those algorithmic processes, to shape and structure how they might think and act in the future. As noted earlier, contemporary techniques of governing seek to position the individual as a 'calculable person' who is both made amenable to calculation by others and endowed with the capacity to be self-calculating. In the current context, learning analytics can be seen as at least partly enmeshed in such techniques. It makes the learner the constant subject of the calculative logic of analytics algorithms, and provides feedback to the learner in the shape of data and visualizations that can then be used as the basis for calculating upon the self in order to improve the self as a lifelong project. This is a generative process of the learner and the database pedagogy constantly co-constituting and reconfiguring each other. The learner is being reconfigured through the feedback loops of learning analytics as a lifelong learner engaged in a ceaseless pedagogic process facilitated by algorithmic forms of power. These pedagogic techniques seek to mould learners for a future in which the algorithmic pedagogic techniques associated with networked and database-driven technologies will be a familiar and everyday feature of governing.

None of this is to suggest that the learner is a passive subject or even 'victim' of such analytics. On the contrary, learning analytics calculates possibilities for learners, activates risk-prevention, and even prescribes relevant personalized pedagogic pathways. Nonetheless, the calculative logic of learning analytics must be understood as introducing into the pedagogic enterprise a particular assumption that the learner can be tracked and modelled through his or her data as a mobile body or a data double, and that the feedback provided by such systems relies on the analysis of this data and on the identification of the learner through it rather than on the embodied expertise of the professional pedagogue. It is the data-based mobile body of the learner that is used as the basis for calculating appropriate pedagogic intervention, and that then becomes the basis for learners' own embodied self-calculations. The boundary brokers promoting such analytics are therefore circulating a particular sociotechnical imaginary which, if operationalized as they intend, would involve the active co-constitution of learners both as the mobile objects of analytics calculations performed 'at a distance' through the calculations designed by analytics companies, and as actively self-calculating subjects mobilizing the data so generated in their own embodied projects of self-improvement.

Conclusion

This chapter has begun to explore how educational governance is being respatialized through the participation of cross-sector boundary brokers in education in England. I have outlined two shifts in the sociospatial configuration of educational governance: first, a shift towards more cross-sectoral, mobile and networked forms of governance, diagrammatically characterized by its intelligent centre and decentralized delivery model, involving public, private and intermediary actors acting within public education; and second, a related shift to imagined new forms of governing through database technologies that are programmed with the algorithmic power to know and act upon the capacities of the individual—or governing through sculpting mobile bodies rather than through governance over the national space of the education system. The governance of the education system and the governing of individuals have become symmetrical projects. As a sociotechnical imaginary shared and stabilized among boundary broker organizations, this respatialized vision articulates a model of how education in the future might be, could be, even should be, and how it might be made attainable through the application of particular technologies. The chapter has attempted to trace some consequences of the operationalization and materialization of such an imaginary for the administrative governance of education and for the governing of learners' conduct and capacities for action through educational data analytics. According to boundary brokers' imaginary, just as the governance of the education system is to be dispersed to heterogeneous authorities and experts from beyond government, the governing of individuals is to be accomplished by making them subjects of a network of digital data practices enacted within the classroom but managed from afar by emerging analytics companies. It is this imaginary that boundary brokers are circulating and stabilizing, and seeking to promote and perform into practice, with significant consequences for how learners themselves are known, understood and acted upon.

The imagined deployment of digital data practices by boundary brokers is intended to accelerate the temporalities of educational governance, making the collection of educational data, its analysis, and its consequences into an automated, real-time and recursive process exercised 'up close' from within the pedagogic apparatus of the classroom rather than 'at a distance' through the governing knowledge generated at expert government centres of calculation (Williamson, 2016). The current growth of learning analytics and the recursivity of data is evidence of how education is imagined as being made governable as a mobile, algorithmic space constituted by information, data, and its analysis, rather than a national space of state government, and infused with the aim of producing lifelong learners for a seemingly mobile, networked and database-led future.

Acknowledgements The research for this chapter was funded by the Economic and Social Research Council (grant ref: ES/L001160/1)

References

Ball, S. J. (2012). *Global Education Inc. New policy networks and the neo-liberal imaginary.* London: Routledge.

Barry, A. (2001). *Political machines: Governing a technological society.* London: Athlone Press.

Beer, D. (2009). Power through the algorithm? Participatory web cultures and the technological unconscious. *New Media and Society, 11*(6), 985–1002.

Beer, D., & Burrows, R. (2013). Popular culture, digital archives and the new social life of data. *Theory, Culture and Society, 30*(4), 47–71.

Beluga Maths. (2013). What is Beluga learning? *Beluga Learning* website. Retrieved November 28, 2014, from http://www.belugalearning.com/index.php/research.

Buckingham-Shum, S. (2013). *Learning analytics.* Moscow: UNESCO Institute for Information Technologies in Education. Retrieved November 28, 2014, from http://iite.unesco.org/pics/publications/en/files/3214711.pdf.

Cairney, P. (2012). *Understanding public policy: Theories and issues.* Houndmills: Palgrave Macmillan.

Cheney-Lippold, J. (2012). A new algorithmic identity: Soft biopolitics and the modulation of control. *Theory, Culture and Society, 28,* 164–181.

Coyle, D. (Ed.). (2009). *Reboot Britain: How the promise of our new digital age can tackle the challenges we face as a country*. London: Nesta.

Davies, J. (2013). Sampling society? The foundations of a new frontier in understanding society. *Nesta* website. Retrieved November 28, 2014, from http://www.nesta.org.uk/blogs/big_data/sampling_society_the_foundations_of_a_new_frontier_in_understanding_society.

Facer, K. (2012). Personal, relational and beautiful: Education, technologies and John Macmurray's philosophy. *Oxford Review of Education, 38*(6), 709–725.

Grek, S. (2009). Governing by numbers: The PISA 'effect' in Europe. *Journal of Education Policy, 24*(1), 23–37.

Grek, S., & Ozga, J. (2010). Re-inventing public education: The new role of knowledge in education policy making. *Public Policy and Administration, 25*(3), 271–288.

Grek, S. (2014). OECD as a site of coproduction: European education governance and the new politics of 'policy mobilization.'. *Critical Policy Studies, 8*(3), 266–281.

Guston, D. H. (2001). Boundary organizations in environmental policy and science: An introduction. *Science, Technology & Human Values, 26*(4), 399–408.

Hampson, M., Patten, A., & Shanks, L. (2012). *10 ideas for 21st century education*. London: Innovation Unit.

Horne, M. (2008). *Honest brokers: Brokering innovation in public services*. London: Innovation Unit.

Hultqvist, K. (2001). Bringing the Gods and the Angels back? A modern pedagogical saga about excess in moderation. In K. Hultqvist & G. Dahlberg (Eds.), *Governing the child in the new millennium* (pp. 143–171). London: RoutledgeFalmer.

Innovation Unit. (2012). *Learning futures: A vision for engaging schools*. London: Paul Hamlyn Foundation/Innovation Unit.

Jasanoff, S. (2015). Future imperfect: Science, technology, and the imaginations of modernity. In S. Jasanoff & S.-H. Kim (Eds.), *Dreamscapes of modernity: Sociotechnical imaginaries and the fabrication of power*. Chicago, IL: University of Chicago Press. Retrieved April 23, 2015, from http://www.harvardiglp.org/wp-content/uploads/2014/10/Jasanoff-Ch-1.pdf.

Kitchin, R., & Dodge, M. (2011). *Code/Space: Software and everyday life*. London: MIT Press.

Lawn, M., & Grek, S. (2012). *Europeanizing education: Governing a new policy space*. Oxford: Symposium.

Leadbeater, C. (2011). *The civic long tail: Big data and the wisdom of the crowd*. London: Demos.

Mackenzie, A. (2012). More parts than elements: How databases multiply. *Environment and Planning D: Society and Space, 30*, 335–350.

Maltby, P. (2015). A new operating model for government. Open Policy Making, March 17. Accessed 18 March 2015. https://openpolicy.blog.gov.uk/2015/03/17/a-new-operating-model-for-government

Margetts, H., & Dunleavy, P. (2013). The second wave of digital-era governance: Quasi-paradigm for government on the Web. *Philosophical Transactions. Series A, Mathematical, Physical, and Engineering Sciences, 371*, 20120382. Retrieved November 28, 2014, from http://dx.doi.org/10.1098/rsta.2012.0382.

Margetts, H., & Sutcliffe, D. (2013). Addressing the policy challenges and opportunities of "Big Data". *Policy and Internet, 5*(2), 139–146.

Mayer-Schönberger, V., & Cukier, K. (2014). *Learning from big data: The future of education*. New York, NY: Houghton Mifflin Harcourt.

McGann, J. G., & Sabatini, R. (2011). *Global think tanks: Policy networks and governance*. London: Routledge.

Mulgan, G. (2005). Reshaping the state and its relationship with citizens: The short, medium and long-term potential of ICTs. In M. Castells & G. Cardoso (Eds.), *The network society: From knowledge to policy* (pp. 225–240). Washington, DC: Johns Hopkins Center for Transatlantic Relations.

Mulgan, G., & Leadbeater, C. (2013). *Systems innovation: Discussion paper*. London: Nesta.

Nesta. (2013a). 13 predictions for 2013. *Nesta website*. Retrieved November 28, 2014, from http://www.NESTA.org.uk/news_and_features/13for2013.

Nesta. (2013b). Decoding learning. *Nesta website*. Retrieved May 28, 2013, from http://www.nesta.org.uk/areas_of_work/public_services_lab/digital_education/assets/features/more_and_better_learning_using_technology.

Ormerod, P. (2010). *N squared: Public policy and the power of networks*. London: RSA. Retrieved April 23, 2015, from https://www.thersa.org/globalassets/pdfs/blogs/rsa_pamphlet-publicpolicy.pdf.

Pea, R. (2014). *Building the field of learning analytics for personalized learning at scale*. Stanford, CA· Stanford University. https://ed.stanford.edu/sites/default/files/law_report_complete_09-02-2014.pdf.

Pykett, J. (Ed.). (2012). *Governing through pedagogy: Re-educating citizens*. London: Routledge.

Rainie, L., & Wellman, B. (2012). *Networked: The new social operating system*. London: MIT Press.

Rizvi, F., & Lingard, B. (2010). *Globalizing education policy*. London: Routledge.

Rose, N. (1996). *Inventing our selves: Psychology, power and personhood*. Cambridge: University of Cambridge Press.

Rose, N. (1999). *Powers of freedom: Reframing political thought*. Cambridge: Cambridge University Press.

Ruppert, E. (2012). The governmental topologies of database devices. *Theory, Culture and Society, 29*(4-5), 116–136.

Ruppert, E., & Savage, M. (2012). Transactional politics. *The Sociological Review, 59*(Suppl 2), 73–92. Special Issue: Sociological Review Monograph Series: *Measure and Value*, edited by L. Adkins & C. Lury.

Siemens, G. (2013). Learning analytics: The emergence of a discipline. *American Behavioral Scientist, 57*(10), 1380–1400.

Thrift, N. (2005). *Knowing capitalism*. London: Sage.

Urry, J. (2007). *Mobilities*. Cambridge: Polity.

Watters, A. (2014). Teaching machines: A brief history of 'teaching at scale.' *Hack Education*, 10 September 2014. Retrieved April 23, 2015, from http://hackeducation.com/2014/09/10/teaching-machines-teaching-at-scale/.

Williamson, B. (2016). Digital education governance: Data visualization, predictive analytics and 'real-time' policy instruments. *Journal of Education Policy, 31*(2), 123–141.

Chapter 4
MOOCs and the Politics of Networked Learning in an Age of Austerity

Chris Jones

The Politics of Networked Learning

There are a small number of papers and articles that address the question of the politics of networked learning directly but the place of values and ethics in networked learning is more widely acknowledged (Greener & Perriton, 2005; Jones, 2001, 2002a; Land, 2006). The wider field of educational technology has recently seen an increasing interest in a critical approach based on the social sciences which has a political focus (see for example Hall, 2015; Selwyn & Facer, 2013). Early work focused on issues raised by technologically determinist accounts and the way that they influenced policy (Jones, 2002b). Technological determinism remains an important issue (Oliver, 2011) and one that has a continuing effect on policy, for example by way of the rhetoric and policy choices informed by the idea of the net generation and digital natives (Jones, 2011). In their brief history of networked learning McConnell, Hodgson and Dirckinck-Holmfeld do not mention politics directly and only refer to policy at an institutional level. Nevertheless their history clearly identifies the role of critical pedagogy and an ethical stance in relation to collaborative learning:

> The various scholars and practices associated with networked learning have an identifiable educational philosophy that has emerged out of those educational theories and approaches that can be linked to radical emancipatory and humanistic educational ideas and approaches. (McConnell, Hodgson, & Dirckinck-Holmfeld, 2012: 15)

Collaboration, cooperation and community are terms referenced frequently in networked learning that have a clear relationship to political and ethical positions and they have received regular critical attention (for example see Fox, 2005).

C. Jones (✉)
Liverpool John Moores University, Liverpool, UK
e-mail: c.r.jones1@ljmu.ac.uk

© Springer International Publishing Switzerland 2016
T. Ryberg et al. (eds.), *Research, Boundaries, and Policy in Networked Learning*, Research in Networked Learning, DOI 10.1007/978-3-319-31130-2_4

Overall, however, networked learning has rarely engaged with the broader political landscape sketched by Selwyn and Facer (2013) and it is arguably a pressing concern in the current period because of the severe pressures placed on higher education by economic conditions.

Following the banking crisis of 2008/2009 governments increased their debt levels to stabilise the financial system and to secure the debts of banks. The crisis that followed has severely affected almost all of the advanced industrial countries (with minor exceptions e.g. Australia), the effect on the BRIC countries and other developing economies has been less sharp and taken longer to develop. By 2014 the immediate pressures had receded but the world economy was far from stable with uneven and slow economic growth expected in the world economy (OECD, 2014). These economic and financial conditions matter because they set the tone of public debate, for example about migration and foreign student numbers, and because they affect public finances and thus directly affect the funding of higher education. This has been shown most starkly in the introduction of £9000 (per annum) fee levels for most university courses in England. This policy change, not signalled in the political parties pre-election manifestos, was driven through under the cloak of austerity and has led to a number of perverse and unanticipated consequences. Indeed the changes may actually cost more than the previous government block grants to universities in both the short and medium term (Chowdry, Dearden, & Wyness, 2010; Crawford, Crawford, & Wenchao, 2014).

> The fall in government spending on teaching grants for these students [those receiving loans for the new fees] is almost entirely offset by the long-run cost associated with providing them with larger loans to cover their increased tuition fees. Furthermore, we estimate that if all fees were to increase by £500, then the average cost per student under the two systems would be roughly equivalent. (Crawford et al., 2014: 51–52)

Austerity and government choices about the way to deal with the aftermath of the financial crisis have set a context for the development of networked learning that is hard to ignore.

Perhaps just as importantly the technologies we use are never neutral and they embodied political choices long before the recession. It is many years since Winner identified the inherently political nature of technologies (1986) and Feenberg argued that:

> … technology is not a destiny but a scene of struggle. It is a social battlefield, or perhaps a better metaphor would be a parliament of things on which civilizational alternatives are debated and decided. (Feenberg, 1991: 14)

Technologies are a site of social struggle and educational technology and networked learning are not exempt from these struggles. Prior to the financial crisis the world had moved away from a long period of stability during the 'cold war' in which the capitalist 'West' faced the Communist 'East' and the others states were either described as part of the 'Third World' or self-organised into the 'non-aligned' movement. During that period military expenditure interacted with the early development of e-learning (Friesen, 2010). In the period that followed neo-liberalism and the 'free' market dominated political development and discourse (Harvey, 2005). In this period the technology corporations developed rapidly and often had a progressive and benign reputation summed up in Google's motto "Don't be evil". This wasn't universally accepted and there were dystopian readings of the global corporations' influences on education from an early date and Google itself has become a recent focus of concern (Brabazon, 2007; Zuboff, 2015). The case being made here is not that politics should not influence networked learning, nor that the technologies we use should or can be separated from political understanding. Rather it is a plea for networked learning to analyse and understand the political forces that are embedded in the technologies we use and to assess the degree to which these political forces enable and constrain the possibilities for networked learning.

The Rise of the MOOCs

The MOOC (Massive Open Online Course) has become a symbol of the potentials and risks associated with the application of digital and networked technologies in the contemporary university. There have been wild claims about the possibility of radical change (Barber, Donnelly, & Ritzvi, 2013) and a widespread public interest which extends to news items and the popular press. Governments and university policy makers feel the need to ingratiate themselves with the new stars in the MOOC universe. There are UK and EU initiatives to develop MOOC platforms to compete with the current North American based offerings (Universities UK, 2013) and recently MOOC providers have begun to extend beyond their home bases in the developed economies with the launch of an edX MOOC based in South Africa.[1] Despite their rapid rise the development of MOOCs in developing countries is still limited and unlikely to be a major influence in the expansion of higher education in these contexts, due to restrictions in terms of access, language and computer literacy, especially in rural areas (Liyanagunawardena et al., 2014). The rise of MOOCs has led to a variety of analogies being drawn with other 'business' sectors using the over used notion of 'disruptive innovation' (Christensen, 2013). One of the more interesting parallels was that drawn between MOOCs and the fast food industry (Baggaley, 2014) suggesting that MOOCs were leading to the McDonaldization of education (Ritzer, 1993).

It is difficult at this time to remember the early development of MOOCs by Canadian academics associated with the idea of networked learning (Daniel, 2012). The early days of MOOCs were not accompanied by the kind of hype that emerged later. The first course ran with 25 on-campus fee paying students and 2300 free of charge on-line participants (Daniel, 2012). Daniel noted that:

> The first course carrying the name MOOC was offered in 2008, so this is new phenomenon. Second, the pedagogical style of the early courses, which we shall call cMOOCs, was based on a philosophy of connectivism and networking. (Daniel, 2012: 2)

This early form of MOOC has not gone away and the term cMOOC was coined to distinguish connectivist MOOCs (Siemens, 2012) from the new forms developed and promoted by a complex of elite universities in the US and private corporate

---

[1] https://www.edx.org/blog/wits-joins-edx-its-first-african

interests, also located in the US. Given the changes that have happened since the early days of MOOC development the current diversity of MOOC designs is perhaps to be expected (Bates, 2014). However it is still worth making the broad distinction between the early style of connectivist MOOCs, 'cMOOCs' and later instructivist models, the so called 'xMOOCs'.

The origins of the educational idea of the MOOC are still contested, although there is certainty about the role of connectivism in the process. Both Daniel (2012) and Clarà and Barberà (2013a, 2013b) link connectivism with the ideas of Ivan Illich, but this link is contested by Downes (2013). The link that has been made between connectivism and Illich relies on the association between network forms and the connections in networks with Illich's notion of learning webs which:

> can provide the learner with new links to the world instead of continuing to funnel all educational programs through the teacher (Ilich, 1970: 73).

Siemens has certainly drawn attention to this relationship between his version of connectivism and these ideas found previously in Illich (Siemens, 2008). I have also linked the ideas of Illich to networked learning, viewing him as a precursor of some contemporary ideas:

> When Ivan Illich wrote about de-schooling society, in the very early days of computing, he imagined being able to network expertise and interests in ways that then seemed technically difficult, using a mix of computer databases, mail and telephone (Ilich, 1970). It is still shocking to read Illich write using the terminology of learning webs, educational objects, skill exchanges and peer matching. These ideas still find their echoes amongst the most technologically forward looking research activities today. (Jones & Dirckinck-Holmfeld, 2009)

Whether or not there is a formal and direct connection between connectivism and Illich there is, as Daniel noted a relationship between the aims of Illich and the aims of cMOOCs, which are:

> to provide all who want to learn with access to available resources... empower all who want to share what they know to find those who want to learn it from them. (Daniel, 2012: 3).

These aims stand in sharp contrast to the xMOOCs that became so prominent, because they largely embody an instructivist approach to education. The timing of the two forms of MOOC might also be of interest in that the cMOOC arose prior to and at the point of the global financial crisis, whereas the xMOOC arose as the recession and austerity began to bite. The utopian aims of cMOOCs gave way to an uncertain but definite focus on business and the need for a 'business model' for MOOCs (Barber et al., 2013).

The emergence of xMOOCs remains quite recent and the range and variety of MOOCs continues to develop. Daniel summed up the development timeline in this way:

> Early in 2012 Stanford University offered a free, chunked course on Artificial Intelligence online and 58,000 people signed up. One of the faculty members involved, Sebastian Thrun, went on to found Udacity, a commercial start-up that helps other universities to offer xMOOCs (Meyer, 2012). MIT (2011) announced MITx at the end of 2011 for a launch in spring 2012. MITx has now morphed into edX with the addition of Harvard and UC Berkeley (edX, 2012). Since then similar initiatives from other well known US universities have come thick and fast. There seems to be a herd instinct at work as universities observe their peers joining the xMOOCs bandwagon and jump on for fear of being left behind. (Daniel, 2012: 3–4)

At around the time Daniel was writing Coursera another for profit platform was also launching a range of courses mainly in the US but with examples in various countries including the UK (Knox, 2014; Moocs@Edinburgh Group, 2013). In the UK Futurelearn was launched, a MOOC platform spun out from The Open University (UK). Futurelearn is 'a private company wholly owned by the Open University' that operates with a number of partners to provide courses including universities, the British Council, the British Library and British Museum. Although clearly a 'British' based offering Futurelearn does include some international partners.[2] The offering is a standard MOOC platform which clearly envisages some forms of accreditation: 'We're also going to be piloting features that let you take exams or buy statements of accomplishment as further evidence of your new skills.'[3] The Open University is also a partner in another MOOC project launched in 2013 OpenupEd.[4] OpenupEd is a European initiative supported by the European Association of Distance Teaching Universities (EADTU). Both these initiatives explicitly reference prior experience of online and distance education and both make mention of open access to resources, although the commitment of Futurelearn is limited: 'Wherever possible, we encourage our partners to make course content open and discoverable…'.[5] These two initiatives illustrate that MOOCs will not remain a North American based phenomena with global reach, because European politicians and policy makers will want to ensure European representation in what they see as a significant development. The question for networked learning will be to what degree the principles that inform MOOCs will be drawn from the longer tradition of Open and Distance learning, including networked learning, and to what degree they will represent a degradation of these principles and a replication of the instructivist model of xMOOCs.

It was this wave of activity that gave rise to a flurry of political, policy and public interest in the issue of MOOCs themselves and in the broader question of an innovative challenge to university structures and institutions based on technological developments. In early 2013 the Institute for Public Policy Research, a generally respected UK think tank produced an essay entitled: "An avalanche is coming: Higher education and the revolution ahead" (Barber et al., 2013). Interestingly the authors are employees of Pearson and the essay is also hosted on the Pearson web site. Pearson describe themselves as the 'world's leading education company'. Pearson also includes the Financial Times Group and Penguin Random House publishers. The IPPR is not a free market right of centre group and the IPPR web site describes its purpose in this way:

> The purpose of our work is to assist all those who want to create a society where every citizen lives a decent and fulfilled life, in reciprocal relationships with the people they care about. We believe that a[6] society of this sort cannot be legislated for or guaranteed by the state. And it certainly won't be achieved by markets alone. It requires people to act together and take responsibility for themselves and each other.

---

[2] https://www.futurelearn.com/about

[3] https://www.futurelearn.com/about/how-it-works

[4] http://www.openuped.eu/

[5] https://www.futurelearn.com/about/our-principles

[6] http://www.ippr.org/about-us

Despite this social market stance the essay proposes an apocalyptic vision as outlined in the Forward by Lawrence Summers the President Emeritus of Harvard University:

> An Avalanche is Coming sets out vividly the challenges ahead for higher education, not just in the US or UK but around the world. Just as we've seen the forces of technology and globalisation transform sectors such as media and communications or banking and finance over the last two decades, these forces may now transform higher education. The solid classical buildings of great universities may look permanent but the storms of change now threaten them. (Barber et al., 2013: 1)

Now this is not the first time such warning of a sudden step change in education have been made. In previous years the same kinds of arguments were based on a technological determinist reading of new technology and young people captured in the terms net generation and digital native (for a critique see Jones, 2011).

The three fundamental challenges the authors identify are:

1. How can universities and new providers ensure education for employability? "Given the rising cost of degrees, the threat to the market value of degrees and the sheer scale of both economic change and unemployment, this is a vital and immediate challenge."
2. How can the link between cost and quality be broken? "in the era of modern technology, when students can individually and collectively create knowledge themselves, outstanding quality without high fixed costs is both plausible and desirable."
3. How does the entire learning ecosystem need to change to support alternative providers and the future of work? (Barber et al., 2013: 6)

The report is suffused with corporate style language such as the 'the new student consumer is king and standing still is not an option' (ibid: 6). This cannot be thought of as a reasoned contribution to a debate, it is a call to action for policy makers across the higher education system and it is couched in neo-liberal business rhetoric.

Costs and the Crisis

The argument, based on new technologies and globalisation, includes a new element, one specifically located in the global crisis:

> the global economy is also dealing with a trauma of the worst crisis in modern times, as the consequences of two decades of irrational exuberance slowly unwind. (Barber et al., 2013: 11)

Leaving aside whether the crisis can be put down to 'irrational exuberance' the link being made to the crisis is clear and it is placed alongside an argument that the costs of higher education are rising in an unsustainable way. This argument, although largely US based, is extended to the UK and explicitly linked to the new English fee regime. Clearly the avalanche, although justified by technological determinist reasoning, is closely related to contemporary economic circumstances. Throughout Barber et al.'s essay there are references to MOOCs as a tipping point, at once both the cause of sudden and discontinuous change and a potential solution to the problems arising from that change. In this way the MOOC moment is a form of the solutionism which has been so ably criticised by authors such as Morozov (2013) in a book ironically published under a Pearson imprint. Solutionism, Morozov argues, is the recasting of complex social situations as either 'neatly defined problems with definite, computable solutions or as transparent and self-evident processes that can easily be optimised' (Morozov, 2013: 5). He goes on to say that this is more than supplying technological fixes to difficult or 'wicked' problems it is finding problems in areas that are not actually problematic at all. The increasing cost of higher education in the IPPR essay is claimed to be a problem for the UK, but the European University Association showed a fall in the percentage of GDP spent on university funding between 2008 and 2013 in 10 EU countries and an increase in eight (EUA, 2013). In the UK (England and Wales) they found that university spending was falling as a proportion of GDP. After rising from 2008 to 2011, expenditure fell to 0.46 % of GDP, with only Hungary, Italy, Portugal and Greece having lower proportional expenditure. This is hardly a problem requiring revolutionary transformation as there has been a nominal change of −10 % between 2008 and 2012, −13 % if inflation is taken into account (http://www.eua.be/publicfundingobservatory)

The drive to lower costs has been picked up by bodies representing universities in the UK and linked directly to the potential of MOOCs.

> MOOCs may also help to restructure and lower the costs of higher education in ways that might be attractive to learners looking for lower cost provision and which presents opportunities for new and existing providers (Universities UK, 2013: 2)

The link made by Universities UK between the 'costs of higher education' and 'lower cost provision' elides two quite different issues. The cost to society of higher education is only loosely connected to the price to the student. Indeed the public provision of higher education has generally meant that the costs to the student were subsidised and the issue of loans and income contingent repayment has often been politically toxic (Barr, 2004). There is another important feature of this debate, the hidden cost of the development of MOOCs (Stanton & Harkness, 2014). Estimates of how much it costs to develop a MOOC vary. Altbach for example offers these estimates:

> Udacity, an American MOOC provider, estimates that creating a single course costs $200,000, and is increasing to $400,000. The University of California, Berkeley, estimates development costs at between $50,000 and $100,000… (Altbach, 2014: 3)

An empirical investigation examining costs in four institutions concluded that the costs for MOOC courses ranged from $38,980 to $325,330 per MOOC, and the costs per student who completed the course were between $74 and $272 (Hollands & Tirthali, 2014). They argue that these costs for MOOCs are lower than for traditional course models but they are not insignificant and they imply that MOOCs might need to be considered financially in the same way that institutions have engaged with online distance learning for many years.

The claim made for MOOCs is that while the cost of preparing a course is high, the marginal cost of the next user is small. This might turn out to be true but it relies on massive course size, and a mechanism to recoup even a small marginal cost. Just as importantly MOOCs require significant start-up capital which narrows the kinds of organisations that have become involved in developing MOOC platforms. All the xMOOCs started with significant capital investment, edX which is a non-profit organisation linked to MIT and Harvard University began with $60 million, Coursera and Udacity which are both for profit began with $22 million and $21.5 million respectively (Yuan & Powell, 2013). The provision of publicly funded education allows low or no cost education for students. In the same way in MOOCs a 'free' education for the learner comes with a cost to the provider and as a consequence the question will arise, 'who bears the cost and how will it be paid?' Fischer (2014: 154) lists the following ways that payment from learners might be garnered in MOOCs:

- Certification: Students pay for a badge or certificate;
- Secure assessments: Students pay to have their examinations proctored, as practiced with Coursera's (2014) Signature Track;
- Applicant screening and employee recruitment: Companies pay for access to student performance records. For example, 3000 students have signed up for Udacity's employer-connection program, allowing their CVs to be shared with 350 companies. Employers pay Udacity a fee for any hires made through this service (Ripley, 2012);
- Human tutoring or assignment marking (for individual students who pay for them) and tutors supporting forums to operate more successfully;
- Hotline services to support learners experiencing problem with content and/or technical issues;
- Selling MOOC platforms to enterprises to use in their courses;
- Sponsorships (third-party sponsors of courses);
- Tuition fees, as illustrated by the experiment of the Computer Science Department of Georgia Tech College of Computing, which has decided to offer a master's degree delivered with MOOCs for a fraction of the cost of a "normal" degree (Georgia Tech College of Computing, 2014).

It should be noted that all these mechanisms assume some sort of market, with the price being paid by students or employers. There is no consideration given to the previously dominant model of the public university funded via general taxation. It is in this way that the MOOC discourse is shifting the frame within which acceptable discussion about funding online distance education takes place from 'public' models of financing to 'free' market business models that fit into a neo-liberal economic paradigm (Harvey, 2005; Mirrlees & Alvi, 2014).

Technologies and Platforms

It was noted earlier that technologies were a site of struggle (Feenberg, 1991). This applies to MOOCs and the technologies that enable them and Daniel (2012) notes that:

At the heart of MOOCs are the platforms that enable the various operations involved in offering a MOOC to be done effectively. (ibid: 7)

While this focus on platform suggests a common technological core Siemens (2012) has argued that the platforms for the two types of MOOC are different because they serve different purposes. Siemens' argued that the cMOOC emphasises creation, creativity, autonomy and learning via social networks and that an ecosystem develops around MOOCs (Siemens, 2013). Because cMOOCs were informed by connectivist views of learning in which knowledge is distributed and learning is the process of navigating, growing and trimming connections. Early cMOOCs began using a Learning Management System (LMS), Moodle, but the interactions on the courses spread across a variety of other platforms including Facebook, Second Life, blogs, and wikis. So cMOOCs emulated other distance learning courses and provided an ecology focused on an LMS platform with the addition of various other services. In contrast the xMOOC model emphasises an instructivist and traditional learning paradigm using presentations via video and testing. The platforms for the xMOOCs are exclusive and it still remains the case, as Siemens has noted, that the xMOOC model has yet to provide good opportunities for non-elite institutions to teach courses on their platforms.

In some ways the rise of the two forms of MOOC mirrors the long standing debate between acquisition and participation metaphors in education (Sfard, 1998). It also carries on the longstanding debate from which the idea of networked learning first arose, between those who saw in digital technologies the possibilities for better and more efficient forms of transmission of educational ideas and those who saw in networked and digital technologies the opportunity to advance a more dialogic and discursive engagement (McConnell et al., 2012). Both cMOOCs and xMOOCS represent a further iteration in the development of technological platforms, but they are not really novel in either educational or business terms. Massive online courses were developed by the Open University at the turn of the millennium and ran with cohorts of up to 12,000 students (Weller, 2000; Weller & Robinson, 2001). Daniel notes how little attention seems to have been paid by those commenting on the MOOC phenomena to previous experiences, either to the university expansion online in the dot com boom or to the open university movement (Daniel, 2012: 9). In addition there is concern that the consideration of MOOCs and their influence is locked into prior debates and misses a key characteristic of MOOCs relevant to educational opportunities, their massiveness (Knox, 2014). Knox draws attention to:

…what happens when thousands of people come together and orient themselves around a specific arrangement of educational material? (Knox, 2014: 165)

He suggests that by viewing MOOCs as either instructivist or constructivist a third possibility is missed and furthermore once MOOCs are viewed in this binary form participants are 'immunised' against other possibilities. I find this argument both important and intriguing because of the potential it holds out for networked learning. Knox draws on Hardt and Negri (2004) for intellectual support and for an elaboration of the additional possibilities in the idea of 'multitude'. The argument Knox makes is that the conception of 'multitude' emphasises plurality as against either a 'people' which is defined by a clear identity or the uniformity implied by the idea of the 'masses'. Knox's concern is to maintain the idea of an irreducible difference and to avoid standardisation and the flattening out of 'students' into a single category. My tentative objection to this idea of the multitude is to emphasise the capacity for self-organisation and the need to be self-aware. Students can develop their own group identities in collective action and still not be reduced to uniformity. As I write a wave of university protests is taking place involving collective action by students and others and these actions point to collective organisation beyond a particular MOOC platform or course (Ratcliffe, 2015). In relation to MOOCs Knox notes how students faced with the overwhelming nature of massive courses look towards community as a support. Knox sees this as part of a process of 'immunisation':

> Whether in the form of the scaled, identical educational broadcast or the construction of an orderly, self-centred personal learning network, MOOCs are frequently designed to rationalise and regulate massive participation into the recognisable guise of the university lecture or the cohesive community. (Knox, 2014: 174)

I do not see this as a negative development and I draw on Marx's notion of classes being able to develop self-consciousness from holding a common position in life (Welton, 2014). While there might be a reactionary 'golden age' inclination in adopting the rhetoric of community it might also signal a positive impulse towards student self-organisation in massive courses. The Open University has organised massive courses in similar ways to other online courses, with students organised into smaller groupings within the large overall cohort of students (Weller & Robinson, 2001). The idea of irreducible difference suggests that such institutionally supported organisation flattens or reduces students to uniformity whereas I see the student capacity to self-organise as a bulwark against uniformity. The organisation in massive courses can provide the starting point and context for a dialogue between necessary pre-organisation by universities and course designers and the self-organising capacity of students.

To summarise, the MOOC 'moment' coincided with the embedding of austerity in advanced industrial countries following the financial crash of 2008. This coincidence proves nothing but it was also marked by a move away from a pedagogy informed by a notion of networked learning with an emphasis on dialogue, participation and the construction of knowledge to a more classically instructivist model based in the transmission of knowledge. The MOOC moment was led by a combination of Silicon Valley expertise and Ivy League elite universities, but it was rapidly taken up by policy makers and advocates of a particular kind of educational reform based on notions of 'disruptive innovation' and 'unbundling' the university. Aaaron Brady writing in the New Inquiry argued that:

> These MOOCs [xMOOCs] are just a new way of maintaining the status quo, of re-institutionalizing higher education in an era of budget cuts, sky-rocketing tuition, and unemployed college graduates burdened by student debt. If the MOOC began in the classroom as an experimental pedagogy, it has swiftly morphed into a process driven from the top down, imposed on faculty by university administrators, or even imposed on administrators by university boards of trustees and regents. From within academia, the MOOC phenomenon is all about dollars and cents, about doing more of the same with less funding. (Brady, 2013)

The idea of a MOOC begins with a notion of educational reform based on principles familiar to those involved in the study of networked learning. My own view of the original formulation in cMOOCs was somewhat sceptical and I was cautious about a lack of connection to previous research and a kind of radical individualism that MOOCs seemed to embody alongside a dismissiveness concerning the institutional form of the university. However the re-invention of the MOOC in the US has been accompanied by a re-hashing of rhetoric based on a technological determinism and intended to support an all too familiar and stale agenda based on individualism, transmissive pedagogy and private interests.

Discussion

Education takes time and resources, in financial terms it costs money. At a time of austerity two questions are posed, how much money can be spent on education and who pays. These are political questions and they are not answered by technological change, even though technologies might make new choices available to educational policy makers. The radical experiment in the UK affecting English students has shifted the burden of costs towards the student in the form of fees, even though the fees are initially paid from state loans. The effect is to change the organising principle away from education as a public good towards making higher education a private concern. Other European governments have moved in a different direction and the final German state government (Länder) has now withdrawn from charging fees (Mechan-Schmidt, 2013). The idea of MOOCs has been enrolled in the debate about the funding of universities and the Campaign for the Public University commented in relation to Futurelearn that:

> …the term 'free' appended to 'online courses' is something of a misnomer. FutureLearn is a private company precisely so that it can attract private venture capital and make money for shareholders from MOOCS. The content is apparently free, but the intention is to find a business model by which it can also be paid for in terms of licensing fees for its use within other degree programmes, or through accreditation. (Campaign for the Public University, 2013)

The context in which MOOCs offer cheaper or free education is one in which governments are changing the overall framework of public expenditure. In the UK this has meant raising a 'pay wall' for students and making higher education a largely private consumer-based transaction and opening up higher education to new (private sector) entrants. The withdrawal of fees in Germany shows that these changes are political choices and they are not an inevitable outcome of either economics or technological change. The politics of networked learning have previously been concerned largely with pedagogy and 'small p' politics and little interest has been shown in political regimes or what might be thought of as high-level politics. This paper argues that this approach is unsuitable for a period of recession in which the politics of austerity are recasting educational technology in a narrow way. The example of the development of idea of the MOOC illustrates the tensions researchers can expect to see emerging.

The public interest is one aspect of education viewed as a site of negotiation between a variety of contending interests. Networked learning has an interest in the kind of higher education that is provided and in the nature of the contemporary university (Goodfellow & Lea, 2013). Networked learning takes place in a network society in which power is dispersed between a variety of economic and state actors but which nonetheless still has key centres of power (Castells, 2009). Castells identifies four key forms of power in a network society:

- Networking power (inclusion or exclusion from networks)
- Network power (standards and protocols of networks)
- Networked power (a dispersed and relational capacity to impose)
- Network making power (constituting, setting goals and forming alliances)
- To these given the recent revelations about the NSA and GCHQ, more longstanding concerns about the Great Firewall in China, and the emergence of surveillance capital in organisations like Google (Zuboff, 2015) we might add:
- Network surveillance power.

Networked learning is concerned with all these forms of power. It is interested in who is included in, and who is excluded from the production, circulation and reproduction of knowledge. Researchers are also interested in the ways standards and protocols, essential to networks, can squeeze out the nonconforming and the ways in which the network mechanisms operate to set these standards. Governing power in digital networks is also deeply embedded in the code that sets up feedback loops which can have a shaping role in networked learning (Williamson, 2015; Chap. 3). Governments at a variety of levels still have a key role to play by imposing legislative frameworks in which networked learning operates, but they exercise this networked power in relation to a wider set of contending powers, e.g. corporations, the press and multi-national actors. Networked learning is also affected by the network making power of those actor-networks that frame the goals, visions and projects that constitute not only existing networks but frame their future development (Fenwick & Edwards, 2010). It is in this kind of actor-network that key power brokers operate, connecting and filtering activity across the network, acting as network 'switches' (Castells, 2009).

In an Epilogue to their exploration of the politics of educational technology Facer and Selwyn set the following challenge:

> …for researchers to take an active role in locating themselves as part of wider movements of resistance alongside those teachers, student groups, civil society, and nongovernmental organisations who are making the case for education as a means of personal and social emancipation (Selwyn & Facer, 2013: 218)

In broad terms this seems like a sensible response to contemporary conditions but I would add that there may be a need to be explicit in including traditional forms of political action via trade unions and political parties. In an age of austerity it is necessary to consider the distribution of resources between different elements in the economy. One of the rationales for the development of MOOCs has been that they allow for the introduction of new entrants into higher education. Multi-national corporations, often engaged directly or indirectly in higher education, can move their profits from one national system to another, using licensing arrangements and transfer pricing, and thus avoid taxation. This enrichment of private corporations at the expense of the public purse either increases the pressure to cut public services or to increase taxation on the wider public. For there to be a public higher education system, within which networked learning can develop, there needs to be resistance to the inclusion of private sector corporations that do not pay their share of national taxes. This might affect corporate provision of cloud computing services and the direct provision of specific services to public higher education (e.g. distance learning) as well as the development of fully private providers. The pressure for private providers to maximise profit is relentless. In the US private universities spend a large proportion of their income on marketing and they focus on the most profitable courses and subject areas (Reuters, 2012). This focus on a narrow range of subjects is mirrored in MOOC offerings (Yuan & Powell, 2013). Public education has a different set of motivations, including the development of an educate citizenry, that are central to the preservation of the pedagogic values associated with networked learning.

Conclusion

The conclusions I draw from the discussion above is that networked learning needs to pay greater attention to formal or 'high' politics if it is to maintain its position in higher education. Communication, collaboration and dialogic methods of education are not exclusive to public education and they can be found in business schools and practiced by private consultancies. However across the full higher education sector the role of public money and the unique place of the university as a protected island of academic freedom is essential for the development of an environment in which networked learning can flourish. The example of the rapid transition from cMOOCs to xMOOCs illustrates the ways in which commercial and financial concerns can affect pedagogic decisions and significantly influence a policy environment.

Secondly in so far as the MOOC moment leads towards the development of the MOOC as a new technical platform networked learning researchers should take a keen interest in the kinds of pedagogies these new platforms instantiate and encourage. Even the xMOOC moment has led to some brave and interesting experiments. The Edinburgh MOOC "E-learning and Digital Cultures", although based on the Coursera platform applied a pedagogy more usually associated with cMOOCs (Knox, 2014; Knox, Bayne, Macleod, Ross, & Sinclair, 2012). The new xMOOC platforms are no more determinist than any other technology and those interested in networked learning should experiment to explore the limits that these platforms allow. The suggestions found in Knox's work certainly provide a starting point with their celebration of the 'irreducible difference' found amongst students. My own inclination is to add to this concern a wish to explore the possibilities for self-organisation among students in massive courses and in education more generally.

References

Altbach, P. G. (2014). MOOCs as neo-colonialism: Who controls knowledge. *International Higher Education, 75*, 5–7. Retrieved November 27, 2014, from http://ejournals.bc.edu/ojs/index.php/ihe/article/view/5426.

Baggaley, J. (2014). MOOCS: Digesting the facts. *Distance Education, 35*(2), 159–163.

Barber, M., Donnelly, K., & Ritzvi, S. (2013). *An avalanche is coming: Higher education and the revolution ahead.* London: IPPR. Retrieved November 27, 2014, from http://www.ippr.org/publication/55/10432/an-avalanche-is-coming-higher-education-and-the-revolution-ahead.

Barr, N. (2004). Higher education funding. *Oxford Review of Economic Policy, 20*, 264–283.

Bates, T. (2014). MOOCs: Getting to know you better. *Distance Education, 35*(2), 145–148.

Brabazon, T. (2007). *The University of Google: Education in a (post) information age.* Aldershot: Ashgate.

Brady, A. (2013). The MOOC moment and the end of reform. *The New Inquiry.* Retrieved November 27, 2014, from http://thenewinquiry.com/blogs/zunguzungu/the-mooc-moment-and-the-end-of-reform/.

Campaign for the Public University. (2013). MOOCs and the University Mission. Retrieved November 27, 2014, from http://publicuniversity.org.uk/2013/09/13/moocs-and-the-university-mission/.

Castells, M. (2009). *Communication power.* Oxford: Oxford University Press.

Chowdry, H., Dearden, L, & Wyness, G. (2010). Higher education reforms: Progressive but complicated with an unwelcome incentive. *IFS Briefing Note* 113. Retrieved November 27, 2014, from http://www.ifs.org.uk/bns/bn113.pdf.

Christensen, C. (2013). *The innovator's dilemma: When new technologies cause great firms to fail.* Boston, MA: Harvard Business Review Press.

Clarà, M., & Barberà, B. (2013a). Learning online: Massive open online courses (MOOCs), connectivism, and cultural psychology. *Distance Education, 34*(1), 129–136.

Clarà, M., & Barberà, B. (2013b). Three problems with the connectivist conception of learning. *Journal of Computer Assisted Learning, 30*(3), 197–206.

Coursera. (2014). *Signature track guidebook.* Retrieved November 27, 2014, from https://www.coursera.org/signature/guidebook.

Crawford, C., Crawford, R., & Wenchao, J. (2014). *Estimating the public costs of student loans.* London: Institute for Fiscal Studies. Retrieved November 27, 2014, from http://www.ifs.org.uk/comms/r94.pdf.

Daniel, J. (2012). Making sense of MOOCs: Musings in a maze of myth, paradox and possibility. *Journal of Interactive Media in Education.* Retrieved November 27, 2014, from http://jime.open.ac.uk/2012/18

Downes, S. (2013). *On the three or four problems of connectivism.* Retrieved November 27, 2014, from http://halfanhour.blogspot.ca/2013/10/on-three-or-four-problems-of.html.

edX. (2012). UC Berkeley joins edX. Retrieved November 27, 2014, from https://www.edx.org/press/uc-berkeley-joins-edx.

EUA (European Universities Association). (2013). EUA's public funding observatory report, Spring 2013. Retrieved November 27, 2014, from http://www.eua.be/Libraries/Governance_Autonomy_Funding/EUA_PFO_report_2013.sflb.ashx.

Feenberg, A. (1991). *Critical theory of technology.* New York, NY: Oxford University Press.

Fenwick, T., & Edwards, R. (2010). *Actor network theory in education.* London: Routledge.

Fox, S. (2005). An actor-network critique of community in higher education: Implications for networked learning. *Studies in Higher Education, 30*(1), 95–110.

Friesen, N. (2010). Ethics and the technologies of empire: E-learning and the US military. *AI and Society, 25*(1), 71–81.

Georgia Tech College of Computing. (2014). Online master of science in computer science. Retrieved November 27, 2014, from http://www.cc.gatech.edu/news/georgia-tech-announces-massive-online-masters-degree-computer-science.

Goodfellow, R., & Lea, M. (Eds.). (2013). *Literacy in the digital university.* London: Routledge.

Greener, I., & Perriton, L. (2005). The political economy of networked learning communities in higher education. *Studies in Higher Education, 30*(1), 67–79.

Hall, R. (2015). For a political economy of massive open online courses. *Learning, Media and Technology, 40*, 265. doi:10.1080/17439884.2015.1015545.

Hardt, M., & Negri, A. (2004). *Multitude: War and democracy in the age of empire.* New York, NY: Penguin.

Harvey, D. (2005). *A brief history of neoliberalism.* Oxford: Oxford University Press.

Hollands, F. M., & Tirthali, D. (2014). Resource requirements and costs of developing and delivering MOOCs. *International Review of Research in Open and Distance Learning (IRRODL), 15*(5), 113–133. Retrieved November 27, 2014, from http://www.irrodl.org/index.php/irrodl/article/view/1901.

Ilich, I. (1970). *Deschooling society.* New York, NY: Harper and Row. Retrieved November 27, 2014, from http://www.preservenet.com/theory/Illich/Deschooling/intro.html.

Jones, C. (2001). Do technologies have politics? The new paradigm and pedagogy in networked learning. Technology Pedagogy and Politics – What next? Mount Royal College, Calgary, AB, Canada, May 4–5, 2001. Retrieved November 27, 2014, from http://oro.open.ac.uk/33381/.

Jones, C. (2002a). The politics of networked learning (Symposium 8). In S. Banks, P. Goodyear, V. Hodgson, & D. McConnell (Eds.), *Networked learning 2002: A research based conference on e-learning in Higher Education and Lifelong Learning.* Sheffield: University of Sheffield. Retrieved November 27, 2014, from http://www.networkedlearningconference.org.uk/past/nlc2002/proceedings/symp/08.htm.

Jones, C. (2002b). Is there a policy for networked learning? In S. Banks, P. Goodyear, V. Hodgson, & D. McConnell (Eds.), *Networked learning 2002: A research based conference on e-learning in Higher Education and Lifelong Learning.* Sheffield: University of Sheffield.

Jones, C. (2011). Students, the net generation and digital natives: Accounting for educational change. In M. Thomas (Ed.), *Deconstructing digital natives: Young people, technology and the new literacies.* London; New York, NY: Routledge.

Jones, C., & Dirckinck-Holmfeld, L. (2009). Analysing networked learning practices: An introduction. In L. Dirckinck-Holmfeld, C. Jones, & B. Lindström (Eds.), *Analysing networked learning practices in higher education and continuing professional development.* Rotterdam: Sense Publishers, BV.

Knox, J. (2014). Digital culture clash: "Massive" education in the e-learning and digital cultures MOOC. *Distance Education, 35*(2), 164–177.

Knox, J., Bayne, S., Macleod, H., Ross, J., & Sinclair, C. (2012). MOOC pedagogy: The challenges of developing for Coursera. Retrieved November 27, 2014, from http://newsletter.alt.ac.uk/2012/08/mooc-pedagogy-the-challenges-of-developing-for-coursera/.

Land, R. (2006). Networked learning and the politics of speed: A dromological perspective. In S. Banks, V. Hodgson, C. Jones, B. Kemp, D. McConnell, & C. Smith (Eds.), *Proceedings of the Fifth International Conference on Networked Learning 2006.* Lancaster: Lancaster University. Retrieved November 27, 2014, from http://www.networkedlearningconference.org.uk/past/nlc2006/abstracts/pdfs/P16%20Land.pdf.

McConnell, D., Hodgson, V., & Dirckinck-Holmfeld, L. (2012). Networked learning: A brief history and new trends. In L. Dirckinck-Holmfeld, V. Hodgson, & D. McConnell (Eds.), *Exploring the theory, pedagogy and practice of networked learning* (pp. 3–24). New York, NY: Springer.

Mechan-Schmidt, F. (2013). Unbridled success: German fees foes claim victory. *Times Higher Educational Supplement.* Retrieved November 27, 2014, from http://www.timeshighereducation.co.uk/news/unbridled-success-germanys-fee-foes-claim-victory/2003928.article.

Meyer, R. (2012). What it's like to teach a MOOC (and what the heck's a MOOC?). Retrieved November 27, 2014, from http://www.theatlantic.com/technology/archive/2012/07/what-its-like-to-teach-a-mooc-andwhat-the-hecks-a-mooc/260000/.

Mirrlees, T., & Alvi, S. (2014). Taylorizing academia, deskilling professors and automating higher education: The recent role of MOOCs. *Journal for Critical Education Policy Studies, 12*(2), 45–73. Retrieved November 27, 2014, from http://www.jceps.com/wp-content/uploads/2014/08/2-JCEPS122-tami-FINAL-17-July-2014.pdf.

MIT (Massachusetts Institute of Technology). (2011). MIT announces online learning initiative. Retrieved November 27, 2014, from http://web.mit.edu/newsoffice/2011/mitx-education-initiative-1219.html.

Moocs@Edinburgh Group. (2013). Moocs@Edinburgh Report #1. Retrieved October 3, 2013, from http://hdl.handle.net/1842/6683.

Morozov, E. (2013). *To save everything click here: Technology, solutionism and the urge to fix problems that don't exist.* London: Allen Lane.

OECD. (2014). *OECD economic outlook, Volume 2014/2.* Paris: OECD Publishing. doi:10.1787/eco_outlook-v2014-2-en.

Oliver, M. (2011). Technological determinism in educational technology research: Some alternative ways of thinking about the relationship between learning and technology. *Journal of Computer Assisted Learning, 27*(5), 373–384.

Ratcliffe, R. (2015). University protests around the world: A fight against commercialisation. The Guardian Higher Education Network. Retrieved April 20, 2015, from http://www.theguardian.com/higher-education-network/2015/mar/25/university-protests-around-the-world-a-fight-against-commercialisation.

Reuters. (2012). U.S. for-profit colleges spend big on marketing while slashing other costs. Retrieved November 27, 2014, from http://www.reuters.com/article/2012/11/28/net-us-forprofitcolleges-analysis-idUSBRE8AR0FJ20121128.

Ripley, A. (2012, October 18). College is dead. Long live College! Time. Retrieved November 27, 2014, from http://nation.time.com/2012/10/18/college-is-dead-long-live-college/print/.

Ritzer, G. (1993). *The MacDonaldization of society.* London: Sage.

Selwyn, N., & Facer, K. (2013). *The politics of education and technology: Conflicts, controversies, and connections.* New York, NY: PalgraveMcMillan.

Sfard, A. (1998). On two metaphors for learning and the dangers of just choosing one. *Educational Researcher, 27*(2), 4–12.

Siemens, G. (2008). *Learning and knowing in networks: Changing roles for educators and designers.* Paper 105: University of Georgia IT Forum. Retrieved November 27, 2014, from http://it.coe.uga.edu/itforum/Paper105/Siemens.pdf.

Siemens, G. (2012). MOOCs are really a platform. eLearnspace. Retrieved November 27, 2014, from http://www.elearnspace.org/blog/2012/07/25/moocs-are-really-a-platform/.

Siemens, G. (2013). Massive open online courses: Innovation in education? In R. McGreal, W. Kinuthia, & S. Marshall (Eds.), *Open educational resources: Innovation, research and practice* (pp. 5–16). Vancouver, CA: Commonwealth of Learning and Athabasca University.

Stanton, J. M., & Harkness, S. S. (2014). Got MOOC?: Labor costs for the development and delivery of an open online course. *Information Resources Management Journal (IRMJ), 27*(2), 14–26.

Universities UK. (2013). Massive open online courses: Higher education's digital moment? Retrieved November 27, 2014, from http://www.universitiesuk.ac.uk/highereducation/Documents/2013/MassiveOpenOnlineCourses.pdf.

Weller, M. J. (2000). The use of narrative to provide a cohesive structure for a web based computing course. *Journal of Interactive Media in Education (1).* Retrieved from http://jime.open.ac.uk/article/view/2000-1/48.

Weller, M., & Robinson, L. (2001). Scaling up an Online Course to Deal with 12 000 Students. *Education, Communication & Information, 1(3).* Retrieved from http://www.mit.jyu.fi/OPE/kurssit/TIES461/Materiaali/Weller_Robinson.pdf.

Welton, M. R. (2014). The educator needs to be educated: Reflections on the political pedagogy of Marx, Lenin and Habermas. *International Journal of Lifelong Education, 33*(5), 641–656.

Williamson, B. (2015). Governing software: Networks, databases and algorithmic power in the digital governance of public education. *Learning, Media and Technology, 40*(1), 83–105.

Winner, L. (1986). Do artifacts have politics? In L. Winner (Ed.), *The whale and the reactor: A search for limits in an age of high technology* (pp. 19–39). Chicago, IL: University of Chicago Press (Reprinted in The Social Shaping of Technology. MacKenzie, D., and Wajcman, J. (eds) (1999) [2nd Edition] London: Open University Press pp 28-40).

Yuan, L., & Powell, S. (2013). MOOCs and open education: Implications for higher education. JISC Cetis. Retrieved November 27, 2014, from http://publications.cetis.ac.uk/2013/667.

Zuboff, S. (2015). Big other: Surveillance capitalism and the prospects of an information civilization. *Journal of Information Technology, 30*, 75–89.

Part II
Boundaries in Networked Learning

Chapter 5
It's Not All About the Learner: Reframing Students' Digital Literacy as Sociomaterial Practice

Lesley Gourlay and Martin Oliver

Introduction

Removing the agency of texts and tools in formalising movements risks romanticising the practices as well as the humans in them; focusing uniquely on the texts and tools lapses into naïve formalism or techno-centrism. (Leander & Lovorn, 2006: 301)

This paper develops a critique of dominant contemporary accounts of "digital literacies". It identifies recent developments in this discourse, and examines the assumptions and characteristics of two widely cited models of digital literacy. These are then considered in relation to two theoretical traditions of work: New Literacy Studies and Sociomateriality. This examination is followed by data from an empirical study that involved longitudinal, multimodal data production and interviews with a dozen students from one Higher Education Institution. The analysis of this data shows that digital literacy cannot be adequately understood from a purely decontextualized, cognitive account of learners, but needs to account for the material and social networks in which practices are enacted.

Digital Literacies

It is generally accepted that the term 'digital literacy' was coined by Glister, who defined it as '...the ability to understand and use information in multiple formats from a wide range of sources when it is presented via computers' (1997: 1). The concept has subsequently been developed by a range of researchers and

L. Gourlay (✉) • M. Oliver
UCL Institute of Education, University of London, London, UK
e-mail: l.gourlay@ioe.ac.uk; m.oliver@ioe.ac.uk

© Springer International Publishing Switzerland 2016
T. Ryberg et al. (eds.), *Research, Boundaries, and Policy in Networked Learning*, Research in Networked Learning, DOI 10.1007/978-3-319-31130-2_5

commentators (e.g. Carrington & Robinson, 2009; Goodfellow & Lea, 2013; Lankshear & Knobel, 2008). It is beyond the scope of this chapter to provide a comprehensive literature view of this complex field; instead we will focus on recent attempts to define student digital literacies, showing how these attempts have relied primarily on taxonomies or lists of features.

Several models of 'digital literacies' have arisen in recent years, and these have been influential in shaping policy, development and research. In many ways, these models represent an advance in mainstream thinking about this very complex area of student practice, in that they have served to shift the focus of work towards the learner, rather than the technology (Bawden, 2008; Glister, 1997). However, this original emphasis on "the ideas and mindsets, within which particular skills and competences operate, and [...] information and information resources, in whatever format" (Bawden, 2008: 19) has since been obscured by other, more technology-oriented definitions, even though "these formulations still tend to focus on technical 'know-how' that is relatively easy to acquire and on skills that are likely to become obsolete fairly rapidly" (Buckingham, 2008: 77).

We argue that this drift towards technical formulations is a mistake, even when it is framed in a 'student-centred' manner. In seeking to define digital literacies in terms of capabilities or features of learners, the field is in danger of losing sight of important aspects of student engagement with technologies as revealed by recent research. In order to explore this issue, we can trace how these discussions have shaped, and in turn been shaped by, national level policies and funding within the UK.

Our point of departure for this discussion is the definition provided by the European Union-funded DigEuLit project, which has proved influential in subsequent attempts to break the concept down into constituent parts:

> Digital Literacy is the awareness, attitude and ability of individuals to appropriately use digital tools and facilities to identify, access, manage, integrate, evaluate, analyse and synthesize digital resources, construct new knowledge, create media expressions, and communicate with others, in the context of specific life situations, in order to enable constructive social action; and to reflect upon this process. (Martin & Grudziecki, 2006: 255)

This is a broad definition, appearing to cover all areas of contemporary digitally-mediated life, as opposed to restricting itself to notions of meaning. In an attempt to encapsulate what is meant by the term, Martin and Grudziecki employ a long list of active verbs related to 'digital resources'. This marks a subtle shift away from Glister's 'information'. However, their emphasis remains on the creation of knowledge and on communication, with an acknowledgement of the connection between this and 'social action'. Once more, however, these practices remain 'free floating'; although there is mention of specific situations, the list given remains ungrounded, unmodulated by the range of ways in which these verbs might be enacted.

Building on this EU definition, Beetham (2010) developed a model as part of a scoping exercise for a large programme of UK government-funded development in universities (JISC, 2011). Because of its position as a foundational point of reference for a programme of funded research, it has become particularly influential in the UK. Beetham provided the following definition: 'Digital literacy defines those capabilities which fit an individual for living, learning and working in a digital society'.

What is striking about Beetham's definition is the continued expansion of its scope, with the term no longer focused on digitally-mediated meaning-making, but on all spheres of activity in 'a digital society'. This may reflect its position in shaping a national-level programme, one that needed to remain inclusive and open at the point of specification. This definition is accompanied by a model structured in four layers. Each layer is seen as resting on the preceding layer (often represented as a pyramid), with 'access' at the base, seen as the first step in "a developmental sequence" (Sharpe & Beetham, 2010: 88), to be followed by 'skills', 'social practices' and finally 'identity'.

This model is insightful in many respects, as it acknowledges the multiple dimensions of this complex phenomenon, and the need for practical access and activities for engagement. It is worth focusing on the continued use of the word 'skills', however. This is a controversial term to employ in a definition of 'literacies': the foundational definition of 'academic literacies' (Lea & Street, 1998) rest on the explicit rejection of the then-prevalent 'skills' model of student communication, which was critiqued as being insufficiently focused on social, disciplinary and individual practices and identities. It is also noteworthy that these elements are constructed as (con) sequential and hierarchical in their nature, with one seen as resting on another in what appears to be a causal configuration. The assumption also seems to be that each of these are steps is taken in ascending order of complexity, with identity appearing almost as a 'product' of the preceding levels of engagement. Whilst this may appeal to common-sense notions of what these concepts denote, it could equally be argued that 'access' flows from identity or cultural capital (Bourdieu, 1986). Indeed, as Bennett argued after working with this model (2014), although academics' identities as teachers might drive engagement with specific social practices, few academics followed a linear progression from seeking access towards the development of a 'digital practitioner' identity.

Additionally, separating 'social practices' from other categories is highly problematic, as this term arguably subsumes all of the others—for example, 'access' (or the lack of it) only makes sense in terms of access to something, for some purpose; in other words, it becomes meaningful as part of social practice. A further point of critique is that identity work permeates all aspects of digital engagement, whether 'basic' or 'advanced'.

Finally, the development of the model from prior empirical work has, arguably, involved category shifts and changes of emphasis that have not been theoretically or empirical driven, but which contribute to the separation of model from specific situated practices. For example, the original derivation of the levels was a response to learners' accounts of enablers and barriers to their development (Sharpe, Beetham, Benfield, DeCicco, & Lessner, 2009: 16)—these were specific, but the specificity is hidden by the abstract terminology of the model. Further, the pinnacle level was expressed in terms of learners' conceptions, and labelled 'creative appropriation' rather than 'identity'. The shift to identity was justified partly in relation to Maslow's

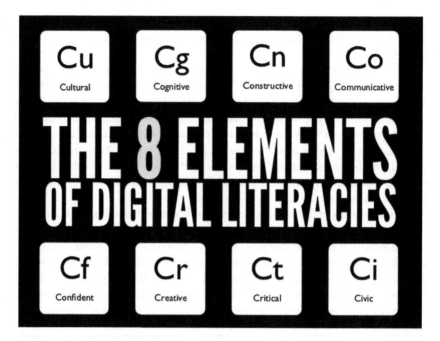

Fig. 5.1 Belshaw's 8 elements of digital literacies

hierarchy of needs by drawing an analogy with self-actualization, with the original label becoming less and less visible over time. This development was not driven nor explicitly informed by theories of subjectivity or identity, however. Consequently, although the model has been influential, and may well be useful heuristically, it remains problematic as an account of students' digital literacies, not least because of the growing drift that can be traced in its development away from specific situated practices.

Another model which has arisen in recent years was formulated by Belshaw (2011). This model proposes that there are 'Eight Elements' of digital literacies, namely: Cultural, Cognitive, Constructive, Communicative, Confident, Creative, Critical, Civic.

The first noteworthy point is that his use of the term 'essential elements' appears to explicitly reference the periodic table of chemical elements, as can be seen this slide taken from a presentation available online (Fig. 5.1; Belshaw, 2012):

Although Belshaw is clearly employing a lighthearted and engaging metaphor, we argue that his choice of metaphor is worth exploring more seriously, since its still influences discussions in this area. It rests on the notion that 'Digital Literacies' is a composite, or a substance made of a combination of all of these elements; consequently the elements are posited as essential, distinct, and amenable to precise definition and delineation. This invites contestation. For example, it could immediately be argued that the concept of 'cultural' contains within it the notion of 'civic'.

Indeed, the terms used in the model are all contestable, blurred and open to multiple definitions—and in that respect are very far from 'essential'.

Linking back to the analysis of Beetham's model, it is also worth noting that the 'elements' all consist of a wide-ranging set of adjectives which refer to qualities often regarded as positive and desirable in students in higher education, none of which are grounded in specific situations. Although it should be recognised that the development of 'the whole person' has long been regarded as an outcome of higher education, these tended to focus on higher-order abilities in academic reasoning and self-expression. In contrast, it can be argued that the contemporary conception of 'graduate attributes' bears a relationship to dominant discourses which place emphasis on the university's role in preparing graduates for the workforce. Viewed through this lens, aspects of the list is reminiscent of rather aspirational 'graduate attributes', and defines literacies in terms of the individual as a bundle of descriptive attributes as opposed to focusing on practices. Such conceptions have been widely contested, both for their coherence and also for the highly political way in which they reposition relationships between Higher Education, employers and wider society; they hinge on the promise of unproblematic transfer of skills between situations (e.g. Atkins, 1999).

Questions can also be asked about the status of practices that incorporate some but not all of the elements. According to this model, for example, an under-confident student writing an essay using online sources may not be engaged in 'digital literacies', as one of the 'essential elements' (confidence) is missing. Whilst it might be possible to use this in a diagnostic way—for example, looking for practices that are more complete than others—the model has not been used in that situated way, and can thus be interpreted instead as an ideological wish-list that positions a student as a particular kind of subject, but does not refer to meaning-making practices—or indeed to 'the digital'—directly.

Common features can be seen in both of these analyses; arguably, these models, and others like them, exhibit several similarities. Firstly, despite having been derived from empirical research, arguably the nuanced nature of the data has been rendered less visible in the move to abstract 'transferable' models. This creates an impression that digital literacies are in some sense quantifiable, relatively stable, generic and transferable entities: i.e. that they are taxonomic, not simply in the sense of being a well-structured classification, but carrying connotations of platonic or transcendental qualities, abstracted away from any specific, situated instance. As a result, such models can create an impression of digital literacies as abstract entities, whose defining features can be identified as residing in the individual. This we would argue is a particular issue when such frameworks come to be associated with neoliberal agendas around 'graduate attributes'.

This idea of learners as individuals carrying stable properties can be further critiqued by drawing on Friesen's analysis of the influence of the US military on e-learning (2010). The close association of military agendas and funding in the development of e-learning as a field are reflected, he argues, in the metaphors 'encoded' within learning systems. He points in particular to the 'closed systems' model that arose from Cold War concerns about the design of systems that demonstrated "survivability". In such models, networks are framed as closed systems in which the learner becomes a component: learners become part of a "man-computer symbiosis".

> The representation of the learner—"student, technician, laborer, professional, warfighter, anyone!"—as a mere organ is perhaps the strongest illustration of this. The human learner is depicted, in effect, as a specialized, functional component interposed in a much larger electronic system. (Friesen, 2010: 77)

As a functional component, the development of 'digital literacies' takes on a very different tone, not as a student-centred expression of agency, but as a concern with re-engineering a substandard component in order to foster the efficient operation of wider technical systems. From this perspective, the creation of a stable, abstract taxonomy of digital literacies takes on clear politics, repositioning graduates as standardised components in corporate systems, not as valued individuals in their own right.

It is also worth noting that models such as those offered by Beetham and by Belshaw are composed of a combination of cognitive acts, attitudinal states, capabilities and attributes. Qualitative adjectives are used, which we would argue feeds the underlying ideology of the graduate as a quality-assured 'product'. Ironically, given that much of the original work was learner-centred, there is then a danger that the ongoing use of such models can result in learners and their situated digital practices being occluded. In order to theorise our critique, we will refer to two bodies of literature and theory in the following two sections—New Literacy Studies and Actor-Network Theory.

New Literacy Studies

The notion of 'academic literacies' was proposed by Lea and Street (1998) as an explicit challenge to the dominant 'skills' paradigm of student writing and communication. This perspective came out of a broader strand of work known as New Literacy Studies (NLS) (Barton, 2007), and sees student writing and other forms of communication as situated social practices centred on meaning-making. Textual practices of all kinds (linguistic, verbal, multimodal involved in reading, writing and speaking) are positioned as central to students' study practices and lives. In this perspective (which has its roots in social anthropology and applied linguistics), cultural, disciplinary and individual practices and texts are seen as fundamentally unstable and in flux. They are also seen as context-specific and under ongoing contestation.

The emphasis within this tradition of research is on social actors, involved in joint engagement via struggles for meaning-making which are seen as co-constitutive of identities and learning. This reflexive relationship between textual media and knowledge practices in higher education has been recognised in media theory (e.g. Kittler, 2004). Since the academic literacies model was developed, the media systems of the university have changed significantly, leading to a situation where the material campus is now largely saturated with digital mediation, and the status of 'face-to-face' as a non-digital category has been placed in radical doubt (e.g. Gourlay, 2012). There has been a recognised need to explore the ramifications of devices and digitally-mediated semiotic practices on meaning making. NLS has responded to this with a series of studies and publications which seek to apply this theoretic perspective to the digital (e.g. Goodfellow & Lea, 2013; Lankshear & Knobel, 2008). An NLS definition illustrates the contrast between this conception and those described above. Gillen and Barton define digital literacies as 'The constantly changing practices through which people make traceable meanings using digital technologies' (2010: 9). The emphasis here is still on situated social practices and meaning-making, rather than decontextualized characteristics of learners.

We will argue with reference to our data that this model reflects more accurately the experiences of students engaged with technologies in their studies, and will propose that this emphasis on situated meaning-making should be present in mainstream definitions and accounts of digital literacies. However, we would like to add a further theoretical strand to this critique. Although the NLS perspective restores the focus on meaning-making and situated practices, arguably, it does not adequately theorise digitally-mediated semiotic practices, in particular the relationship between the student, text and device, the multiply-distributed nature of digital literacies and the materiality of literacy practices (Gourlay, Lea, & Hamilton, 2013).

Sociomaterial Perspectives

Work on the materiality of practice has been developed within the context of Actor-Network Theory. For example:

> If you can, with a straight face, maintain that hitting a nail with and without a hammer, boiling water with and without a kettle…are exactly the same activities, that the introduction of these mundane implements change 'nothing important' to the realisation of tasks, then you are ready to transmigrate to the Far Land of the Social and disappear from this lowly one. (Latour, 2005: 71)

In this quote, Latour prompts us to notice the crucial but often overlooked role of material objects—or 'nonhuman actors'—in everyday processes. These material assemblages are similarly overlooked in educational theory, as Fenwick et al. point out:

> Humans, and what they take to be their learning and social process, do not float, distinct, in container-like contexts of education, such a classrooms or community sites, that can be conceptualised and dismissed as simply a wash of material stuff and spaces. The things that assemble these contexts, and incidentally the actions and bodies including human ones that are part of these assemblages, are continuously acting upon each other to bring forth and distribute, as well as to obscure and deny, knowledge. (Fenwick, Edwards, & Sawchuk, 2011: vii)

Latour sees technologies as 'mediators', rather than as intermediaries. This distinction is important in explaining both the distinctive status of 'digital literacies' as a category of practices, but also in explaining why attempts to abstract from social practices to taxonomic categories are problematic.

For Latour, an intermediary is '…what transports meaning or force without transformation: defining its inputs is enough to define its outputs', while mediators 'transform, translate, distort, and modify the meaning or the elements they are supposed to carry' (Latour, 2005: 39). Latour notes the tendency of groups to position tools as intermediaries when they wish to draw attention away from their operation, naturalising them; whereas he argues that intermediaries are "not the rule, but a rare exception that has to be accounted for" (40). This is as important in academic practices as it is elsewhere.

> Almost all of our interactions with other people are mediated through objects of one kind or another. For instance, I speak to you through a text, even though we will probably never meet. And to do that, I am tapping away at a computer keyboard. At any rate, our communication with one another is mediated by a network of objects – the computer, the paper, the printing press. And it is also mediated by networks of objects-and-people, such as the postal system. The argument is that these various networks participate in the social. They shape it. In some measure they help to overcome your reluctance to read my text. And (most crucially) they are necessary to the social relationship between author and reader. (Law, 1992: 380)

This perspective offers theoretical purchase on the materiality of devices and technologies in a way NLS has not done until now (see Gourlay, Hamilton, & Lea, 2013). This allows us to see digital literacies as emergent through networks of human and nonhuman actors (collectively referred to as actants) and constitutive of 'context', spaces and places. It is this perspective that motivated and informed the study that follows.

Methodology

In order to study students' use of digital technologies in their studies, a nested design was adopted, as part of a JISC-funded project undertaken at a large UK postgraduate institution specialising in Educational research. The student body at the institution is predominantly mature and postgraduate, and many combine study with work and family responsibilities. Students are from diverse countries of origin and a broad range of education cultures. Most have been out of formal education for several years. Consequently, they may never have used the kinds of digital technologies that are regarded as mainstream in higher education, although they have well-established repertoires of digital practices developed in personal or professional settings.

The first phase of research, a secondary analysis of existing data on student satisfaction, identified preliminary areas of practice and concern, but lacked detail. However, it highlighted differences in experience between groups of students following distinct programmes of study. This was used to design the second phase: four focus groups, one each with students following PGCE courses (the UK qualification to teach in compulsory education), taught Masters courses, taught Masters courses studied at a distance, and doctoral students. Participants were recruited to ensure diversity of gender; age; home/EU or international and full-time/part-time status. All participants were studying education-related topics (including pedagogy,

Table 5.1 Participants in the journaling study

Pseudonym	Category	Gender	Nationality
Bokeh	Distance Masters	M	British
Danny	Distance Masters	M	British
Django	PhD	F	British
Faith	PGCE	F	Taiwanese
Frederick	PhD	M	German
Juan	Masters	M	British
Lara	Distance Masters	F	British
Louise	PGCE	F	British
Nahid	Masters	M	Bangladeshi
Polly	PGCE	F	British
Sally	PhD	F	British
Yuki	Masters	F	Japanese

the economics of education, educational development, etc.). Each focus group opened by inviting students to sketch the places in which they studied and the resources they used; this formed the point of departure for the focus group discussions. Transcripts from the focus groups were analysed thematically, revealing that study took place in diverse settings; using a broad array of technologies; and involved extensive use and production of (multimodal) texts, with the University library playing an important role in the provision of these. This was used to structure the third phase of work, which forms the basis of the analysis offered in this paper.

The final empirical phase of the project was a longitudinal study. Three students from each group (see Table 5.1) assembled multimodal journal records of their day-to-day practices and interactions with texts and technologies in a range of settings, producing images, videos and textual notes of everyday objects and processes. These were discussed in an iterative series of 3–4 interviews, over a period of around 9 months, so that the images and artefacts served not only as objects of analysis, but also as stimulus for in-depth exploration of subjectivities, challenges and issues, following an 'Interview plus' approach (Mayes, 2006). (Students studying at a distance were interviewed over Skype, with discussions referring to previously-shared digital resources.) Participants were encouraged to focus on the 'messy' micro-level day-to-day lived activities, networks and the material/spatial aspects of practice. This was meant to help them move beyond neat, decontextualised accounts of the kind that can be generated in stand-alone interviews, where interviewees can find themselves making abstractions rather than retelling specifics (Gourlay, 2010).

The first interview explored students' current practice, invited a 'digital biography' covering historical uses of technology for learning and introduced the devices to be used for data collection. The 'Interview plus' component for this initial discussion involved asking students to draw maps of their study practice, building on the approach used for the focus group, and then developing this through the interview by asking questions about the networks and devices used in different domains; the associations between spaces, tasks and times; the resources drawn upon; feelings of support, control or frustration; and so on. The subsequent interviews focused on themes and issues identified in the focus groups, including use of the VLE and the library, and the consumption and production of study-related texts. Across the course of the interviews students took increasing responsibility for curating, presenting and analysing their own data, adding a layer of interpretation to the dataset. The interviews were transcribed, and transcripts were mapped to the images, videos and resources that students discussed. This multimodal dataset was analysed thematically, drawing on visual methodologies (e.g. Rose, 2012) to interpret images and videos further. The study received institutional ethical clearance and followed approved procedures for informed consent, including guarantees of anonymity and confidentiality, and the right to opt out at any point.

Findings

Not Free-Floating

Students' interviews provided powerful accounts of the ways in which their ability to act in meaningful ways were impeded by the situations in which they were placed. For example, one PGCE student described how her ability to print materials for a class was impeded not through some lack of skill, but through issues of professional identity (and the cultural capital that represents) that set priorities for access:

> In my school […] our staff room was equipped… one, two, three, four, five, six, seven… seven computers now we can use and only one of them attached with a printer. So, actually we've got six PGC students over there, so it's, kind of, everybody wants to get to that computer where you can use the printer. […] So, it, kind of, sometimes feels a bit crowded. And when the school staff want to use it, well, okay, it seems like we are the invaders, intruders? (Faith, Interview 2)

In terms of the models reviewed earlier, 'access' here was problematic, rendering irrelevant Faith's 'skills', by denying her the material resources required for her to enact social practices. Rather than being hierarchical, this situation cut across the foundations of the 'pyramid' model. Belshaw's model appears to fare better, in that this situation appears to fail in terms of 'cultural' or perhaps 'civic' elements; however, Faith's solution (to use a printer in the school library intended for pupils) arguably demonstrates digital literacy, without repairing either of those broken elements.

Not Taxonomic

Participants identified a wide range of technologies used to support study. These included:

- Office tools (primarily Microsoft, plus Google docs and Prezi)
- Institutional VLEs (Moodle and Blackboard)

- Email (institutional, personal and work-based)
- Synchronous conferencing services (Skype, Elluminate)
- Calendars (iCal, Google)
- Search engines and databases (including Google, Google Scholar, library databases, professional databases such as Medline, etc.),
- Social networking sites (Facebook, Academia.edu, LinkedIn) and services (Twitter)
- Image editing software (photoshop, lightbox)
- Endnote
- Reference works (Wikipedia, online dictionaries and social bookmarking sites such as Mendeley)
- GPS services
- Devices (PCs at the institution and at home, laptops including MacBooks, iPhones, iPads, Blackberries and E-book readers)

Importantly, however, no participant used everything from the list. Each worked with a subset that was relevant to them, and moreover, used different technologies at different points in their studies. (Data analysis tools were an obvious example of this, only becoming relevant during and after empirical work.)

This means that any simple functional, taxonomic list would be partial (other students may well use different resources and services), over-inclusive (for example, GPS was relevant to students undertaking fieldwork but not others), plagued by problems of granularity (should Facebook, Academia.edu and Twitter all be counted as 'social networking', or classified separately?) and time-bound (expertise in earlier versions of SPSS was no guarantee of being able to use current versions). Lists may therefore make sense in relation to a particular data set, or provide some heuristic value, but their status as taxonomies cannot be justified.

Not Just Human

The use of maps and images to ground the interviews generated rich accounts of a range of actants that were attributed with agency in relation to their studies.

> My third half of my brain is Google scholar. (Frederick Interview 2)

This kind of example led to rich descriptions of the kinds of heterogeneous networks that students relied upon—and were implicated in—in order to study successfully.

> ...It's not necessarily the working with, sort of, the traditional practices, but much more about the, you know, our physical bodies in space, rather than... And thinking about online environments as being... the iPhone, or whatever it is, connected to a projector, or working then with the iPad, and connecting, so you've got this kind of circuit within a physical space. (Django Interview 1)

Following the principle of symmetry, not all such actants were viewed positively; some participants provided accounts of struggles or dependency rather than enhancement.

> I think they (the technologies) control me as well, because I can't really do anything without them (Faith Interview 1)

Some participants went so far as to describe technologies as malevolent, raising particular concerns about the ways in which they would take and distribute personal information, for example.

> I feel like, also that Google is equally watching you. You know, they're all watching you, they're all trying to sell you things [...] You know, I don't want my friends to spy on me, I don't want my friends to know what I listen to on YouTube. (Sally Interview 1)

Not Just Digital

Whilst students' accounts presented a picture of study as digitally saturated, non-digital resources remained important. Some students found that they supported particular practices, such as annotation, better than digital technologies currently do; they also carried emotional resonance for them.

> My favourite way of studying something is sitting down with a book and…a pen and some yellow paper and taking notes…. And then I will use the technological side as well, because… Yes, I like combining the two, but I also like to be… the demarcation lines between them, you know, if I, if I have a reading to do then I can, then I almost, I invariably print it off and highlight. (Juan, Interview 1)

This 'demarcation' was important: moments at which texts passed from printed to digital, and from digital to print, were important in the study process. These included shifts in practice (such as moving from skimming to reading in depth) and in status (such as from raw data to a form suitable for analysis; or from draft to final, bound and submitted dissertation).

Nor were the networks that students created made purely of material resources and tools; other people played important parts in supporting studying, too. Participants identified tutors, librarians and fellow students as contributing to their studying, in ways that ranged from formal feedback to informal encouragement.

> The student bar we would go to quite often, because it would be the same group of people that usually all work in a library. [...] You know it was fluid enough that people who worked in different places, but you would invariably bump into people, and sort of go how's it going? How's your dissertation? So that event I think was really important. A sort of peer support, whatever, but it being still quite informal, quite casual. (Juan, Interview 4)

Again, accounts that focus purely on individuals in isolation risk ignoring important roles that others play in studying successfully.

Fig. 5.2 A students' curated image data showing the variety of places where they study

Co-constituted Spaces

The sketched maps and images created as data by participants drew attention to the range of spaces that they used for study. As with texts, both digital and physical spaces remained important, with moves between the two signalling important moments of transition. Again, participants described emotional responses to different environments.

> I'll only work at the computer usually to actually do the final part of writing an essay. I enjoy... the image of being, sort of, in a dusty, you know, sort of, wooden shelved, kind of, old library, where it's, sort of, cosy and warm, that's, you know, I like that and that's a part of the experience of studying that I enjoy. (Juan, interview 1)

A recurrent theme was well summed up by the title one participant gave to her montage of images (Fig. 5.2): "less bound by place".

For some of the participants, the portability of devices meant that they could create spaces for study in lots of different locations; this led to a romanticising of the digital as transcending the physical.

> That's really interesting how much I use the iPad for a start everywhere and anywhere... And I have the information there all the time constantly, and I just feel as though I don't have to be anywhere physical at all anymore... (Django, Interview 3)

However, as the frequent accounts of studying on public transport demonstrated, students were not 'free' of spaces; instead, they were better able to create study spaces, to engineer the conditions they needed to study. This usually involved digitising or collating texts, carrying them around, then unpacking them in new locations (e.g. getting out an iPad on a train) so as to make use of them. This sense of being "less bound" was achieved through careful preparation and the purchase of devices (iPads, laptops, ring binders) that helped curate resources. Moreover it was not always successful; participants who used cloud-based file storage were not always able to access this whilst on the move, for example.

Discussion

The cases presented above show some of the complexity of students' study practices, and importantly, demonstrate that simply considering individuals in isolation cannot explain whether or not they should be classified as 'digitally literate'. Existing models of digital literacies do go some way towards recognising this complexity—for example, Beetham's model recognises that access is important, pointing to some degree towards the materiality of social practice; similarly, Belshaw's elements draw attention to the positioning of practice within wider social contexts.

However, drawing on a sociomaterial perspective may help to draw attention to the ways in which students work to create heterogeneous networks of things and people in order to study. The distributed, often private, nature of studying made conventional ethnographic approaches to "follow the actors themselves" (Latour, 2005: 12) impractical to implement, but the rich, longitudinal and multimodal narratives that participants provided allowed such trajectories to be recreated in sufficient detail to appreciate the complexities of their practices. This has demonstrated that technologies do indeed act as mediators, rather than intermediaries, for the academic texts with which students are working. Whether this was the convenience and connectivity that iPads provided, the seriousness and focus that learners associated with research libraries, or the way that post-it notes and marker pens were used to layer meanings onto printed copies of articles, the spaces, tools and technologies that learners worked with contributed to the kinds of texts they were able to produce.

As a result, it is unsurprising that some participants saw their academic self as partially constituted by the technologies, space and services that they drew upon. Rather than 'identity' emerging as an epiphenomenon above a layer of social practice, learners such as Fredrick described themselves as enmeshed with technologies in a manner more akin to Harraway's cyborgs (1991) than to the military, command-and-control circuits that Freisen critiques (2010). This has implications for the unit of analysis for research on digital literacies. As Bhatt and de Roock have argued, focusing on "digital literacy events" rather than on individuals in the abstract may make more sense of the complex, emergent sociomaterial practices that constitute studying, even if it does little to aid in the production of standardised, quality-assured graduate 'components'.

Conclusions

The importance of learning and cognition is undeniable in seeking a comprehensive account of how learners move into new contexts and apply and adapt literacies. However, mainstream accounts of digital literacy tend to create an impression of learners as 'free floating', idealised agents, unencumbered by material concerns. These accounts have been valorised as learner-centred. While this focus on learners is undoubtedly important, the critiques advanced in the first section of this paper, drawing on NLS and Actor-Network Theory, suggest that accounts that ignore the settings in which learners try to study can risk inadvertently promoting a neo-liberal agenda that frames graduates as individualised products. By contrast, taking a sociomaterial perspective provides a fine-grained characterisation of social practices, one that reveals the situated complexity of acting in a digitally literate way.

The study presented here used qualitative data generated by and with students, which in our analysis we argue undermines the validity of such decontextualised accounts. Analysing these empirical cases using concepts drawn from sociomaterial theory demonstrated that, for these students, successful study involves the creation and coordination of sociomaterial assemblages that span material and digital alike. This was particularly visible in the acquisition, curation, destruction and creation of texts, especially as part of assessed work. While existing spaces (the library, home) were confirmed as important sites for study, participants' accounts of the adaptation of existing spaces — whether a seat on a train, a laptop on a sofa or books on a library desk — emphasised the dynamic, improvised and even ephemeral nature of these achievements.

In doing so, it demonstrates that learner-centeredness need not lead to neglect of sociomaterial considerations.

This has implications for future work: close study is needed of students' experiences, including the resources they work with and the settings they create.

References

Atkins, M. (1999). Oven-ready and self-basting: Taking stock of employability skills. *Teaching in Higher Education, 4*(2), 267–280.

Barton, D. (2007). *Literacy: An introduction to the ecology of written language* (2nd ed.). Oxford: Blackwell.

Bawden, D. (2008). Origins and concepts of digital literacy. In C. Lankshear & M. Knobel (Eds.), *Digital literacies: Concepts, policies and practices* (pp. 17–32). New York, NY: Peter Lang.

Beetham, H. (2010). Review and Scoping Study for a Cross-JISC Learning and Digital Literacies Programme. JISC. Retrieved from www.jisc.ac.uk/media/documents/funding/2011/04/Briefingpaper.pdf.

Belshaw, D. (2011). What is 'digital literacy'? A pragmatic investigation. Doctoral Thesis, Durham University. Retrieved from http://neverendingthesis.com/doug-belshaw-edd-thesis-final.pdf.

Bennett, L. (2014). Learning from the early adopters: Developing the digital practitioner. *Research in Learning Technology, 22*, 1–13.

Bourdieu, P. (1986). The forms of capital. In *J.G. Richardson's handbook for theory and research for the sociology of education* (pp. 241–258). New York, NY: Greenwood Press.

Buckingham, D. (2008). Origins and concepts of digital literacy. In C. Lankshear & M. Knobel (Eds.), *Digital literacies: Concepts, policies and practices* (pp. 73–89). New York, NY: Peter Lang.

Carrington, V., & Robinson, M. (2009). *Digital literacies: Social learning and classroom practices*. London: Sage.

Fenwick, T., Edwards, R., & Sawchuk, P. (2011). *Emerging approaches to educational research: Tracing the sociomaterial*. London: Routledge.

Friesen, N. (2010). Ethics and the technologies of empire: E-learning and the US military. *AI and society, 25*(1), 71–81.

Gillen, J., & Barton, D. (2010). *Digital literacies: A research briefing by the technology enhanced learning phase of the teaching and learning research programme*. London: London Knowledge Lab. http://www.tlrp.org/docs/DigitalLiteracies.pdf.

Glister, P. (1997). *Digital literacy*. New York, NY: John Wiley and Sons.

Goodfellow, R., & Lea, M. (2013). *Literacy in the digital university: Critical perspectives on learning, scholarship and technology*. London: Routledge.

Gourlay, L. (2012). Cyborg ontologies and the lecturer's voice: A posthuman reading of the 'face-to-face'. *Learning, Media and Technology, 37*(2), 198–211.

Gourlay, L., Hamilton, M., & Lea, M. (2013). Textual practices in the new media digital landscape: Messing with digital literacies. *Research in Learning Technology, 23*, 1–13.

Haraway, D. (1991). *A cyborg manifesto: Science, technology, and socialist-feminism in the late twentieth century. Simians, cyborgs and women: The reinvention of nature*. London: Routledge.

Kittler, F. (2004). Universities: Wet, hard, soft and harder. *Critical Inquiry, 31*(1), 244–255.

Latour, B. (2005). *Reassembling the social: An introduction to actor-network-theory*. Oxford: Oxford University Press.

Law, J. (1992). Notes on the theory of the actor-network: Ordering, strategy, and heterogeneity. *Systems Practice, 5*(4), 379–393.

Lea, M., & Street, B. (1998). Student writing in higher education: An academic literacies approach. *Studies in Higher Education, 23*(2), 157–172.

Leander, K., & Lovorn, J. (2006). Literacy networks: Following the circulation of texts, bodies and objects in the schooling and online gaming of one youth. *Cognition and Instruction, 24*(3), 291–340.

Martin, A., & Grudziecki, J. (2006). DigEuLit: Concepts and tools for digital literacy development. *Innovation in Teaching and Learning in Information and Computer Sciences, 5*(4), 249–267.

Mayes, T. (2006). LEX – Methodology report. Glasgow Caledonian University and Open Learning. Retrieved from http://www.jisc.ac.uk/media/documents/programmes/elearningpedagogy/lex_method_final.pdf.

Sharpe, R., & Beetham, H. (2010). Understanding students' uses of technology for learning. In R. Sharpe, H. Beetham, & S. De Freitas (Eds.), *Rethinking learning for a digital age: How learners are shaping their own experiences* (pp. 85–99). London: Routledge.

Sharpe, R., Beetham, H., Benfield, G., DeCicco, E., & Lessner, E. (2009). Learners experiences of e-learning synthesis report: Explaining learner differences. Unpublished project report, Oxford Brookes University. Retrieved from https://wiki.brookes.ac.uk/display/JISCle2f/Findings.

Chapter 6
Artefacts and Activities in the Analysis of Learning Networks

Peter Goodyear, Lucila Carvalho, and Nina Bonderup Dohn

Introduction

The main aim of this chapter is to help people who design for networked learning reflect on their ways of thinking about connections between learning activity and the physical world (places, tools and other artefacts etc., digital, material and hybrid). The empirical work informing this chapter is part of a 5-year programme of research into the architecture of learning networks (Carvalho & Goodyear, 2014; Carvalho, Goodyear, & De Laat, 2016; Goodyear & Carvalho, 2013).

Underpinning our approach is the view that *learning networks* are worthy of research in their own right—taking their place as researchable phenomena alongside more familiar topics like learner experiences, learning outcomes, pedagogy, moderation strategies, etc. We take a learning network to be a heterogeneous assemblage of people and things connected in activities that have learning as an explicit goal or as a significant side effect. Coherence among the activities helps resolve the learning agenda of the network, which, in turn, helps trace the limits of the network. As Jones (2004) has pointed out, calling something a network can be seen as bringing the network into being. We agree that calling something a network is an analytic choice. It entails a claim that—for certain sets of research purposes—it is helpful to see something as taking the form of a network, rather than a hierarchy, or a community, or a space or a set of market relations. But, in our view, once some aspects

P. Goodyear (✉) • L. Carvalho
Centre for Research on Computer Supported Learning and Cognition, Faculty of Education and Social Work, University of Sydney, Sydney, NSW, Australia
e-mail: peter.goodyear@sydney.edu.au; lucila.carvalho@sydney.edu.au

N.B. Dohn
Department of Design and Communication, University of Southern Denmark, Copenhagen, Denmark
e-mail: nina@sdu.dk

© Springer International Publishing Switzerland 2016
T. Ryberg et al. (eds.), *Research, Boundaries, and Policy in Networked Learning*, Research in Networked Learning, DOI 10.1007/978-3-319-31130-2_6

of a network have been labelled, many of its other characteristics are real rather than arbitrary. (For example, once one defines what constitutes a link between nodes in a network, one cannot arbitrarily prune the network.) Seeing something as a network necessarily focuses on node-link structures, foregrounding connectivity and topology and backgrounding such things as spatial relations.

Our approach to analysing learning networks is driven by a commitment to identifying reusable design ideas. In other words, our main goal is to understand how existing learning networks function, in order to inform the design practice of people who help learning networks to flourish. A commitment to generating knowledge that can be useful in design means having a sharp eye for what *can* be designed, and what is necessarily emergent (Goodyear, 2000, 2005; Goodyear & Dimitriadis, 2013). We find that it is useful to focus on five main aspects of learning networks: learning outcomes, learning activities, tasks, physical settings and divisions of labour (Goodyear & Carvalho, 2014). The last three of these are (partially) designable; the first two are emergent. The influence of the physical setting (digital and material) on learning activity is often important, but is under-researched and under-theorised: it is often taken for granted. Yet designers need to have some principles, or at least some rules of thumb, to link the physical setting to learning activity. In other words, the design vocabulary for networked learning needs to include a number of terms that can connect the qualities of a learning place, and/or tools, artefacts and other kinds of physical things, to intended learning activities: to suggest what needs to "come to hand" for the activity to proceed successfully. The idea of "affordance" is one such term, but it is quite rightly contested and is insufficient on its own (Dohn, 2009).

Every learning network has an architecture, in which structural relations can be traced, at a number of scale levels, between designable elements and emergent activities and outcomes (Carvalho & Goodyear, 2014, esp. Chapters 1–3 and 16). In other words, (a) any individual activity holds together, and is shaped by, an assemblage of task (epistemic), physical and social entities, and (b) these entities are often nested (e.g. tasks have sub-tasks, places contain tools, etc.). The knowledge needed for design includes understanding the possibilities and constraints held in connections between physical things and physical things (T-T), human beings and human beings (H-H) and human beings and physical things (H-T) (Hodder, 2012; Yeoman & Carvalho, 2014). This is in addition to understanding such matters as the experience of learning and connections between learning activities and likely outcomes (the classic domain of learning theory). Some construals of the world (ontologies) are good for explaining and predicting T-T relations; others are better for understanding human experience and H-H relations. Our focus in this chapter is on H-T relations, but we also comment on whether and how designers can work with multiple, apparently contradictory, ontologies. It turns out that while dualist ontologies (which deal separately with the human and the physical) can be useful in understanding T-T and H-H, they struggle with H-T. To understand the implications of connections between humans and things (H-T), one needs a relational rather than a dualist ontology: for example, an affordance of a thing for a person depends on qualities of the thing relative to capabilities of the person (skills, perceptual acuity, etc.).

Creating richer understandings of the relations between physical things and human activity is a core concern for social science researchers interested in materials and materiality: notably, researchers involved in archaeology and anthropology (see e.g. Boivin, 2008; Hodder, 2012; Ingold, 2011; Malafouris, 2013; Miller, 2010). "Digital things" are not well covered in most of this literature, and since some of the attributes of (tangible) material things do not apply to non-material technological things, such as software (Faulkner & Runde, 2011), we use the term "physical" to include both the material and the digital. There is some work that speaks from this broad position to address the use of digital technologies: e.g. Suchman (2007), Orlikowski (2007) and Leonardi, Nardi, and Kallinikos (2012). Sorensen (2009) and Johri (2011) provide introductions to materialist perspectives in educational technology, and Fenwick, Edwards, and Sawchuk (2011) offer such a treatment for education more generally. The elements sketched above also draw on aspects of activity theory (e.g. Engestrom, Miettinen, & Punamaki, 1999), though a limitation of activity theory for the work at hand is that it is strangely uninterested in tracing the implications of qualitative differences in materials.

Design for Networked Learning

Much of the networked learning literature about teaching focuses on teaching as a facilitation or moderation activity (Feenberg, 1987; Mason & Kaye, 1989; Salmon, 2000). We are particularly interested in a complementary, upstream and relatively neglected aspect of teaching—*teaching as design*: the kind of educational work that sets things in place prior to a learning activity. It is thoughtful, creative, time-consuming work that entails solving complex problems and balancing (or resolving tensions between) multiple competing demands. Amongst other things, this needs a repertoire of explicit design constructs to link design decisions to intended learning activities and outcomes (Conole, 2013; Goodyear, 2005; Goodyear & Dimitriadis, 2013; Goodyear & Retalis, 2010; Laurillard, 2012). Investing time in design pays better returns for the teacher (and learners) than having subsequently to spend time animating, repairing and redirecting activities. A provocative question, worth asking at this point, is whether it is actually possible to design for someone else's learning. From where can a teacher-as-designer gain some confidence that what they help set in place is likely to have a beneficial effect on what learners subsequently do? What kinds of knowledge can they draw upon to connect designable things to valued learning? If designers cannot provide a structured argument that connects the outputs of their design work to desired learning activities and outcomes, how can they defend what they do?

Connecting Design Ideas

We want to capture some of the ways in which design for networked learning can position itself as a worthwhile, intellectually defensible activity. This involves delimiting what can be designed and identifying some of the analytical connectors that can be used by teacher-designers to think about links between what they design and what learners are likely to do. In short, we want to identify some of the intellectual resources that can be used in creating design rationales—articulating what has been termed the logic of designs (Nash, Plugge, & Eurelings, 2000; Sandoval, 2014). Placing the knowledge needs of the teacher-designer centre stage also creates a useful hook on which to hang research-based ideas, and indeed can help orient and motivate future research. What can be designed, and what cannot? Are these designable things all of one kind, or is a taxonomy needed? In what ways do people (learners) respond to designed things, of various kinds—what types of *connectors* can provide the analytical structure for a design rationale and/or for design thinking? (Overdijk, Diggelen, Kirschner, & Baker, 2012).

In earlier work, we have shown that a distinction needs to be drawn between learner's *activities* (what they actually do) and the *tasks* that are set for them (Goodyear, 2000). The labels are not important, but acknowledging the likelihood of slippage between the task as set and the actual activity is vital. Teachers usually want learners to exercise some autonomy and creativity in responding to the tasks they are set. This allows them to customise a task to suit their own needs and interests, and provides an opportunity for them to strengthen their self-regulation skills. Unless learning is very closely supervised and directed (which it rarely is), there will usually be some slippage between task and activity, for good and bad reasons. This is important to acknowledge, when designing, because what people learn is a consequence of their actual activity, and therefore only *indirectly* a result of the task set for them (see Fig. 6.1).

Tasks are designable, activities are not—they are emergent. In addition to tasks, there are two other major design components, reflecting the fact that learning activity is both socially and physically situated (Lave & Wenger, 1991; Sawyer & Greeno, 2009). We do not have room here to talk about social design (H-H: assigning roles, divisions of labour etc.), so we turn directly to the physical setting (H-T and T-T). This third design component includes digital, non-digital (material) and hybrid entities. Design entails thinking about the kinds of learning places, tools and other resources that students are likely to find helpful, for any particular task, while recognising that students may not follow the recommendations inscribed in designs. They will often make their own choices about tools to use, where to work, what to read, etc.

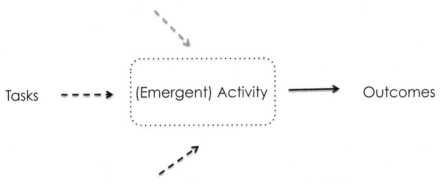

Fig. 6.1 Activity as physically, socially and epistemically situated (adapted from Goodyear & Carvalho, 2014: 59)

Expansive Conceptions of Learning Networks

Like many researchers in the networked learning field, we have a broad understanding of "learning"—one which does not restrict the definition to formal education courses and which also embraces informal, self-directed, vocational and/or interest-based learning, as well as learning that occurs as a by-product of engaging in activity which has some other purpose, such as organisational change, community or political action, or participation in collective scientific and artistic work. Even in tightly circumscribed formal education settings, goals and activities tend to presume fields of application beyond "the (virtual) classroom". Learning is meant to be connected to (the rest of) life. It leaks into, and becomes inextricably entangled with, other activities, as people go on with their lives. We believe a similarly expansive conception is needed of the tools and other resources that are used, and the places that are involved. In the early days of networked learning, research tended to focus on computer-mediated (online) discussions (see e.g. Goodyear, 2014; Henri, 1992; Mason & Kaye, 1989). At the risk of over-simplifying, one might say that people involved in networked learning were generally assumed to be experiencing remote interaction with others: while sitting down, using a desktop computer or terminal; in periods of time they had allocated specifically for that activity; coloured by a sense of slow and/or fragile, unreliable telecommunications links; through reading text that other participants had written and through crafting carefully considered written responses.

Twenty years later, changes in technology, media habits and expectations mean that this sedentary, exotic, keyboard-tethered image of networked learning is no longer tenable. Mobile, personal, voice-enabled multifunctional devices such as laptops, tablets and smartphones have made it possible to participate in networked learning 24/7 from almost any location, including in workplaces, the home, the bus and the street. Exponential growth of web-based information resources and increased use of social media have also reshaped expectations about access to knowledge and people. Networked learning typically now involves heterogeneous digital tools and resources, used in ways that interweave with the other activities of life. It is no longer exotic (Goodyear, 2014; Hodgson, De Laat, McConnell, & Ryberg, 2014). Approaches to researching networked learning have not quite kept pace with changes in the social practices of technology use. Or perhaps we might say that the dominant images of the objects of our research do not yet reflect the extent to which learning networks now consist of heterogeneous assemblages of tasks, activities, people, roles, rules, places, tools, artefacts and other resources, distributed in complex configurations across time and space and involving digital, non-digital and hybrid entities.

The most important thing in a network is what people actually do (i.e. their activity). That said, our main practical purpose in analyzing networks is to extract reusable design ideas. Activity *emerges*—not in an arbitrary, random, free-floating way, but as a response to tasks (explicit and implied), and shaped by the physical and social context. The physical context is constituted by material and digital tools and other artefacts, including those that are bearers of texts. Some of these *things* appear singly (T), others in more complex assemblages (T-T), including assemblages to which one might apply labels like 'room', 'building', 'place' or 'infrastructure'. Activity includes the purely mental, but—more often than not—it is tightly coupled to things. It involves moving things around, moving around among things, and modifying or composing new assemblages.

Identifying the physical elements of a learning network must go beyond the obvious—beyond the shared digital spaces that historically have been seen as the core of a learning network. Insofar as the activity of networked learning participants connects with the material spaces they inhabit, then the characteristics of those spaces are important. This must be so, because these material spaces offer opportunities for action and impose constraints that can be consequential for learning and its application. For example, in one of our case studies (Robinson & Metcher, 2014), the physical spaces in which some network participants wanted to *apply* their learning were not connected to the Internet. The design team made it easier for them to create printable versions of some of their work—paper providing a very useful interface when sharing ideas and resources with people who do not participate directly in the network. A key point here is that an *expansive* sense of a learning network allows a more complete analysis of the relations between things and human activity: one can "follow the things" as they connect activities into a more coherent whole. In turn, this needs an understanding, in both analysis and design, of the strengths and

weaknesses of different ways of conceptualizing things, humans and their relations—a topic to which we now turn.

Framing Relations Between Things and People: Ontology

If designers are to have a sound base on which to make analytical connections
between things that can be designed and human activities, then they need to consider the strengths and limitations of the main ontological positions open to them.
We review these here, before moving on to look at some connecting constructs.
Simplifying ontology somewhat, one may say that there are *dualistic* and *relational*
positions.

Dualistic Perspectives

Dualistic positions fundamentally build on a clear distinction between (1) the physical (rocks, buildings, cars, computers, etc.) and (2) the human (minds, feelings,
perceptions, activities). Precisely how the distinction is drawn varies, i.e. which
phenomena are seen as the basic 'opposing' categories, with traditional Cartesian
dualism focusing on *res extensa* versus *res cogitans* ['extended', material things
versus thinking things], Cartesian heirs opposing physicality and so-called qualia
(e.g. Dennett, 1991; Jackson, 1982; Nagel, 1986; Rorty, 1980), Husserlian phenomenology emphasizing human intentionality as that which sets us fundamentally
apart from the material world (Husserl, 1950), and others contrasting the domain of
physical, causal relations with the domain of agency and/or (self-)interpretation
(Hacker, 2009; Taylor, 1985; Winch, 1990). On all of these dualisms, however, bodies, information, knowledge, texts and software prove to be awkward terms because
they in one way or another cut across the opposed constructs, having both physical/
material/causal properties and thinking/intentional/qualia/agency aspects. On the
one hand they refer to obvious, hard-to-dispute phenomena, but on the other hand
they require quite a lot of easy-to-dispute theorizing to fall into category (1) or (2).

Dualistic positions have inspired two basic contrasting traditions or perspectives—one which focuses on the physical and tends towards the use of positivist
methods and explanations, and one which focuses on the human and tends towards
the use of interpretive methods to understand personal subjective experiences.

(1) Physical/Positivist/Objectivist
    This perspective has the methodological advantage of being concerned with
    publicly available phenomena and therefore of building on what seemingly are
    objective, reproducible data. The construction of theories on the basis of such
    data holds the promise of supplying general, overarching laws rich in both
    explanatory and predictive power and scope. Philosophically, the approach has

the advantage of enabling—at least in principle—an account of the world where humans are included among other natural phenomena, i.e. where no special ontological and methodological status is given to humans. A limitation to the approach is that it has no room for a concept of *meaning* and therefore—in principle—it cannot capture the phenomenological level of what matters most to us in our everyday life. It can only account for a third person view—from outside the world, from no-where—but not the first person view from within the world—the view of now-here—with which we are all most familiar at the outset (Nagel, 1986). Any overarching laws which can be postulated for the field of design for learning can therefore not grasp the *significance* of activities and experiences *for the learner*. Instead, they are restricted to behavioristic predictions and explanations. Furthermore, any proposed overarching predictive law intended to capture how people will behave may lead people to react *to* the predictions by deciding to behave contrary to them, thus leading to the falsification of the law (Bhaskar, 1986; Popper, 1972).

(2) Human/Subjective/Interpretivist

In contrast, the flip-side approach which focuses on personal subjective meaning is very much concerned, from its theoretical and methodological outset, with personal significance—the first person view. Within the field of design for learning, it focuses on how learners report their experiences of learning, aided by different designs. It is well suited to explaining what the objectivist approach cannot— namely how overarching, predictive laws fail for humans because of their capacities for interpretation and reflection and their ability to change their actions on the basis thereof. However, precisely because of this focus on the first person view, the approach has problems when it comes to accounting for influences (from things and other people) *of which the person is unaware*, and of explaining phenomena such as deception and self-delusion. Philosophically, the approach risks falling into relativism: accepting any sincerely presented account as 'the truth of the matter for that person' (e.g. Sfard & Prusak, 2005). Meta-methodologically, the approach grapples with ideas of objectivity and truth, proposing other ways to construe these concepts than the positivist ones (e.g. as 'inter-subjectivity' and 'coherence', respectively), and with the risk of gaining interpretive depth at the cost of explanatory and applicatory scope. Methodologically, it has problems even at the level of verifying informants' claims to sincerity. In terms of designs for learning, the approach struggles to validate the effect of different designs, beyond what learners believe and are able to say.

Relational Perspectives

Both the dualist approaches suffer from the inherited Cartesian philosophical problem of how to "bridge" between the two postulated worlds. That is, both approaches struggle to answer questions about how a person combines subjective mind and physical body in activity in the world. Dualist science therefore has a hard time investigating this connection—e.g. how subjective meanings are projected into the physical world; how the natural sciences and the human and social sciences relate; and how they may inform each other. Many philosophical attempts to remedy this predicament have been advanced over the centuries, with Hegel and Marx as very prominent examples, looming also in the background of the contemporary phenomenological and materialist approaches to be discussed below. Characteristic of these contemporary approaches is a non-dualistic starting point from where the phenomena concerned are viewed as *relational*—neither objective nor subjective, or perhaps both at once, to paraphrase Gibson (Gibson, 1986: 129). Without dualism the question of how to bridge between the perceptions of the mind and the events of the "outside world" does not arise. Recently, a number of theories have been advanced within the field of social inquiry, inspired by thinkers such as Latour and Suchman, which give serious attention to the relations between physical/material things and human activity. Thus, Orlikowski has argued for the *constitutive entanglement* of the material and the social, maintaining that "Humans are constituted through relations of materiality — bodies, clothes, food, devices, tools, which, in turn, are produced through human practices. The distinction of humans and artifacts, on this view, is analytical only; these entities relationally entail or enact each other in practice." (Orlikowski, 2007: 1438). Carrying the argument even further, Ingold (2012) talks of an *ecology of materials* which views humans and materials not as preexisting entities connected in a network, but as always in entangled becoming— "perpetually on the threshold of emergence"—in a meshwork of movement; "the web of life itself" (435).

The strength of these new relational-materialist positions is, firstly, their appreciation of the complexity of material situations, in particular of the way a range of material artefacts, physical structures and "natural occurrences" come together to constitute the significance of any one of the material objects in the given situation. This is in contradistinction to most accounts of the "affordance" of a thing which concentrate on the too-simple question of the relationship between one artefact and a user, thereby neglecting the role which *other* things (T-T) have, not only in determining the affordance of the thing, but in making it what it is. A further strength of this approach is its dynamically emergent view of the relationship between humans and things, avoiding as it does the risk of both social and physical determinism as well as the positing of a gap-to-be-bridged between the mental and the physical. It also emphasizes the fundamental flux of *being* as opposed to the static view presupposed by dualism. It thereby builds on the basic phenomenological point made by Heidegger (1986) and Merleau-Ponty (1962) that humans are always already in the world and that the gap between mind and material comes about only as an abstraction, secondary and derivative, from this "being-in-the-world".

In comparison with the two dualist views, the new "materialist turn" thus allows for a treatment of humans and non-humans within the same ontological framework (a strength of the physicalist side of dualism) whilst also ascribing a central role to the "meaning" of situations, thereby accommodating to our everyday experience of living (a strength of the interpretive side of dualism). In effect, relational-materialism therefore "combines the strengths" of the two dualisms, without combining the positions (or even bits of the positions), by taking a non-dualistic starting point, and recognizing meaning as a basic category. More specifically, the concept of meaning is transformed from a first-person category into a relational, third-person one and things and people are recognized as having "meaning", not only to people, but to things as well. That is, significance is always already inscribed in the world in the relation between the entities there (human and non-human). Or more accurately, significance is the ever-changing result of the dynamic co-constitution of the entities in the world. As Hodder (2012) puts it, humans need things, but also some things need humans (e.g. for their repair), and some things also need other things (e.g. a roof needs a wall; a word-processing package needs a computer).

We agree with the relational perspective of the materialist turn. Still, for other purposes, we do find it necessary to stress that the *way* things have meaning to humans is different in important respects from the way things have meaning to things. The recognition of a basic non-dualist ontological framework should not lead one to the opposite extreme, i.e. to an unqualified postulate of symmetry between humans and things in all matters concerned. There is room, for instance, for differences in epistemological predicaments: Though humans certainly seldom, if ever, 'fully understand' the meaning of a situation, they do on the other hand have the possibility of understanding in a way which things do not. This is important in designs for learning because learners not only use tools, but *learn* to use tools, use tools *to learn*, and understand that this is what they (have to) do. Although the designer must become much more aware of the entanglement of things and humans than is the case today, still, at the heart of designing for learning there is an asymmetry: human learning is qualitatively different from the ways in which things adapt to people.

Constructs to Connect Things and People

How then, can designers plan to connect physical things to human activity? This question begs three further questions. Who is doing the learning? What kind of learning is entailed? What is it reasonable for designers to try to do, to help participants in a learning network? These questions can be tackled in a variety of ways, but we think the most pressing issues are captured in Figs. 6.2 and 6.3.

Figure 6.2 is an elaboration of Fig. 6.1 and its function is to draw attention to the fact that how one conceives of the relations between the physical world of places and things (T) and human activity (H) depends in part on one's conception of the human: of the person engaged in learning, in this case. There are, of course, many positions that can be taken on this question and Fig. 6.2 simply offers one contrast, albeit a very significant contrast in the literatures of networked learning, human computer interaction (HCI) and theories of action and the mind. On the left hand side ('goal directed action') we indicate what might be thought of as a classic paradigm in cognitive psychology and HCI, reflecting the assumption that most human

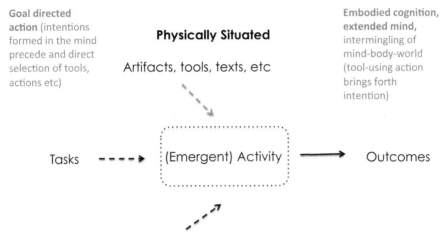

Fig. 6.2 Understanding physical situatedness, and T-H relations, depend upon how one understands the learner

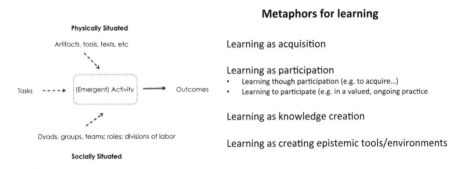

Fig. 6.3 Understanding physical situatedness, and T-H relations, depend upon how one understands learning

action, including that which involves the use of tools (digital and otherwise) can be understood as a working out, in the physical world, of plans formed, prior to action, in the mind (see, for example, Card, Moran, & Newell, 1983; Newell & Simon, 1972; Proctor & Vu, 2009). It is, *par excellence*, a dualist model with a clear separation between the human mind (as the locus of intention and intelligence and the source of action) and the physical world. As Suchman (1987, 2007), Turnbull (1993, 2002), Ingold (2011, 2013) and others have eloquently argued, it is a mistake to insist on always, or generally, understanding human action in the physical world as the enactment of prior mental plans. There exists a range of alternative views, but many of these foreground: the role of tight, fast, perception-action loops in skilled human action; intentions *emerging* from situated action and perception, and a blurring of boundaries between mind, body and world.

> ...cognition is worked out in the practices of engaged daily practices with things. (Hodder, 2012: 37)

> ... equipment affects how things are seen because how we act on the world, and the tasks we perform, shape how we perceive (Kirsh, 2013: np)

> ... our ways of thinking are not merely causally dependent upon but constituted by extra-cranial bodily processes and material artifacts (Malafouris, 2013: 227)

> ...Our intelligence is not only inside the mind, but in its multi-faceted networking connections and downloaded to various peripherals, i.e., artifacts that can be understood as cognitive prostheses that expand and augment human creativity and intelligence when integrated with the cognitive architectures of the participants' minds (Ritella & Hakkarainen, 2012: 242)

The position sketched on the right hand side of Fig. 6.2 acknowledges both an embodied or grounded perspective on human cognition and a notion of the mind as extended—a so-called 'person plus' or 'human-machine symbiosis' perspective.

> Human-machine symbiosis, I believe, is simply what comes naturally. It lies on a direct continuum with clothes, cooking ('external, artificial digestion'), bricklaying and writing. *The capacity to creatively distribute labour across biology and the designed environment is the very signature of our species*, and it implies no real loss of control on our part. For who we are is in large part a function of the webs of surrounding structure in which the conscious mind exercises at best a kind of gentle, indirect control. (Clark, 2003: 174)

While Fig. 6.2 raises questions about the nature of the H(uman) who is doing the learning, Figure 6.3 reminds us of the availability of different conceptions *of* learning. Here we draw on Anna Sfard's influential suggestion and mention four *metaphors* for learning Sfard, 1998). On Sfard's account, the two most widely used metaphors for learning are 'learning as acquisition' and 'learning as participation'. The first of these sees learning as an individual cognitive accomplishment, in which learning results in a person *gaining* new knowledge, skills, etc. which become theirs and which they can take from context to context. 'Learning as participation' sees learning from a sociocultural viewpoint and equates learning with acts of participation in the social practices of a community. This second metaphor has been widely appropriated within formal education, for example, in the adoption of 'community of practice' pedagogies. Close inspection reveals some ambivalence, within written accounts of such CoP pedagogies, about whether participation in community activities is actually a method for fostering the personal acquisition of knowledge, or is fundamentally about learning to participate in valued social practices. These two metaphors for learning throw up some stark differences with respect to the T-H relations. On the *acquisition* view, tools and other artefacts (T) are the *means* to achieve personal cognitive change: accumulating new knowledge. On the *participation* view, social (or rather, socio-material) practices necessarily involve tools (etc.), so learning to participate includes learning to master the tools that are bound up in the practices of the community (Lonchamp, 2012). Tool use is part of participation, not merely a means to the end of acquiring personal knowledge. Paavola, Lipponen, and Hakkareinen (2004) have extended Sfard's work to add a third, *knowledge creation* metaphor. On this view,

> Learning is not conceptualized through processes occurring in individuals' minds, or through processes of participation in social practices. Learning is understood as a collaborative effort directed toward developing some mediated artifacts, broadly defined as including knowledge, ideas, practices, and material or conceptual artifacts. (Paavola et al., 2004:569–70)

The H-T relation compatible with this knowledge creation view places T as both a means of creating new knowledge and as embodiments of newly created knowledge. That is, the shared practices of knowledge creation depend, in part, on the use of tools (etc.) but they also create new things in which new knowledge is inscribed: such as conceptual artefacts that have a material existence. Finally, Figure 6.3 offers a further elaboration of the knowledge creation metaphor, in which learning is also seen as involving the creation of new tools and physical environments (T) that are themselves tailored to, and intended for, the creation of new knowledge: *epistemic* tools and environments. (See Markauskaite & Goodyear, 2016).

How designers for networked learning choose to understand learners and learning is, in large part, a personal and professional choice. Theorists cannot compel designers to subscribe to all or any of the viewpoints sketched above. However, we *do* want to assert that any account of H-T relations that is meant to be useful to such designers needs to be comprehensive and nuanced enough to capture the range of issues flagged in Figs. 6.2 and 6.3. Furthermore, such an account needs also to be able to deal with more specific relations between H-T, such as the idea of affordance that we mentioned earlier.

Design of the physical (T) can focus attention and provide scaffolding, helping the participant (H) direct scarce mental resources to the areas that benefit from careful thought. In Goodyear and Carvalho (2013), we argued that the notion of "affordance" works best when it is seen as engaging with the almost automatic cognitive "System 1" described by Kahneman (2011): thought which is fast, intuitive, emotional, if error prone. For example, "affordance" can describe a relationship in which computer interface elements, layout and so on make it easy for people to navigate to the point/place where they need to engage "System 2", which is slower, more deliberate and logical. In a similar vein, Hodder (2012) talks about non-reflective and reflective engagement with things. Such scaffolded navigation depends, in turn, on the skills, perceptual acuity, working memory capacity, etc. of the participant—affordance being a relation between person and thing(s). An assemblage of things does not have affordances *per se*; rather, it has affordances in relation to the capabilities of the people who use them. These evolve over time as people become better at working with the assemblage. Affordance and skill must be understood, not as pre-given, but as co-evolving, emergent and partly co-constitutive (Dohn, 2009). In a learning situation, the interface designers' motto of "don't make me think" is inappropriate. It should be, "don't make me think, until I get to those points where thinking will help me learn".

Second, design of the physical can help the participant find answers to the question: "what is on offer here?" Not all activity is closely goal-directed. In digital spaces, just as in material spaces, people sometimes wander around, exploring, waiting to see what will happen, or where a path will take them. Notions of "place legibility" are appropriate here: being able to come to at least a partial understanding of the layout and character of a place (online or otherwise) is important if people are to be invited to explore.

Third, design of the physical can help ensure that the tools and other resources needed for satisfactory completion of a task will come to hand when the participant requires them. This is a matter of furnishing learning places with appropriate tools, artefacts, etc. In a similar vein, design might help alert participants to the fact that they will need certain kinds of things at a later point in a sequence of tasks: so that they can set in place the things they will need. Whichever way this is done, design needs to be informed by an ergonomic sense of the match between tasks, activities, things and the capabilities of the participant(s).

In each of these cases, the connecting constructs that give a design its rationale are *relational* constructs. They do not speak about the qualities of a thing *or* the capabilities of a person: both are involved, simultaneously. Extending this idea, one also needs to recognize that the relations are rarely between one thing and one person. Things come in crowds—as assemblages rather than as discrete entities. Gibson made this point when first introducing the concept of affordance: "the *affordances* of the environment are what it *offers* the animal, what it *provides* or *furnishes*, either for good or ill." (Gibson, 1986: 127). Gibson's focus is on a relationship between an animal and the *whole environment* in which the animal is situated. Yet the way the term has been used within the interface design and networked learning communities has almost always been with a focus on individual artefacts, tasks, or social organization structures—or even just features hereof—not on the "environment" or "context" as such. There are several reasons for this, some relating to the history of the term, some to design pragmatics. Despite Gibson's broad introduction of the term, his own examples concern singular things, e.g. a seat, a surface, and a mailbox. Norman (1989), who introduced the term to the field of design, focused still more narrowly on such things as door knobs and Lego blocks. These theoretical beginnings have influenced later usage of the word. When designing new things—a door knob, a button on the user interface, or a collaboration script—it is of course perfectly reasonable to focus on getting the details right and thus on singular aspects of the artefact to be designed. However, in the context of understanding the relationship between things and humans in networked learning, and more particularly in the context of designing the *physical setting* for learning networks, the single-item-approach is far too simplistic. Instead, we must focus on the assemblages of things which make up the environment and on the way they jointly co-constitute a range of affordances for the learners. (Our insistence on a relational understanding of the constructs connecting things to human activity also extends to tasks and to the social design of networked learning. That is to say, the connection between a person and a tool is not the same for all tasks or all divisions of labour.)

We recognize the danger that insisting on seeing things, tasks and people as coming together in complex assemblages may make design look impossibly complex. If everything is connected to everything else, then where does one begin? How does one avoid an exponential growth in interdependencies? We do not have a complete answer, but we will bring this discussion to an end with three parts of an answer. First, design is a practice that has succeeded in managing complexity in many other fields. Second, an aspect of design expertise is knowing how to find the zones of relatively low connectivity within a richly interconnected system—"carving nature at the joints". Third, development work on educational design patterns is providing ways of representing designs that allow for nesting of design components and for specifying the conditions under which a design may be workable (see e.g. Voigt, 2010). Design for networked learning will need to become more sophisticated if it is to thrive in the midst of complexity, change and uncertainty—but good practical tools and ideas are there for the taking.

Acknowledgements Peter Goodyear and Lucila Carvalho acknowledge the financial support of the Australian Research Council (Laureate Fellowship Grant FL100100203), as well as stimulating ideas and generous feedback from the other members of the Laureate team. Nina Bonderup Dohn acknowledges the financial support of Lundbeckfonden which contributed to making possible her stay as a Visiting Scholar at the University of Sydney in 2013.

References

Bhaskar, R. (1986). *Scientific realism and human emancipation.* London: Verso.

Boivin, N. (2008). *Material cultures, material minds: The impact of things on human thought, society and evolution.* Cambridge: Cambridge University Press.

Card, S., Moran, T., & Newell, A. (1983). *The psychology of human-computer interaction.* Hillsdale, NJ: Erlbaum.

Carvalho, L., & Goodyear, P. (Eds.). (2014). *The architecture of productive learning networks.* New York, NY: Routledge.

Carvalho, L., Goodyear, P., & de Laat, M. (Eds.). (2016). Place-based spaces for networked learning, New York, NY: Routledge.

Clark, A. (2003). *Natural-born cyborgs: Minds, technologies, and the future of human intelligence.* Oxford: Oxford University Press.

Conole, G. (2013). *Designing for learning in an open world.* Berlin: Springer.

Dennett, D. (1991). *Consciousness explained.* New York, NY: Little, Brown and Co.

Dohn, N. (2009). Affordances revisited. Articulating a Merleau-Pontian view. *International Journal of Computer Supported Learning, 4*(2), 151–170.

Engestrom, Y., Miettinen, R., & Punamaki, R.-L. (Eds.). (1999). *Perspectives on activity theory.* Cambridge: Cambridge University Press.

Faulkner, P., & Runde, J. (2011). The social, the material, and the ontology of non-material technological objects. Paper presented at the 27th EGOS (European Group for Organizational Studies) Colloquium, Gothenburg. http://webfirstlive.lse.ac.uk/management/documents/Non-MaterialTechnologicalObjects.pdf. Accessed 25 March 2016.

Feenberg, A. (1987). Computer conferencing in the humanities. *Instructional Science, 16*, 169–186.

Fenwick, T., Edwards, R., & Sawchuk, P. (2011). *Emerging approaches to educational research: Tracing the sociomaterial*. Abingdon: Routledge.

Gibson, J. J. (1986). *The ecological approach to visual perception*. Hillsdale, NJ: Lawrence Erlbaum.

Goodyear, P. (2000). Environments for lifelong learning: Ergonomics, architecture and educational design. In J. M. Spector & T. Anderson (Eds.), *Integrated and holistic perspectives on learning, instruction & technology: Understanding complexity* (pp. 1–18). Dordrecht: Kluwer Academic Publishers.

Goodyear, P. (2005). Educational design and networked learning: Patterns, pattern languages and design practice. *Australasian Journal of Educational Technology, 21*, 82–101.

Goodyear, P. (2014). Productive learning networks: The evolution of research and practice. In L. Carvalho & P. Goodyear (Eds.), *The architecture of productive learning networks*. New York, NY: Routledge.

Goodyear, P., & Carvalho, L. (2013). The analysis of complex learning environments. In H. Beetham & R. Sharpe (Eds.), *Rethinking pedagogy for a digital age: Designing and delivering e-learning*. New York, NY: Routledge.

Goodyear, P., & Carvalho, L. (2014). Framing the analysis of learning network architectures. In L. Carvalho & P. Goodyear (Eds.), *The architecture of productive learning networks*. New York, NY: Routledge.

Goodyear, P., & Dimitriadis, Y. (2013). In medias res: Reframing design for learning. *Research in Learning Technology, 21*, 19909. Retrieved September 28, 2013, from http://dx.doi.org/10.3402/rlt.v21i0.19909.

Goodyear, P., & Retalis, S. (2010). Learning, technology and design. In P. Goodyear & S. Retalis (Eds.), *Technology-enhanced learning: Design patterns and pattern languages* (pp. 1–28). Rotterdam: Sense.

Hacker, P. (2009). Agential reasons and the explanation of human behaviour. In C. Sandis (Ed.), *New essays on the explanation of action* (pp. 75–93). Houndmill: Palgrave Macmillan.

Heidegger, M. (1986). *Sein und Zeit*. Tübingen: Max Niemeyer Verlag.

Henri, F. (1992). Computer conferencing and content analysis. In A. Kaye (Ed.), *Collaborative learning through computer conferencing: The Najaden papers*. Berlin: Springer.

Hodder, I. (2012). *Entangled: An archaeology of the relationships between humans and things*. Chichester: Wiley-Blackwell.

Hodgson, V., De Laat, M., McConnell, D., & Ryberg, T. (2014). *The design, experience and practice of networked learning*. Dordrecht: Springer.

Husserl, E. (1950). *Husserliana: Edmund Husserl - Gesammelte Werke*. The Hague/Dordrecht: Nijhoff/Kluwer.

Ingold, T. (2011). *Being alive: Essays on movement, knowledge and description*. Abingdon: Routledge.

Ingold, T. (2012). Towards an ecology of materials. *Annual Review of Anthropology, 41*, 427–442.

Ingold, T. (2013). *Making: Anthropology, archaeology, art and architecture*. Abingdon: Routledge.

Jackson, F. (1982). Epiphenomenal qualia. *The Philosophical Quarterly, 32*, 127–136.

Johri, A. (2011). The socio-materiality of learning practices and implications for the field of learning technology. *Research in Learning Technology, 19*, 207–217.

Jones, C. (2004). Networks and learning: Communities, practices and the metaphor of networks. *ALT-J: Journal of the Association for Learning Technology, 12*, 81–93.

Kahneman, D. (2011). Thinking, fast and slow. New York: Farrar, Straus and Giroux.

Kirsh, D. (2013). Embodied cognition and the magical future of interaction design. *ACM Transactions on Computer-Human Interaction, 20*, 1–30.

Laurillard, D. (2012). *Teaching as a design science: Building pedagogical patterns for learning and technology*. Abingdon: Routledge.

Lave, J., & Wenger, E. (1991). *Situated learning: Legitimate peripheral participation*. Cambridge: Cambridge University Press.

Leonardi, P., Nardi, B., & Kallinikos, J. (2012). *Materiality and organizing: Social interaction in a technological world.* Oxford: Oxford University Press.

Lonchamp, J. (2012). An instrumental perspective on CSCL systems. *International Journal of Computer-Supported Collaborative Learning, 7,* 211–237.

Malafouris, L. (2013). *How things shape the mind: A theory of material engagement.* Cambridge: MIT Press.

Markauskaite, L., & Goodyear, P. (2016). *Epistemic fluency and professional education: Innovation, knowledgeable action and working knowledge,* Dordrecht: Springer.

Mason, R., & Kaye, A. (Eds.). (1989). *Mindweave.* Oxford: Pergamon.

Merleau-Ponty, M. (1962). *Phenomenology of perception.* London: Routledge and Kegan.

Miller, D. (2010). *Stuff.* Cambridge: Polity Press.

Nagel, T. (1986). *The view from nowhere.* New York, NY: Oxford University Press.

Nash, J., Plugge, L., & Eurelings, A. (2000). Defining and evaluating CSCL projects. *European Conference on Computer Supported Collaborative Learning (ECSCL 2000),* Maastricht, Netherlands.

Newell, A., & Simon, H. (1972). *Human problem solving.* Englewood Cliffs, NJ: Prentice Hall.

Norman, D. (1989). *The design of everyday things.* New York, NY: Basic Books.

Orlikowski, W. (2007). Sociomaterial practices: Exploring technology at work. *Organization Studies, 28,* 1435–1448.

Overdijk, M., Diggelen, W., Kirschner, P., & Baker, M. (2012). Connecting agents and artifacts in CSCL: Towards a rationale of mutual shaping. *International Journal of Computer-Supported Collaborative Learning, 7,* 193–210.

Paavola, S., Lipponen, L., & Hakkarainen, K. (2004). Models of innovative knowledge communities and three metaphors of learning. *Review of Educational Research, 74*(4), 557–576.

Popper, K. (1972). *Objective knowledge: An evolutionary approach.* Oxford: Clarendon.

Proctor, R., & Vu, K.-P. (2009). Cumulative knowledge and progress in human factors. *Annual Reviews of Psychology, 61,* 623–651.

Ritella, G., & Hakkarainen, K. (2012). Instrumental genesis in technology-mediated learning: From double stimulation to expansive knowledge practices. *International Journal of Computer-Supported Collaborative Learning, 7,* 239–258.

Robinson, L., & Metcher, J. (2014). Professional learning and a national community of practice for teachers leading local curriculum change. In L. Carvalho & P. Goodyear (Eds.), *The architecture of productive learning networks* (pp. 109–124). New York, NY: Routledge.

Rorty, R. (1980). *Philosophy and the Mirror of Nature.* Oxford: Basil Blackwell.

Salmon, G. (2000). *E-moderating: The key to teaching and learning online.* London: Kogan Page.

Sandoval, W. (2014). Conjecture mapping: An approach to systematic educational design research. *Journal of the Learning Sciences, 23,* 18.

Sawyer, K., & Greeno, J. (2009). Situativity and learning. In P. Robbins & M. Aydede (Eds.), *The Cambridge handbook of situated cognition* (pp. 347–367). Cambridge: Cambridge University Press.

Sfard, A. (1998). On two metaphors for learning and the dangers of just choosing one. *Educational Researcher, 27*(2), 4–12.

Sfard, A., & Prusak, A. (2005). Telling identities: In search of an analytical tool for investigating learning as a culturally shaped activity. *Educational Researcher, 34*(4), 14–22.

Sorensen, E. (2009). *The materiality of learning: Technology and knowledge in educational practice.* Cambridge: Cambridge University Press.

Suchman, L. (1987). *Plans and situated actions: The problem of human-machine communication.* Cambridge: Cambridge University Press.

Suchman, L. (2007). *Human-machine reconfigurations: Plans and situated actions.* Cambridge: Cambridge University Press.

Taylor, C. (1985). *Philosophical papers. Vols. 1 and 2.* Cambridge: Cambridge University Press.

Turnbull, D. (1993). The ad hoc collective work of building Gothic cathedrals with templates, string, and geometry. *Science, Technology, and Human Values, 18,* 315–340.

Turnbull, D. (2002). Performance and narrative, bodies and movement in the construction of places and objects, spaces and knowledges: The case of the Maltese megaliths. *Theory, Culture and Society, 19*, 125–143.

Voigt, C. (2010). A pattern in the making: The contextual analysis of electronic case-based learning. In P. Goodyear & S. Retalis (Eds.), *Technology-enhanced learning: Design patterns and pattern languages*. Rotterdam: Sense Publishers.

Winch, P. (1990). *The idea of a social science and its relation to philosophy*. London: Routledge.

Yeoman, P., & Carvalho, L. (2014). Material entanglement in a primary school learning network. In Bayne, S., Jones, C., de Laat, M., Ryberg, T., & Sinclair, C. (Eds.). *Proceedings of the 9th International Conference on Networked Learning 2014*, Edinburgh, April 7–9.

Chapter 7
Transitioning Across Networked, Workplace and Educational Boundaries: Shifting Identities and Chronotopic Movements

Sue Timmis and Jane Williams

Introduction

Transitions are part of the experience of Higher Education. These include beginnings, endings and also frequent movements across physical and online settings. There has been a lot of attention on transitions into and out of higher education (Ecclestone, Biesta, & Hughes, 2009; Knight & Yorke, 2013; Reay, Crozier, & Clayton, 2010). However transitions are also particularly important for students on professional programmes such as teaching, law, medicine, social work or nursing where continual movements between work-based placements and university environments are commonplace, crossing in and out of different settings and spaces regularly. Such transitions involve both physical and online boundaries and always involve cultural changes and adaptations. This chapter explores the role of networked learning in mediating the boundary crossings that take place when students are working across contexts and seeks to understand the nature and influence of chronotopes or space:time configurations (Bakhtin, 1981) in making such contexts and transitions meaningful and in shaping identities.

Most students in higher education are frequent users of the Internet, social networking and multiple digital tools (Dahlstrom, Walker, & Dziuban, 2013) and this involves working across boundaries in formal and informal settings (Timmis, 2012). Ellis and Goodyear (2010) argue that undergraduates should become more adept at understanding their own learning needs and develop as 'apprentice knowledge workers', using tools and media efficiently in their various 'learnplaces'. As students

S. Timmis (✉)
Graduate School of Education, University of Bristol, Bristol, UK
e-mail: sue.timmis@bristol.ac.uk

J. Williams
Centre for Medical Education, University of Bristol, Bristol, UK
e-mail: j.williams@bristol.ac.uk

© Springer International Publishing Switzerland 2016
T. Ryberg et al. (eds.), *Research, Boundaries, and Policy in Networked Learning*, Research in Networked Learning, DOI 10.1007/978-3-319-31130-2_7

move across different 'learnplaces' as part of their daily routines, they will encounter new social and cultural repertoires in different settings and adaptations and adjustments will be needed to accommodate such changes. This is even more critical for those who have chosen a programme of study that involves both work-based and university based elements where networked environments are often designed to support the educational programme elements but do not necessarily cross the boundaries into work-based settings where different online environments and systems must be accessed and used.

Grounded in a sociocultural perspective, we understand learning as a socially, culturally and historically mediated activity where tools and artefacts, including digital media and creations are part of the cultural production of the community (Säljö, 2010; Vygotsky, 1978; Wertsch, 1991). Learning can also be understood as a matter of identity building (Wenger, 1998) and a creative process emphasising knowledge construction and meaning making (Kumpulainen, Mikkola, & Jaatinen, 2014; Lillejord & Dysthe, 2008). This chapter argues that such transitions can be regarded as chronotopic movements. A chronotope (Bakhtin, 1981) is a space:time configuration where time and space are dialectically related and where such relationships help to make transitions meaningful. In the next section, the concepts of space and time and their relationships to learning, meaning making and identity are first discussed.

Chronotopes: Space:Time Configurations

> Our sense of place, whether immediate or virtual, is made cumulatively and progressively as we act in and move through spaces, affording ourselves of their opportunities to perceive, feel, use, act, and move. (Lemke, 2004: 1)

Lemke (2004) argues that space is typically understood metaphorically in western cultures to be a container waiting to be filled or simply as emptiness and that time is often considered as fixed and immutable, flowing independently of our lives and actions. In contrast, he argues that spatiality and temporality are related to action or material processes and that we experience space and time as we construct them. Bakhtin (1981) writing about literature and narrative in the 1920s adapted the idea of a chronotope to explore how different forms of narrative move the scene of action from place to place and how events unfold over time. The word *chronotope* is from the Greek *chronos* meaning time and *tope* meaning space.[1] Lorino (2010) expands on its origins by referring to two different Greek words for time:

> Scholars who analyze time in organizations sometimes use the distinction between two concepts of time as defined by ancient Greeks: Kairos and Chronos. Chronos is the physical

---

[1] Bakhtin usually referred to these as time:space in line with the Greek ordering in the word chronotope. For Bakhtin's purposes in understanding the construction of the narrative within literary forms, this makes sense; within the context of networked learning and online and offline dynamics, we refer to them as space:time configurations to foreground the significance of space and for consistency. However, given that they are mutually constituting and defining, the order is not highly significant.

linear time, measured in equivalent units, characterized by regular periodicity (day and night, seasons). Kairos is not linear; it is the time of opportunity and of favourable occasions. It rather qualifies the specific depth of certain moments: "now is the right time to act". It is appraised, not through a measurement tool like a watch, but through feelings. But it is worth noting that originally the Greek word "kairos" has a spatial meaning. It designates a particular point of discontinuity in a structure, some opening or cut. (Lorino, 2010: 5)

Thus it would appear that there has long been a deep connection between the temporal and spatial and that some early understandings of time were both spatial and affective. Both time and space are concepts that deserve more attention in understanding how we make sense of our actions, the events that we participate in and the experiences we have. For Bakhtin (1981), time and space are inextricably linked to each other. Space is always created through time and vice versa so that they are dialectically related. A dialectical relationship (usually depicted as a connected pair, e.g. space:time) is where one dimension presupposes the other, they both determine and oppose each other (Timmis, 2014). Such mutual, yet conflicting relationships can be seen for example in university networked environments or spaces such as virtual learning environments or wikis. These are spaces that have a relation to time that is determined by their design and by the way in which activities are designed and enacted within the space. Yet constraints may arise where insufficient time is available, where people are not working synchronously or where the availability of space and time are misaligned. Bakhtin was perhaps more attentive to time than space because of his main concern with literary narratives but as we have seen by understanding their relations through the idea of a mutually constituting pairing, we can see how they are deeply connected to the way we organise and make sense of our lives.

The concept of a chronotope has been adopted recently in theorising on learning across contexts (e.g.Kumpulainen et al., 2014; Lemke, 2004; Ligorio, Loperfido, & Sansone, 2013). In particular, it is argued that chronotopes give accounts of actions and discourses through which people make meaning and could be described as 'chronotopes in action' (Ligorio et al., 2013: 353). A chronotope is therefore a typical pattern of organisation and activities across space and time where "space becomes a place when, over time, it is attached with socially meaningful affordances" (Kumpulainen et al., 2014: 4). We would add to this by arguing that chronotopes are characterised in learning across contexts primarily as *movements through both space and time*. Space:time configurations are not static, they are dynamic and subject to multiple influences. Networked learning can also be understood chronotopically, by analsysing the shifting and evolving forms of digital and physical space that are constructed through time and changes in culture.

Bakhtin (1981) was interested in how space:time relationships are configured, used and conventionalized differently by different authors, genres and generations. This can give us insight into how cultural groups' instantiate the typical forms of activities as trajectories across different places and over time.

> As in art, so also in life. The cultural practices and norms of our society, or any society, and the ways these are embodied in the habitus of our bodies, our dispositions for action, the tools we are provided, and the architectures we live in also tend to conventionalize, if not

routinize, the ways in which we act in different places, move from place to place and setting to setting in the course of a day, a week, or longer, and make use of place and experience space and time in and across these settings. (Lemke, 2004: 2)

In considering these ideas in relation to students in higher education who are undergoing transitions between physical and online places and contexts, we suggest that understanding how space:time configurations are conventionalized and become part of our personal and cultural repertoires (and where and why they don't) can help us understand and make sense of the experience of transition and cross-contextual working.

We also argue that working across different space:time configurations is always a matter of identity transition as new spaces and cultures are experienced. When crossing the boundaries between workplace and educational settings which require different cultural repertoires, students must shape their identity in relation to new norms and practices as they encounter them, both in the physical and online environments they come across. Holland and colleagues have argued that identities are constructed through our encounters with different 'figured worlds' and identities can be either figurative or positional. Figurative identities are bound up in 'the stories, acts and characters that make the world a cultural world' (Holland, Lachicotte, Skinner, & Cain, 1998: 127). Positional identities are those that are constructed in relation to power, deference and entitlement and 'with the social-interactional, social-relational structures of the lived world' (ibid: 127). This suggests that identities develop through the dynamic interplay between aspirational possibilities and political positioning and are constructed through our actions in overcoming conflicts and adapting to new social-relational structures or improvisations. Identity building can therefore be considered as both creative improvisations and positional adjustments which are performed in relation to time and space as we cross boundaries and encounter new contexts, power relations, behaviours and cultures (ibid).

In summary, space:time configurations or chronotopes are a useful way of understanding and analyzing transitions across physical and virtual boundaries within education-related settings and their dialectical, interconnected relations. The term *chronotopic movements* helps us to clarify further that chronotopes are not static 'things' but dynamic changes that occur across temporal and spatial dimensions. This helps us to understand how transitions are managed and the way time and space can be mobilised as resources to help learners solve transitional or boundary-related problems. Finally, we discussed the influence of chronotopes on learner identities as they move across different figured worlds where they may be required to adapt their identities according to new positions and possibilities that they encounter. Different spaces both digital and physical have different expectations and practices associated with them and will make different demands, which may present problems and challenges, for example communications, expected behaviours and control of the space. In the following section, we introduce a recent study, its aims and methodology before discussing relevant findings that help to illustrate this argument.

Study of Learning on Clinical Placements

In this section, space:time configurations are examined in relation to the findings from a recent study which aimed to investigate how digital tools and resources can contribute to the development of undergraduate medical students' learning in diverse educational, clinical and online settings.

Research questions were:

1. How do students make sense of working across educational and workplace boundaries?
2. What kinds of digital resources, tools and spaces are students using to support their studies across physical and online settings when on work-based placements?
3. How, when and where are they mobilized to support learning?

Methodology

A co-researcher methodology (Timmis & Williams, 2013) was adopted in this study, where all members of the team participated in the research. Student co-researchers explored their experiences firsthand, investigating their use of digital technologies in everyday situations, choices and decisions. This ensured commitment from students who were actively involved in the research design, planning and execution. Participants were medical students studying at a research intensive university in the UK. They were in their third year when students are fully immersed in clinical practice after 2 years of formal class-based teaching located within the university. Teaching from year 3, takes place in geographically dispersed academies, attached to hospitals across the region and students only return to the university sporadically throughout the year for whole cohort teaching. Digital tools and online resources were reported by the university to be one way of redressing variations in teaching and learning and ensuring equality of access. The distributed model of medical education in this case study is not necessarily typical of other models of professionally oriented degree programmes, although many students on professional programmes are involved in work-based placements where they are required to work across a number of different settings, physical and online spaces.

Data Collection and Analysis

Students were invited to participate and six students from three academies, following different specialisms took part. Data collected was longitudinal and collected over 6 months. Informed consent was sought and agreed and an initial research plan was negotiated with students involved. Using handheld cameras, each student maintained a video diary from February to July 2010, recording entries approximately weekly. Students recorded over 100 entries, totalling over 500 min. Diaries included observations, demonstrations (of resources), contextual information and reflections on data (Altrichter & Holly, 2005). They described and demonstrated (on camera) how they used digital tools and resources including problems and resolutions. The longitudinal, video-based design enabled comparisons across time and contexts and facilitated collaborative analysis (Büscher, 2005). The video data was independently transcribed as verbatim transcripts and checked for accuracy. Initial thematic analysis of the diaries was conducted collaboratively through regular group analysis sessions, where groups of students and researchers worked together on thematic coding of other students' diaries, working towards a hierarchy of themes. The themes and sub themes were then discussed as a whole group in order to agree and stabilize categories and validate category assignment. During group discussions, students commented on and discussed the findings of the video diary analysis and their experience in relation to it, providing a further level of insight into the initial outcomes from the data. Data was subsequently analyzed as space:time configurations and trajectories across temporal and spatial sites of activity through analysis of the relationships between space, time and activity in video diary entries and data from group discussions.

Transitioning Across Workplace and Educational Contexts

The major themes that emerged relating to chronotopes or space:time configurations were:

- Cultures, specialisms and settings
- Access to and management of resources
- Creating and repurposing tools and artefacts.

However, it is important to note that because space and time are fundamental and cross cutting, these are interlinked and all contributed to the development of new chronotopes. The findings from these three, related areas will now be discussed.

Cultures, Specialisms and Settings

The medical students in this study were in their third year and were working mainly in clinical settings, returning to the university for a few days each term. They were found to be moving continually between different clinical and educational cultures and practices for example, different hospital departments, primary, mental health and social care settings, university education environments and home. Each day might consist of teaching or clinical practice in three to four distinct space:time configurations which students moved between. Each of these involved different activities, ways of working, access to and use of digital and physical spaces. For example:

> At 8 o clock this morning I had a tutorial in the Respiratory department. This involved some case presentations, [...] then the tutor finished by showing us some x-rays and CT scans of a patient of his. I then went to my home ward to clerk a patient and then at 11 o clock I had some case presentation teaching with one of the endocrinology professors. (Student 1, video 2)

The culture of the subject specialism (e.g. psychiatry, orthopaedics) meant that students had to improvise and adjust their practices and develop hybrid roles as the students were no longer just medical students but neither were they fully qualified doctors engaging in practices associated to both. Staff expectations of students also differed across specialisms. When considering that students moved between many settings and specialisms, these changes in culture and practice become more significant because of the requirement for improvisation and adaptation. The digital environments were also discipline and specialism dependent, including access arrangements and when they were available. Students needed to be flexible in managing time and space to ensure they could access and use these specialist tools at different times of the working week.

> In general I think the PACS system is a brilliant aid for learning but I find it quite frustrating as we are completely reliant upon the doctors or the mentors to log us into this system. (Student 4, video 6)

The PACS system is a radiology system that is widely available in the NHS and very comprehensive but access for medical students is not consistent. Equally, there are constant changes in timetabling and teaching arrangements:

> Since starting in hospitals this year, I've realised how useful and important it is to have portable access to your emails. And seminars are constantly being, you know, allocated, changed, cancelled. The bedside teachings sometimes has to be cancelled because certain wards are shut and I've found that having my iPhone on me and having my emails, you know, with me most of the time has saved me a lot of wasted time. (Student 4, video 1)

> I also found, from not checking my emails, that I turned up to a teaching session that had been cancelled the day before. (Student 1, video 8)

Not everyone in the group had smart phones and access to emails, but there appeared to be an expectation that students would be able to react to changes very quickly and that when a last minute email is sent, it will be read within the same timeframe. Tutors and administrators actions seemed to show a lack of awareness of the particular challenges of moving contexts and to make assumptions about connectivity, though it should be acknowledged that this study is investigating the students' understandings and these actions may have been interpreted differently by others. However, another challenge for students in managing last minute changes is that network access is not always straightforward in clinical settings:

> One quite frustrating thing is that in the DHBR, which is our common room, there is a lack of reception, so sometimes I have to go outside to check my emails (Student 4, video 1)

Students also had to learn whilst 'on the move' and needed to transport work with them. Being peripatetic made access to the internet and digital resources location dependent and not always under their control, creating further spatio-temporal tensions, as the following quote shows:

> It is a bit annoying if you don't have much time and you think you might want to take it with you. You are stuck- you are bound to your computer and you do need the Internet for it, which is a bit of a pain. (Student 3, video 23)

Practices such as emailing oneself were used to manage transitions and create stability across settings.

> I went to the study room in [...] and did some more work on my clerking portfolios. And then the work I had done, I just emailed those documents to myself so that I'd be able to access them at home and print them off. (Student 1, video 14)

Access to and Management of Resources

Aside from the work conducted in the placement settings, students were also managing university assessments and work activities alongside. Access to space for working with others was a challenge for students moving from setting to setting and the desire for designated physical workspace that they could call their own was noted by some of the students, who found 'homes' where they could, as this quotation makes clear.

> Today I practised vignettes and other important aspects of the curriculum with a friend in the multimedia room that's based at [hospital] in the Learning and Research Centre. The multimedia room provided a really good space for us to be able to work and talk out loud without disrupting other students who were working independently in the rest of the library. We didn't actually use any ICT facilities on this occasion, but there were facilities in the room, had we chosen to use them. And I just thought it was really important that spaces such as this are provided for us when we are based at the academies because coffee shops aren't always the best place or the most conducive to work. But this room really was ideal (Student 2, video 9)

Clearly the need for physical space and face to face interaction were important and in this case, networked environments or online interactions were not considered as ways of resolving the lack of a space to work in with others, because in the context of moving from one clinical space to another, alongside other students, where time was limited for attending to educational work, a space:time configuration that fitted in between these existing commitments was needed.

Students also found that online communications help them move around less often and helped them to make a more stable and dependable working environment:

> The benefits of using emails was that it meant I could continue to work at home, with all my books and information and computer there, without having to cart everything around to the wards to find him [doctor], and I wasn't even sure where he would be. (Student 5, video 7).

Carrying out assessed university work whilst on clinical placement represented another form of space:time configuration. Access to printers and printing was often temporally and spatially challenging for those based primarily in hospital or community medicine environments. Adapting to these challenges involved workarounds and improvisations.

> Also had a bit of a problem with the email because I wanted to send my ISSC project to the Students Union print shop in order to get some copies printed off so that I can give copies of the brochure to members of the tutor group and some friends that wanted a copy. But, I tried to send it twice from different email accounts and I got a delivery failure notification sent back to me on both occasions. So I had to cycle up to the SU today to take it to them in person, which was very annoying because then I had to wait for ages in a queue of people printing off dissertations. (Student 1, video 8)

This student found that relying on online systems for assessed work was risky and she had to improvise to resolve a potentially critical deadline and submission, mobilising both time and space to solve her problem.

Creating and Repurposing Tools and Artefacts

In addition to transitioning and adapting to different cultures and practices, students stabilised and made sense of the multiple influences on their work by constructing new digital artefacts involving online tools and resources (e.g. internet sites, online journals, online tutorials, recorded lectures, their own notes, videos and images) in combination with printed sources to help them make sense of their experiences. Students reported that online resources felt ephemeral and they wanted ways of making transitionary knowledge more tangible and personal. Multiple levels and kinds of resources, from academic scholarly journals through to Wikipedia were brought together through patchworking practices (Bonderup Dohn, 2009), synthesising knowledge and creating their own study-related artefacts. These were often transformed into new multimodal documents which were frequently adapted, printed or annotated further. Printing and annotating added further levels of meaning and made artefacts more transportable.

> I actually decided to make a bank of, sort of, photos in Microsoft Word based on the pictures that came up in the tutorial, because I just wanted something to refer to, so I'm going to get them printed off tomorrow. (Student 2, video 7)

> Now I've got a copy of it I can annotate it and highlight it and stuff. And I find reading off the Internet for long periods of time quite hard to do. My eyes go funny. So… it's different when you're typing for some reason, when you're like staring, and trying to write down something I can't- I don't seem to be able to do it very well. So I prefer having like a piece of- having it on like a handout so I can go away and read it. (Student 6, video 7)

Making their learning tangible and transportable across contexts appeared to be critically important for these students, ensuring resources would not disappear and helping to stabilise learning in transition. These chronotopic strategies demonstrate how both resourcefulness and improvisation helped students make sense of the different spaces and places they were encountering and how they developed their own forms of conventions to manage trajectories across and between the different space:time configurations or chronotopes that they encountered.

In the discussion sessions, students also frequently reported directly on the challenges of transition and of being in the workplace and being a student at the same time and working across different spaces and cultures. They confirmed that managing space and time were critical to navigating transitions and that the adaptations they made helped them in working across boundaries and shifting their identities from student to practitioner, from specialism to specialism, from online to offline. Transition is a different journey for everyone, however, and will always involve challenges that need to be creatively overcome and it is these improvisations that help shape emerging identities.

Discussion

This study has shown that being on clinical placement is pressurised; the students in the case study were working across multiple settings where patient care takes priority. They were learning to become professional practitioners alongside continuing to operate as undergraduate students with the traditional expectations and requirements. Multiple space:time configurations were operating traversally so that students experienced daily transitions across, within and between disciplinary contexts, physical and online settings and home, clinical and educational environments. Networks can be conceptualised as operating horizontally rather than vertically and networked learning environments assisted in managing the fluidity and changes in space and time across different clinical and educational cultures and contexts. Such environments also helped students make sense of the experience of different spaces and through this creating their own 'places'. Networked learning environments afforded opportunities for connecting and hybridising spaces, stabilising practices and creating artefacts and new discourses (Lemke, 2004), helping to instantiate the idea of 'space becoming place' through the meanings that are attached to it (Bakhtin, 1981; Kumpulainen et al., 2014).

Yet, the culture and practices of networked learning are not fixed, they too, are in transition and subject to chronotopic and cultural variation. Lorino (2010: 5) refers to the second meaning of time in ancient Greek as 'Karios' or the 'time of opportunity and favourable occasions' but networked learning environments are not always favourable or offering opportunities, they can be themselves be destabilising or add to the complexities. In this study there were examples of this when the availability of space and time were misaligned through system failure or where the cultural expectations of the speed of responses and actions in networked environments were not matched by actions. Contrary to the prevailing discourse of constant connectivity, Internet access is still not universal or seamless, especially when working and studying across large organisations with differing priorities, rules and systems, as most of those on professional programmes with work-based elements find. Working in physical spaces without networked resources or the Internet's social memory (Säljö, 2010) remains a critical part of students' studying practices and further to this, an increasing requirement to manage the spatio-temporal tensions between working online and offline and across multiple networked spaces. Working and studying across all these different intersecting chronotopes can make it more difficult to know how, when and where to go in order to achieve what is required or desired.

Chronotopes always constitute a dialectical relationship; space and time are held in tension, both opposing and mutually defining one another (Timmis, 2014) and they do not take place in isolation. Other dialectical relations operate alongside and are mutually intertwined such as physical:virtual, online:offline, individual:community, workplace:university. The concept of 'the university' and 'the workplace' are therefore not clear cut or necessarily separate physical spaces. Equally digital tools such as mobile devices and tablets cross the boundaries between the physical and the virtual and offer new hybrid spaces and time uses. Networked digital tools open up the possibilities for new space:time configurations, including being constantly connected and working offline. Students in this study found that smart phones helped them with transitions by helping to shape what counts as 'institutional space' by being connected to the university network when working elsewhere. Where students didn't have smartphones, this was often challenging as important information was assumed by academic staff to be read immediately and resulted in missed appointments and opportunities. Since the study in 2010, this online:offline dynamic has become more critical as ipads and tablet use has increased and with the emergence of the 'App'. Students create their own digital 'place' but this is offline. The medical students in this case study were also working individually and communally in tandem, where they must become enculturated into different specialisms in the workplace and were also working as individual students, developing their identities as 'becoming doctors'.

Other spatio-temporal conflicts emerged through the necessity of mobility when working in transit, where the students felt they had to take things with them which was not always possible. Because they were constantly on the move, students also felt that online resources were less tangible and less permanent. Through creating their own artefacts and devising workarounds they sought to even out the space:time disruptions and extend the reach of existing spaces over time and forming new chronotopic trajectories (Lemke, 2004). We have shown how time and space are inseparable and mutually constituting and that temporal or spatial challenges have to be managed in relation to one another as well as in relation to other dialectical tensions. Improvisation is part of the practices associated to identity construction and performance where new identities (both positional and figurative) can emerge through both action and resistance (Holland et al., 1998). Working across boundaries and in new space:time configurations involves frequent adaptations to new cultures which include power relations and working practices, where agency and resourcefulness are critical. Students in the study had to develop hybrid, transitionary identities to accommodate the multiple digital and physical spaces, cultures and communities encountered and these were sometimes in conflict with their existing roles as individual medical students, new roles as 'becoming doctors' (Monrouxe, Rees, & Hu, 2011) and the expectations of staff in how students manage new or transitionary roles, adapting to variations in status. Digital spaces formed part of students' identity performances as they moved through and between these different 'figured worlds' (Holland et al., 1998). As we have shown, these improvisations helped in adapting and overcoming multiple or conflicting space:time transitions and forming new identity performances whilst also adding additional complexities and discontinuities (Lorino, 2010). Overcoming such challenges requires agency on the part of students, employing resourcefulness and improvisation in solving problems and working around the space:time constraints they encounter.

Conclusions

Since this study in 2010, technology has moved on, in particular the increased concentration of tablets and mobiles devices in use amongst higher education students, making the findings and discussion in this paper, we argue, even more relevant. Furthermore, the same issues associated to transitions, sense-making and stabilization are still faced by medical (and other) students today working in workplace and educational settings. Networked learning environments offer distinct and dynamic chronotopes that assist in managing the physical:virtual, online:offline, individual:community and workplace:university dialectical tensions that such transitions involve and allow new forms of practice and discourse to emerge which are critical for students' sense making when transitioning between contexts and cultures. Being in transition is always challenging and transformative. We conclude that learning in transition between workplace and formal educational spaces requires students to construct new chronotopes in order to make sense of their education and manage the continual changes of culture and identity necessitated by transitions. Chronotopes therefore act as resources for mobilizing human agency. Digital learning environments afford distinct chronotopes that can both stabilise and reconfigure time and space, enabling a place for identity working, improvisation and sense making.

Finally, we conclude that the dynamics of fluid, shifting boundaries of space and time are amongst the key changes that networked environments and the Internet have made possible for the practices of working and studying in higher education. Networked learning environments offer distinct and dynamic chronotopes, allowing new forms of practice, discourse and identity to emerge which are critical for students' sense making when transitioning between contexts and cultures. Yet they also present their own challenges as the possibilities of online:offline, multi spatio-temporal working increases and not all such transformations are positive for learners. The concepts of space:time configurations or chronotopes and chronotopic movements can give us insights into researching how spatiality and temporality frame our actions as they unfold and help to make sense of such actions, including the resultant tensions and intersections. This has the potential to provide a rich seam for further research and investigation of higher education student learning and experience, particularly when this involves transitions between workplace and educational contexts.

Acknowledgements We would like to thank the following doctors who were student co-researchers on the research project discussed above for their invaluable contribution to earlier work on this topic and their participation in the original study: Amy Hardeley, Joanne Lee, Charlotte Mann, Camilla Milner-Smith, Catherine Trappes-Lomax, Laura Tyler.

References

Altrichter, H., & Holly, M. J. (2005). Research diaries. In B. Somekh & C. Lewin (Eds.), *Research methods in the social sciences* (pp. 24–32). London: Sage.

Bakhtin, M. M. (1981). *The dialogic imagination: Four essays* (C. Emerson & M. Holquist, Trans.). University of Texas Press.

Bonderup Dohn, N. (2009). Web 2.0: Inherent tensions and evident challenges for education. *International Journal of Computer-Supported Collaborative Learning, 4*, 343–363.

Büscher, M. (2005). Social life under the microscope? *Sociological Research Online, 10(1)*. Retrieved from http://www.socresonline.org.uk/10/1/buscher.html.

Dahlstrom, E., Walker, J., & Dziuban, C. (2013). The ECAR study of undergraduate students and information technology (Vol. 2010). Louisville, KY. Educause Center for Analysis and Research. Retrieved from http://www.educause.edu/ecar.

Ecclestone, K., Biesta, G., & Hughes, M. (2009). *Transitions and learning through the lifecourse*. London: Routledge.

Ellis, R., & Goodyear, P. (2010). *Students' experiences of e-learning in higher education: The ecology of sustainable innovation*. Abingdon: Routledge.

Holland, D., Lachicotte, W., Jr., Skinner, D., & Cain, C. (1998). *Identity and agency in cultural worlds*. Cambridge, MA: Harvard University Press.

Knight, P., & Yorke, M. (2013). *Learning, curriculum and employability in higher education*. London: Routledge.

Kumpulainen, K., Mikkola, A., & Jaatinen, A.-M. (2014). The chronotopes of technology-mediated creative learning practices in an elementary school. *Learning, Media and Technology, 39*, 53. Retrieved from 10.1080/17439884.2012.752383.

Lemke, J. L. (2004). Learning across multiple places and their chronotopes. Paper presented at the AERA 2004 Symposium, San Diego, CA. Retrieved from http://www-personal.umich.edu/~jaylemke/papers/aera_2004.htm.

Ligorio, M. B., Loperfido, F. F., & Sansone, N. (2013). Dialogical positions as a method of understanding identity trajectories in a collaborative, blended university course. *International Journal of Computer Supported Collaborative Learning, 8(3)*, 351–367. Retrieved from http://link.springer.com/article/10.1007%2Fs11412-013-9174-3.

Lillejord, S., & Dysthe, O. (2008). Productive learning practice - A theoretical discussion. *Journal of Education and Work, 21(1)*, 75–89.

Lorino, P. (2010). The Bakhtinian theory of chronotope (spatial-temporal frame) applied to the organizing process. *Proceedings of International Symposium on Process Organization Studies. Theme: Constructing Identity in and around Organizations*. June 11–13, 2010, Rhodes, Greece Retrieved from http://www.alba.edu.gr/sites/pros/Pages/acc_papers.aspx.

Monrouxe, L. V., Rees, C. E., & Hu, W. (2011). Differences in medical students' explicit discourses of professionalism: Acting, representing, becoming. *Medical Education, 45*(6), 585–602.

Reay, D., Crozier, G., & Clayton, J. (2010). 'Fitting in' or 'standing out': Working class students in UK higher education. *British Educational Research Journal, 36*(1), 107–124.

Säljö, R. (2010). Digital tools and challenges to institutional traditions of learning: Technologies, social memory and the performative nature of learning. *Journal of Computer Assisted Learning, 26*, 53–64.

Timmis, S. (2012). Constant companions: Instant messaging conversations as sustainable supportive study structures amongst undergraduate peers. *Computers and Education, 59*(1), 3–18.

Timmis, S. (2014). The dialectical potential of cultural historical activity theory for researching sustainable CSCL practices. *International Journal of Computer Supported Collaborative Learning, 9*, 1556. Retrieved from http://link.springer.com/article/10.1007/s11412-013-9178-z.

Timmis, S., & Williams, J. (2013). Students as co-researchers: A collaborative, community-based approach to the research and practice of technology-enhanced learning. In E. Dunne & D. Owen (Eds.), *The student engagement handbook: Practice in higher education*. Bingley: Emerald.

Vygotsky, L. S. (1978). *Mind in society: The development of higher psychological processes*. Cambridge, MA: Harvard University Press.

Wenger, E. (1998). *Communities of practice: Learning, meaning and identity*. Cambridge: Cambridge University Press.

Wertsch, J. V. (1991). *Voices of the mind: A socio-cultural approach to mediated action*. Cambridge, MA: Harvard University Press.

Part III
Researching Networked Learning

Chapter 8
Field Activity and the Pedagogy of Simultaneity to Support Mobile Learning in the Open

Michael Sean Gallagher and Pekka Ihanainen

Introduction

Learning in the open, the process of learning generated outside classrooms or lecture halls amidst the materials, constructions, and negotiated practices of the everyday, is of critical importance to the development of the field of education. It resides in the spaces outside, but often supporting or applying the knowledge gleaned from, formal education. Learning in the open accounts for the vast majority of time and activity that takes place outside the classroom. Learning in the open can be positioned through a conceptualization adapted from mobile learning and activated through field activity, the subject of this chapter. Mobile learning, defined by Sharples, Taylor, and Vavoula (2007), accounts for learning that occurs across space, across time, across topic, and through a myriad of evolving contexts mediated by technology. Wali, Winters, and Oliver (2008) advances this definition further by suggesting a focus on learning practices directed towards the same objectives occurring across multiple contexts. It is within these definitions that the pedagogy and field activities outlined in this chapter emerged.

The purpose of this chapter is to present a type of mobile learning that engages the learner in field activities, which are defined for the purpose of this chapter as activities designed to authentically enact disciplinary learning or informal learning engagement. Field activities (and the associated concepts of fieldwork and field

M.S. Gallagher (✉)
Hankuk University of Foreign Studies, Seoul, South Korea
e-mail: gallagher.michaelsean@gmail.com

P. Ihanainen
HAAGA-HELIA University of Applied Sciences, Helsinki, Finland
e-mail: pekka.ihanainen@haaga-helia.fi

© Springer International Publishing Switzerland 2016
T. Ryberg et al. (eds.), *Research, Boundaries, and Policy in Networked Learning*, Research in Networked Learning, DOI 10.1007/978-3-319-31130-2_8

methods) are appropriated for this chapter as a means of enacting a disciplinary or informal observation, data collection, analysis, and composition process through the medium of mobile technology. The field in question is the 'lived world' outside the classroom, which serves as both as the subject of inquiry and the learning context, a model complementary to existing practice in both the field sciences and the humanities. Mobile technology represents a technological tool in this larger process of coming to know in a disciplinary space (Säljö, 1999) by providing capacity for performing data collection, analysis, and composition tasks, as well as providing capacity for media and metadata creation. Learners and teachers in these field activities are in a constant process of coming to know through the manipulation of tools and context. Mobile learning becomes a transformation of habitus, or the learner's mindset (Kress & Pachler, 2007) towards their discipline or field. The learning spaces enacted through these field activities are highly ephemeral and contested, requiring a perpetual construction of context on the part of the learner and the teacher.

Yet, mobile learning, particularly mobile learning that occurs in open space, remains undertheorized. Leander, Phillips, and Taylor (2010) suggest that mobilities and their relation to learning within education are still understudied and undertheorized; Baran (2014) reiterates this call for more research in relation to mobile learning and teacher training. Wali et al. (2008) argue for a repositioning of mobile learning towards learning practices and negotiated contexts, and away from communicative patterns of technology and social activity. This chapter looks to address several of these undertheorized areas by providing a model for mobile learning as a contextual issue of simultaneous practice, and a practical model for teachers and learners to reasonably implement.

The simultaneity referred to repeatedly in this chapter is defined in respect to the variety of learning activities, conscious or subconscious, being undertaken by the learner at any given moment. Simultaneity establishes that learners are perpetually cycling through different learning activities across different time, place and social combinations. Research charting simultaneous learning has been undertaken in linguistics (Warriner & Wyman, 2013), education (Brookshaw, Fuller, & Waters, 2012), and in psychology and physiology (Virsu, Oksanen-Hennah, Vedennaa, Jaatinen, & Lahti-Nuuttila, 2008). Mobile learning and field activity, when combined, represent a complex space of simultaneous activity. Learners are engaging their physical environments, their disciplinary subjects, their technological capacity, their media literacy and their social collaborations across time and space intervals. These are highly ephemeral constructions of context, volatile in their capacity for supporting many perspectives and combinations. This is learning in the open and it can be chaotic. This chapter advances the belief that mobile learning in the field requires a pedagogy that embraces these simultaneous layers of time, place, and social presence and transforms them into learning layers of trust, discussion, and collage (Gallagher & Ihanainen, 2013).

Field Activity Generating Mobile Learning

For this chapter, field activity refers to acts, performances and behavior in which people perceive, examine and make meaning for their current and future understanding in their natural environments (disciplinary activity and daily events of living and working). Fieldwork itself has a long and rich history in formalized learning, both as a methodology as well as an object of investigation (Gupta & Ferguson, 1997). It involves the application of theory to the natural field sciences or the lived world (humanities, anthropology, etc.).

These field activities can be inspired and guided by formal settings such as lessons at school, or they can relate to informal or practical learning opportunities, such as professional development, workplace activities, or personal learning activities. There are many instances of mobile technology supporting fieldwork and field activities (Colley & Gibbs, 2012; Haapala, Sääskilathi, Luimula, Yli-Hemminki, & Partala, 2007; Hwang, Tsai, & Chen, 2012; Sääskilathi, Sippola, Partala, & Luimula, 2010, in their work on using mobile technology in informal learning, field science, and archaeology). Mobile learning enacted in these activities blurs the traditional fieldwork processes of observation and data collection in the field followed by analysis and composition at 'home' or in the classroom. Mobile technology allows for these processes to occur seamlessly and in immediate, if not overlapping, succession. Learners can observe, collect, compose, and disseminate findings in the context of the activity itself.

In this space, the learner is constantly moving between states of informal and formal activity. It can be called everyday learning, which means that learning is present in all natural activities done at the workplace and at home, in hobbies and other leisure activities. Informal learning is not purposefully goal-oriented, but it can happen while working, which itself is targeted activity (building a summer cottage, for example). Informal learning activity is present in formal settings as well, e.g. during class breaks, extra-curricular activities, and through other informal emerging social settings. These mobile learning field activities can also refer to facilitated action in authentic work and job environments, i.e. construction worksites, nursing homes, daycare centers, media companies, etc., in which on-the-job learning, internships, practical training, and apprenticeships take place. Additionally, field activities can take place in the environments of learners' choosing, for instance in cities, suburbs, and rural areas. These field activities can later be interpreted, drawn together, assessed and produced as learning resources in workshops in between field activities.

The disciplinary, formal variety of these mobile learning field activities can take place in the humanities as well (Gallagher, 2013a). Field activity is already a core method of many of the sciences and social sciences (Gupta & Ferguson, 1997); these mobile learning field activities merely extend, or augment, that method further into these disciplines. They foreground media literacy (Marty et al., 2013), collective memory and representation (Jacucci, Oulasvirta, & Salovaara, 2007), and collaborative disciplinary learning (So, Tan, & Tay, 2012). Further field activities might include learning walks (Robinson & Sebba, 2010) as a means of investigating a place informally, or evoking flanerie as a learning activity (McFarlane, 2010). Flanerie in this instance (adapted from Benjamin, 1999; Shields, 2006; Hollevoet, Jones, & Nye, 1992), is a method of learning involving moving through open spaces with or without predefined learning objectives, collecting troves of multimodal data (audio, video, imagery, GPS data, text, etc.) based on emerging interests or curiosities. This data is then collected for individual multimodal compositions documenting or representing learning in urban space. These learning methods can be made more interactive through the incorporation of geocaches as a means of engaging the learner in the investigation and composition of place (Jones, Scanlon, & Clough, 2013). Learners can embed geopositioned metadata into the compositions generated from these field activities, thereby providing a social and intellectual bridge to the next set of learners engaging in that activity in that place. These learners are essentially embedding their learning into the field itself for future discovery.

Compositions generated from this activity are diverse. They can include the traditional text-based essay or scientific dataset, as well as multimodal compositions. They can include collages, mosaics, montages, maps, and models, anything that reveals the meaning and relevance of the learner's understanding. Yet it is most important to foreground the idea that these compositions are never complete; in these activities, learners are "engaged in an iterative, evolutionary process aimed at the gradual improvement" (Bruns, 2007) of learning content. These compositions are active constructions of meaning in a shifting context; the learners are "discovering" meaning through the creation of their compositions (Gallagher, 2013a). This process is not unlike a writer not fully knowing the outcome of a story until having written it; purpose can often emerge as one progresses through the composition. The focus on the field, on life and understanding in the open, further complicates and emboldens this effort: the learners change, the locations change, the research questions, social interactions, and disciplinary contexts will all change, each and every time the learner engages with the location. This complexity forces an examination of existing pedagogy to support such learning. In the following section, we present the salient characteristics of this kind of mobile learning as well as a pedagogy that encompasses them.

Structure of Activity: Helsinki, Seoul, and Talinn (formal) and London, Edinburgh, and Jyväskylä (informal)

The authors have conducted several field activities from 2013–2014 in both formal contexts (workshops for teachers held in Helsinki and Talinn; field activity with undergraduate students in Seoul, Korea and informal contexts (learning walks with authors and colleagues in London, Jyväskylä, Finland, and Edinburgh. Much of what is discussed in this chapter was gleaned from these activities; the pedagogy outlined in this chapter emerged and was refined from these contexts.

The formal workshops were two-day events designed to familiarize teachers with the theoretical underpinnings of mobile learning (particularly as positioned by

Kress & Pachler, 2007; Sharples et al., 2007; Wali et al., 2008), as well as to provide a structure for initiating field activities with their own students. Participants, using the Helsinki workshop as an example (Otavan Opisto, 2013), met to discuss their experiences with mobile learning individually and in an instructional capacity. Instruction was provided on possible frameworks and participants were asked to identify several methods for the observation and data collection activities, which involved using mobile technology to record impressions of Helsinki through a disciplinary lens (architecture, sociology, theology, urban planning, history). Participants collected media through mobile technology, discussed the significance of that media for disciplinary understanding, and then assembled this media into compositions of mobile media that were presented to the other participants at the concluding session the following day. The activity challenged learners to re-examine their understanding of the accepted modes of disciplinary interaction, accepted forms of evidence to present that understanding (media), and accepted containers for that presentation (collages, montages, maps, as opposed to strictly textual essays). Compositions generated from these workshops included interactive tram maps, videos, collages, and montages (Gallagher, 2013b).

Reflective practice was embedded throughout the workshop as participants were asked to reflect on issues related to technology affordances and constraints, media selection and assembly, disciplinary focus and structure, and presentation and dissemination questions. This reflective practice is grounded in the work of Sengers, Boehner, David, and Kaye (2005) on reflective design, Verpoorten, Westera, and Specht (2012) on reflective triggers, and Ifenthaler's (2012) work on reflective prompts. The authors believe it is critical to embed reflective practice into mobile learning in the field due to the highly ephemeral nature of the learning contexts being generated there.

The informal mobile learning that took place London, Edinburgh, and Jyväskylä were not rigorously defined or structured as such, but were walks through these locations in which learning emerged by what was encountered, rather than answering a predefined objective. These activities were acts of urban and rural exploration towards understanding the individual's experience of space (Harvey, 2007). They involved the documentation of the location through mobile technology (primarily audio, video, and images) as well as text and related metadata (notes, GPS, KML files, etc.). The data collected on these walks was pooled for potential use by all the participants and was then assembled into collages spanning the learning gleaned from the activity (Gallagher & Ihanainen, 2014).

Emerging Themes and Lessons Learned

The themes emerging from both these formal and informal learning activities suggested some practical alterations to the structure that would augment their potential impact. To begin, we discovered the importance of diversifying the data collection methods for the field activity. Participants were encouraged to collect specific types of data (video and imagery, specifically); this was adjusted in later workshops to include all types of data whether digital (through mobile technology) or physical (notes, notebooks, sketches, drawings on paper). This broadening of data types provides advantages in the composition and reflection stages as it adds a layer of complexity to the overall process. Not only does the participant have to consider the learning presented in the overall composition, but also what data is going to be used to demonstrate that learning. The variety of data types adds opportunity for narrative experimentation and cohesion. The participants are generating a narrative of intentional state entailment (Bruner, 1991), which can be defined in this context as a process of narrating their own understanding and utilization of open space. As reflexivity is embedded into each stage of this open learning process, learners are forced to reflect on their understanding of that space, their intentional use of tools and materials to construct meaning in that space, and the compositions generated to present that understanding. This reflexivity is essentially a method of narration; the reflections and iterations made as a result of these reflections generates a narrative of the learner's transformation of open space into learning space. By giving them opportunities to choose from a variety of data types, to articulate why they chose those data types, and asking them to compose across data types provides extensive opportunity for a narrative to emerge, opportunities that might not exist as prevalently if the data was limited to a particular type (for example, text only).

Related to this broadening of data collection is a further adjustment to the composition stages of the field activity (referred to in the pedagogical discussion in subsequent sections as collage). The means for composing and disseminating the learning gleaned from these activities was modeled in the workshop ahead of the actual data collection. Examples from the authors' own work were discussed and potential environments for dissemination were reviewed ahead of the actual field activity. While this might be necessary with participants who would not self-identify as technically competent, or with younger students who might respond to greater structure and process orientation, we adjusted this approach to maintain ambiguity in the structure throughout the workshop. Ambiguity in this respect is defined in terms of not modeling output, but rather merely theory, process and reflection. In this adjustment, participants are free to explore across geographies (participants choose the locations they want to document), across media (they choose the media and data they wish to collect), and across compositional structures (they choose the form of composition generated from this activity).

The role of the facilitator in this respect shifts away from the materiality of the field activity (location, data, media, composition) towards process and reflection. The facilitator challenges participants to identify method but not necessarily form or output, to reflect on selections made and not made and their aggregation into an overall learning experience. Facilitation in this approach is itself an act of trust that learners will organize, execute, compose, and reflect on their own learning. As such, it presents challenges to teachers working in formal, or highly assessed, educational environments. These activities generate learning that can be assessed summatively, but they remain inherently formative learning approaches. This requires consideration when designing workshop and field activities; teachers, in particular, need opportunity to resolve this approach with existing teaching practice and assessment.

One such resolution might be using these mobile field activities as precursors, or data collection and research methods, to supplement classroom learning activities. For example, having learners explore and generate data related to particular neighborhoods or urban spaces as a precursor to interdisciplinary classroom activities related to the sociology, history, or architecture or a particular space. Many such iterations exist, depending on how they are balanced with the existing curriculum.

More than the pragmatic adjustments suggested, the open spaces and learning processes presented here suggest the need for pedagogy to efficiently make use of them. These continuums of activity, defined as learning movements through open space, are outlined in the next section, along with a discussion on the pedagogy generated to support them. These continuums of activity are by no means exclusive; there are undoubtedly many more ranges of activity not considered here. The continuums presented here are merely categorizations created from activity emerging from the informal and formal learning activities described in previous sections (Fig. 8.1).

Characteristics of Mobile Learning for Creating a Pedagogical Model

Mobile learning generated through field activity is highly contextual, which can be characterized by movement through the following ranges of activity. They are the first step to understand how mobile learning field activity can progress into an education called Pedagogy of Simultaneity. Learning in movement means at least three things, which are orientation, structure and human presence of learning. In the Pedagogy of Simultaneity they are the learning and pedagogical context.

- serendipity and intentionality continuum in terms of orientation
- informal and formal continuum in terms of structure
- initiative-seduction-sense of intervals continuum in terms of presence

Serendipity-Intentionality Continuum

Serendipity means that learning encounters are filled with possibility. Some of these encounters or possibilities become consciously visible, yet many if not most remain at the subconscious level to be revealed as a potential learning activity at a later date, if at all. A serendipitous learning orientation refers to a trust in the potential for serendipity to reveal itself and its learning potential, as well as an open mind for registering this serendipity.

Intentionality means that we as learners and teachers try to proceed within and execute purposeful encounters to learn, to benefit from and enjoy this learning and the people they include. This intentionality can be manifested through teaching or

Fig. 8.1 An image designed to evoke many of the continuums of activity being engaged simultaneously in open environments. The open learner is responsive to serendipity, yet simultaneously performing intentional learning acts; the open learner shifts between states of informal and formal learning activity (the informal and playful sketching over the open environment as in the above illustration, followed by a formal consideration of how these open spaces can be approached from a disciplinary perspective); moving between initiative in their approaches to space, and seduction in how space approaches them. It is important to pedagogically consider these continuums of activity when designing field activity (Gallagher & Gallagher, 2013a)

learning settings, professional meetings and all kinds of mutual and multilateral social encounters. An intentional orientation is a conscious and goal-oriented readiness to act to realize learning potential. The serendipitous and intentionality continuum points to an emergence of a learning orientation that moves back and forth between these states of serendipity and intentionality. This serendipity-intentionality orientation is a trust argument for the Pedagogy of Simultaneity, and it is assumed for the purposes of this chapter that learning, especially mobile learning field activity is a shifting process of learning by intention and learning by serendipity. Intentionality is codified in much of our activity-based pedagogy, such as experiential learning (Kolb, 1984), while serendipitous learning has been investigated extensively in e-learning and mobile learning scenarios (Buchem, 2011; Vavoula & Sharples, 2002). Orienting the learner towards both sides of this continuum is valuable for maximizing the learning benefits of mobile learning field activities.

Informal-Formal Continuum

The informal and formal structures are presented as the artifacts of a learning context; these are combined into learning structure in an endless variety of forms. Informal structures are those everyday settings, activities, places, and people that are present in workplaces and at home, in hobbies and other leisure activities, that are not enacted purposefully. Formal structures include goal-oriented physical and virtual working environments, school and corresponding layouts, curriculum-based content, and methods used in teaching and study resources made available for learning activities. The complexity of these structures across the formal and information continuum suggests a dynamic of simultaneous engagements and presence. Learners can and often engage in many of these informal and formal structures simultaneously to make meaning, consciously or otherwise. In these engagements the discussion argument for the Pedagogy of Simultaneity becomes visible. The interplay between the informal and formal is activated and made visible by the discussion and collaboration forums made available for learning.

Initiative-Seduction-Sense of Intervals Continuum

Initiative and seduction are presented to account for the learner's engagement with their learning, whether it is through a deliberate initiative (learner autonomy) or through a seduction (a contextualization of learning more often presented to them by a teacher). Initiative is an open and public conscious performance in a social environment, while the seduction is an indirect and tacit activity. The sense of intervals is connected to the understanding and respect of the existence of tacit occurrence and knowledge, a phase of 'quiet water' inside human activity. Initiatives, seductions and senses of intervals form a human presence aura for learning activities. This humaneness constitutes a collage argument for the Pedagogy of Simultaneity.

Pedagogy of Simultaneity Model

The Pedagogy of Simultaneity is a narrative of the intersecting time, space and social layers constituting learning in interplay of layers of trust, discussion and collage (Gallagher & Ihanainen, 2013). The activity layer of this pedagogy is composed of three variables: the serendipitous and intentional orientation being a root and argument for trust; informal and formal meeting structures constituting a discussion argument; and initiative- seduction-sense of intervals based presences giving a human atmosphere for collage. Supporting this activity are the background layers of time, place and social presence in general. These three layers, including simultaneity in three forms, i.e. confluence (time), coexistence (place) and pervasiveness (social presence), and their emergent, complex and humane quality are so multidimensional and rich that only through the trust, discussion and collage approaches of the Pedagogy of Simultaneity can they be fully and successfully met. The Pedagogy of Simultaneity represents an attempt to capture and make use the simultaneous activities and engagements employed by learners to make meaning in the complex and volatile spaces targeted in these mobile learning field activities.

Time, Place and Human Presence: Space Itself

There are many different layers of time the mobile learner engages with to make meaning. Time itself is one of these layers. It is possible to speak about pointillist and cyclical time along with linear time. Learners sporadically return to discrete moments of learning (pointillist) or engage in learning through process (cyclical). These layers of time often intertwine with one another to produce overlapping time (Ihanainen & Moravec, 2011). In addition, duration can be included in time layers as a means of registering the length of the learning activity (Railly, 2012). Linear time is familiar: yesterday, today, tomorrow; at 12, 6 pm and 1 am. Pointillist time exists in separate points. For instance, tweets are this kind of produced and experienced time point; they exist in and of themselves in time. Cyclic time suggests a more intensive burst than pointillist time. Traditionally, it was experienced in the seasons of a year. During the industrial era a corresponding cyclic activity can be seen in the rhythms of work and leisure time periods. A burst of activity is visible in online discussion, which includes both strong, intense flows of activity and slower, quieter participation sequences. The content of the conversations found in the field activity workshops presented in this chapter proceeded in these cycles.

Overlapping time refers to the simultaneous overlaps of linear, pointillist and cyclical time; overlapping time is experienced as friction (the general deterioration of the self experienced over time) and conversely as an empowering time constituent. It is important to foreground that learners engage in these time layers simultaneously and continuously to establish a context to make meaning. In the field activities presented in this chapter, learners are constantly engaging in pointillist (data collection, geopositioned images or other media, tweets, etc.), cyclic (online discussion, chatting, reflection, composing, blogging) and overlapping time layers.

Another characteristic of these field activities are their engagements with multiple places simultaneously. Physical-social places are the personal spaces of people constituted by the actual physical and social context. The shared places of people like cafes, cities, workplaces and cultures are physical-social spaces. Nature, such as forests, seas, and skies, are positioned here as physical places. Modern physical-social places often overlap with virtual spaces. We exist in these spaces persistently through technology and this persistence has revealed patterns of learner engagement and online spatial orientations (see Bayne, Gallagher, & Lamb, 2014 in relation to the enactment of this space online in formal higher education). More and more of this engagement is generated by mobile technology. Virtual spaces can be presented through textual narratives, written stories and descriptions; they can be multimodal assemblies, compositions and exchanges.

Both physical and virtual places are social. The sociability of these places is realized by the fact that people share information with each other. People permeate these places with their presence; in turn, this presence allows for the emergence of hybridized practices and modes of interaction. As mobile technology further embeds itself in the everyday and we search for learning theories to embrace this transformation (Polson & Morgan, 2010), the boundaries between discrete physical, virtual, and social places have blurred. There are only hybridized places, which are simultaneously physical, virtual and social. They coexist in the places of today and in mobile learning field activities. Sociability is a characteristic of being human as it is embedded in time, place and other occurrences. Sociability is a phenomenon that is often experienced simultaneously in groups (multiple people experiencing a similar social reality) or individually (a person experiencing multiple social engagements simultaneously). This simultaneity is a social presence, a process of engaging with multiple social realities simultaneously, whether visible or invisible, understandable or incomprehensible (Shotter, 2011). It can most readily be described as pervasiveness.

Social presence emerges from and between individuals. Social presence between people can be listening, empathetic, and dialogic or conversational. It can also be non-listening, non-empathic and non-conversational. The latter means in practice a form of social absence, but it still has a strong impact in an actual social situation. In short, non-participation in a social activity is still a social presence. Social presence and non-presence is illustrated in these mobile learning field activities through activities that move freely between isolated or individualistic orientations (Park, 2011) that pass through communities of non-presence, (such as data collection, observations and media creation with or around non-peers) to highly socialized ones (discussion, composition, dissemination of findings or reflections with peers).

Social presence can be seen as a shared cognitive, emotional and intentional mental state or mood. Formal learning is pedagogically designed to stimulate a cognitive social presence, but includes all the other states of social presence as well. Informal and familiar meetings of people are more emotionally-based than cognitive, yet the cognitive layers are present. An intentional social activity is constituted by conscious aims to achieve something, whether a formal or informal event. Mobile learning field activities engage many of these types of social presence routinely and simultaneously.

Trust, Discussion, and Collage

The Pedagogy of Simultaneity, having both the background and activity layers described above, is crystallized in the dynamic of trust, discussion and collage. In a pedagogical sense one has to trust in learning executed in expressions and acts, make possible forums for (re)creation in discussion and collaboration, and recognize the importance of collage to both generate and identify emerging collages of aggregated meaning. In the context of field activity, trust is made visible through empowering learners to identify their own focus and learning process to enact that focus. In short, learners choose the topics of their own field activity, either within a disciplinary context (for formal learning) or within a specific perceived need (for informal learning). Trust begins with topic selection.

Trust generates individual learning, the discussion and negotiation of mutual understanding and the pooling of shared resources and compositions. Discussion emerges from trust and social presence; these field activities are oriented to a collective negotiation of meaning and composition. Discussion is critical in establishing not only the collective negotiation of meaning, but also to developing an understanding of how these collages of meaning will be received by the learner's social or learning community (colleagues, classmates, friends, or even the broader online community). Collage is the stitching together of meaning through compositions, representations, reflections, or any output generated from the field activity. The commitment of the Pedagogy of Simultaneity explicitly to trust, discussion and collage emphasizes the capacity of the individual to process and make use of open space. Through trust, mutual collaboration, and creation, open and lifelong learners are developed.

Trust also means that pedagogically, the teacher must avoid or meaningfully compose control and comparative measurement structures into their learning. The teacher must engineer respect, attention, and patience into their learning design, providing opportunity for the learners to construct their own learning paths through the field activity. Trust is present in all kinds of online and offline gatherings of people. The organic energy and activity in these gatherings is discussion, but it can evolve into multilateral collaborations. The basic pedagogical task is to notice and make possible discussion informally and formally at schools, workplaces, through networks both online and offline, in all places, both virtual and physical, where learners meet. This includes the field activities being presented in this chapter.

However, the authors freely admit that trust is problematic as a trait to be developed, maintained, and ultimately assessed. Trust as a pedagogical trait will vary considerably in particular contexts; Finland, for example, will vary dramatically from South Korea in terms of the role of formalized assessment in the learning process. Trust is problematic in terms of how it is developed and maintained in a learning community, and preceding that, how it is activated in the first instance.

In formal education, trust emerges as a result of the interplay between the relationships of student and student; and teacher and student. It is further governed by a set of structuring variables: disciplinary norms for meaning making, the culture of the organization, broader sociocultural norms for communication and expression, etc. Yet, in formally assessed contexts, trust parallels self-efficacy, or the extent of the learner's belief in their ability to complete learning tasks. Trust builds on self-efficacy by accounting for learning activity in which the task itself is not defined, even when the relationships (student-student, and teacher-student) as well as the supporting structures (disciplinary norms, socio cultural influences, etc.) are present as they are in formal education. Trust, in this formal context, becomes an act of navigating these relationships and structures *after* navigating the potential and the structure of open space. Once open learning has been constructed in open space it is *then* adapted into the formal learning space (the classroom, for example). Once inserted into the formal learning space, assessment focuses not on trust itself, but rather on the knowledge representations that emerged from that trust (compositions or collages constructed from open learning are then formalized or adapted to classroom practice). This positioning remains problematic in terms of providing extrinsic motivation for students to engage in this open learning process, but it tacitly positions trust in the learning process. As a teacher, I trust that my students will engage their open spaces deliberately; as a student, I trust that all open environments are fruitful for exploration.

There is precedent for positioning trust, and self-efficacy, as a pedagogical trait at the center of the learning process. There is evidence to suggest that trust can be positioned as a pedagogical trait (for example, in DeMeulenaere, 2012); that it influences knowledge sharing itself (presented through the context of OERs in Van Acker, Vermeulen, Kreijns, Lutgerink, & Van Buuren, 2014) within learning communities; and within the process of providing feedback in higher education (Carless, 2012). Knowledge sharing and feedback are at the core of many productive social learning communities and, in turn, their assessment practices; positioning trust so explicitly in this process acknowledges that they (knowledge sharing, feedback, and a host of other learning processes) are influenced to a large degree by the level of trust that exists.

Collages as Impressions and Compositions

Collages first appear as aggregates of separate fragments, but then—after aesthetic orientation—they emerge by themselves as reflective wholes. They are intuitive facts, which yet are perpetually being defined. In practice all mashups, collections, summaries and other aggregates can be seen as collages. Collages are never external truths but personal and inviting, constructed to help the individual see and understand their environments. Yet they are communal resources, like cubist artwork in a gallery to be interpreted and used for remixing by later use by visitors. In the Pedagogy of Simultaneity context it is important to note the collage quality of OERs (open educational resouces) emerging from trust and discussion; the trust and discussion depend on the openness of open educational resources. In the contexts of the informal and formal learning activities in Edinburgh, Helsinki, London, and Seoul in particular, the data collected (audio, video, text, image, GPS metadata, etc.) was pooled amongst the participants for open use; the compositions (or collages) created were made openly accessible as well. Participants were free to select data to

Fig. 8.2 An image encapsulating many of the learning processes occurring simultaneously in open environments. The learner is responsive to both the serendipitous and intentional aspects of the immediate environment as learning is both presented and sought after. The reality is simultaneously being recorded and composed, disseminated and discussed through both mobile and other technologies. The pedagogical components of trust (in the ability of the learner to find learning in this open space), discussion (represented by the social functionality of the mobile technology) and collage (represented by the emerging outlined composition taking place over the visual space) are all present (Gallagher & Gallagher, 2013b)

compose as they saw fit; reflective practice was inserted throughout this process to consider the affordances of particular media, or how they 'spoke' to the other pieces of data in the larger collage. In this way, these OERs become more than personal representations of learning on a particular location; they become social material for composing meaning. Further, they enact the pedagogical principle of trust not only in the teacher-student dynamic, but also amongst learners themselves. The Pedagogy of Simultaneity is an attempt to make all this visible and usable in both formal and informal learning contexts (Fig. 8.2).

Conclusion

The kind of learning being enacted in mobile learning field activities is often complex and chaotic, where meaning is being perpetually constructed and context evolves as a response to it. This learning is a heady, complex process of employing intellectual, social, emotional and technological tools towards a process of coming to know (Säljö, 1999). This process of coming to know is accelerated by mobile technology; mobile learning, as a result of this acceleration, is an environment of overlap and simultaneity, where layers of time, social presence, and place are engaged with repeatedly by the learner to generate meaning.

This environment of overlaps and simultaneity challenges educators to generate pedagogically appropriate responses and designs for mobile learning in field activities. The Pedagogy of Simultaneity is one such response that is explicitly designed to account for the simultaneity of purpose, place, social presence, and layers of time present in mobile learning. It acknowledges that the intersections of these simultaneities are fertile learning spaces; in response to this complexity, the Pedagogy of Simultaneity emphasizes methods that are distinctly human: trust, discussion, and collage. It emphasizes learners that "artfully engage their surrounding to create impromptu sites of learning" (Sharples et al., 2007) through social interaction and creative composition; learners that transform their habitus (Kress & Pachler, 2007) in response to both intentionality and serendipity. It is a pedagogy specifically designed for the simultaneity being generated in mobile learning.

The pedagogical approaches outlined in this chapter are designed to address the particular learning environments as outlined in these mobile learning field activities, but we believe they are not exclusive to mobile learning. Indeed, the authors believe that this pedagogy has application to digital education and informal learning. The field activities presented in this chapter are merely one example of where this complexity is enacted and made visible; indeed, the same rich intersections of open space, learner engagement, and compositional practices occur across the educational spectrum. This is learning in the open and it requires a pedagogically appropriate response, one that seeks to understand and make use of these sophisticated learning engagements.

References

Baran, E. (2014). A review of research on mobile learning in teacher education. *Journal of Educational Technology and Society, 17*(4), 17–32. Retrieved September 20, 2014, from http://www.ifets.info/journals/17_4/2.pdf.

Bayne, S., Gallagher, M. S., & Lamb, J. (2014). Being 'at' university: The social topologies of distance students. *Higher Education, 67*(5), 569–583.

Benjamin, W. (1999). The return of the flâneur. *Selected Writings, 2*, 1927–1943.

Brookshaw, R., Fuller, A., & Waters, J. L. (Eds.). (2012). *Changing spaces of education: New perspectives on the nature of learning*. London: Routledge.

Bruner, J. (1991). The narrative construction of reality. *Critical Inquiry, 18*, 1–21.

Bruns, A. (2007, June). Produsage. In *Proceedings of the 6th ACM SIGCHI conference on Creativity & Cognition, Association of Computing Machinery (ACM)* (pp. 99–106), Washington, DC, June 13–15, 2007.

Buchem, I. (2011). Serendipitous learning: Recognizing and fostering the potential of microblogging. *Form@ re-Open Journal per la formazione in rete, 11*(74), 7–16.

Carless, D. (2012). Trust and its role in facilitating dialogic feedback. In *Feedback in higher and professional education* (pp. 90–103). London: Routledge.

Colley, S., & Gibbs, M. (2012). *Capturing archaeological performance on digital video: Implications for teaching and learning archaeology.* Retrieved May 1, 2015, from http://pripati.library.usyd.edu.au/bitstream/2123/8673/1/ColleyGibbsDigitalVideoEdSC20Sep12.pdf.

DeMeulenaere, E. (2012). Toward a pedagogy of trust. In *Places where ALL children learn: The power of high expectation curricula with low achieving students* (pp. 28–41). New York, NY: Teachers College Press.

Gallagher, M. (2013a). *Incessant motion through space: Mobile learning field activities in the humanities.* Retrieved August 20, 2013, from http://michaelseangallagher.org/wp-content/uploads/2015/02/Incessant-Motion-Through-Space.pdf.

Gallagher, M. (2013b). *mLearning workshop in Helsinki: Documenting the city through architecture, religion, sound, habitus.* Retrieved October 1, 2013, from http://bit.ly/1g2jpII.

Gallagher, M., & Gallagher, J. (2013a). *London street scene: PoS.* Retrieved September 1, 2014, from http://michaelseangallagher.org/wp-content/uploads/2015/02/Incessant-Motion-Through-Space.pdf.

Gallagher, M., & Gallagher, J. (2013b). *Parisian cafe scene: PoS.* Retrieved September 1, 2014, from http://michaelseangallagher.org/wp-content/uploads/2015/02/Incessant-Motion-Through-Space.pdf.

Gallagher, M., & Ihanainen, P. (2013). *Pedagogy supporting the simultaneous learning processes of open education: Pedagogy of Simultaneity (PoS). Open Education 2030: Higher Education.* Ispra: European Commission, Joint Research Centre: Information Society Unit.

Gallagher, M., & Ihanainen, P. (2014). *Pedagogy of simultaneity: Compositions.* Retrieved November 1, 2014, from http://www.pedagogyofsimultaneity.org/?page_id=16.

Gupta, A., & Ferguson, J. (Eds.). (1997). *Anthropological locations: Boundaries and grounds of a field science.* Oakland: University of California Press.

Haapala, O., Sääskilathi, K., Luimula, M., Yli-Hemminki, J., & Partala, T. (2007, June). Parallel learning between the classroom and the field using location-based communication techniques. In *World conference on educational multimedia, hypermedia and telecommunications* (pp. 668–676), 2007.

Harvey, B. (2007). The twentieth part: Virginia Woolf in the British Museum Reading Room. *Literature Compass, 4*(1), 218–234.

Hollevoet, C., Jones, K., & Nye, T. (1992). *The power of the city: The city of power* (Vol. 1). New York, NY: The Museum.

Hwang, G. J., Tsai, C. C., & Chen, C. Y. (2012). A context-aware ubiquitous learning approach to conducting scientific inquiry activities in a science park. *Australasian Journal of Educational Technology, 28*(5), 931–947.

Ifenthaler, D. (2012). Determining the effectiveness of prompts for self-regulated learning in problem-solving scenarios. *Journal of Educational Technology and Society, 15*(1), 38–52.

Ihanainen, P. (2013). A zone between formal and informal learning. In K. Aaltonen, A. Isacsson, J. Laukia, & L. Vanhanen-Nuutinen (Eds.), *Practical skills, education and development - Vocational education and training in Finland.* Helsinki: HAAGA-HELIA University of Applied Sciences.

Ihanainen, P., & Moravec, J. (2011). Pointillist, cyclical, and overlapping: Multidimensional facets of time in online education. *The International Review of Research in Open and Distance Learning, 12*(7), 27–39.

Jacucci, G., Oulasvirta, A., & Salovaara, A. (2007). Active construction of experience through mobile media: A field study with implications for recording and sharing. *Personal and Ubiquitous Computing, 11*(4), 215–234.

Jones, A. C., Scanlon, E., & Clough, G. (2013). Mobile learning: Two case studies of supporting inquiry learning in informal and semiformal settings. *Computers and Education, 61*, 21–32.

Kolb, D. A. (1984). *Experiential learning: Experience as the source of learning and development* (Vol. 1). Englewood Cliffs, NJ: Prentice-Hall.

Kress, G., & Pachler, N. (Eds). (2007). *Mobile learning: Towards a research agenda*. WLE Centre, Occasional Papers in Work-based Learning 1.

Leander, K. M., Phillips, N. C., & Taylor, K. H. (2010). The changing social spaces of learning: Mapping new mobilities. *Review of Research in Education, 34*, 329–394.

Marty, P. F., Alemanne, N, D,, Mendenhall, A., Maurya, M., Southerland, S. A., Sampson, V., ... Schellinger, J. (2013). Scientific inquiry, digital literacy, and mobile computing in informal learning environments. *Learning, Media and Technology, 38(4)*, 407–428.

McFarlane, C. (2010). The comparative city: Knowledge, learning, urbanism. *International Journal of Urban and Regional Research, 34*(4), 725–742.

Otavan opisto. Retrieved October 1, 2013, from http://apaja.otavanopisto.fi/kurssit/pedagogy-simultaneity.

Park, Y. (2011). A pedagogical framework for mobile learning: Categorizing educational applications of mobile technologies into four types. *The International Review of Research in Open and Distance Learning, 12*(2), 78–102.

Polson, D., & Morgan, C. (2010). Towards an intelligent learning system for the natural born cyborg. *Journal of the Research Center for Educational Technology, 6*(1), 185–193.

Railly, M. (2012). Bold schools: Part I - Learner as knowmad. Retrieved December 10, 2013, from http://maryannreilly.blogspot.fi/2012/01/bold-schools-part-i-learner-as-knowmad.html.

Robinson, C., & Sebba, J. (2010). Personalising learning through the use of technology. *Computers and Education, 54*(3), 767–775.

Sääskilahti, K., Sippola, O., Partala, T., & Luimula, M. (2010). Location-based communication techniques in parallel learning between the classroom and the field. *International Journal of Continuing Engineering Education and Life Long Learning, 20*(1), 21–39.

Säljö, R. (1999). Learning as the use of tools. In K. Littleton & P. Light (Eds.), *Learning with computers: Analysing productive interaction*. Hove: Psychology Press.

Sengers, P., Boehner, K., David, S., & Kaye, J. J. (2005). Reflective design. In *Proceedings of the 4th decennial conference on Critical computing: Between sense and sensibility* (pp. 49–58). Washington, DC: ACM.

Sharples, M., Taylor, J., & Vavoula, G. (2007). A theory of learning for the mobile age. In R. Andrews & C. Haythornthwaite (Eds.), *The sage handbook of eLearning research* (pp. 221–247). London: Sage.

Shields, R. (2006). Flanerie for cyborgs. *Theory, Culture and Society, 23*(7-8), 209–220.

Shotter, J. (2011). *Getting it: Withness-thinking and the dialogical--in practice*. New York, NY: Hampton Press.

So, H. J., Tan, E. B. K., & Tay, J. (2012). *Collaborative mobile learning in situ from knowledge building perspectives*. Retrieved May 1, 2015, from http://www.webinar.org.ar/sites/default/files/actividad/documentos/Aper-06%20So,%20Tan%20&%20Tay_FINAL.pdf.

Van Acker, F., Vermeulen, M., Kreijns, K., Lutgerink, J., & Van Buuren, H. (2014). The role of knowledge sharing self-efficacy in sharing open educational resources. *Computers in Human Behavior, 39*, 136–144.

Vavoula, G. N., & Sharples, M. (2002). KLeOS: A personal, mobile, knowledge and learning organisation system. In *IEEE International Workshop on Wireless and mobile technologies in education* (pp. 152–156). New York, NY: IEEE.

Verpoorten, D., Westera, W., & Specht, M. (2012). Using reflection triggers while learning in an online course. *British Journal of Educational Technology, 43*(6), 1030–1040.

Virsu, V., Oksanen-Hennah, H., Vedennaa, A., Jaatinen, P., & Lahti-Nuuttila, P. (2008). Simultaneity learning in vision, audition, tactile sense and their cross-modal combinations. *Experimental Brain Research, 186*(4), 525–537.

Wali, E., Winters, N., & Oliver, M. (2008). Maintaining, changing and crossing contexts: An activity theoretic reinterpretation of mobile learning. *ALT-J: Research in Learning Technology, 16*(1), 41–57. Retrieved September 20, 2014, from http://journals.co-action.net/index.php/rlt/article/viewFile/10884/12557.

Warriner, D. S., & Wyman, L. T. (2013). Experiences of simultaneity in complex linguistic ecologies: Implications for theory, method, and practice. *International Multilingual Research Journal, 7*(1), 1–14.

Chapter 9
A Practice-Grounded Approach to 'Engagement' and 'Motivation' in Networked Learning

Nina Bonderup Dohn

Engagement and Motivation: Widespread, Yet Unclear Concerns

A recurrent issue within the literature on ICT-mediated learning is how to engage or motivate learners to participate in the tasks of educational programs. Salmon's much-used guides to e-learning for this reason have large sections devoted to the discussion of how student motivation and engagement in participation may be promoted (Salmon, 2003, 2013). Her articulations of the issue and how to deal with it are quite typical:

- Quote 1: *To succeed in fully engaging the participants and promoting their active involvement…* (Salmon, 2003: 34).
- Quote 2: *The participant needs information and technical support to get online, and strong motivation and encouragement to put in the necessary time and effort* (Salmon, 2003: 31).

Similar formulations are found in papers from the Networked Learning conferences, e.g.:

- Quote 3: *The main reason for using Web 2.0 discussions was as a means to involve all students and force [sic] them to engage in a more active and reflective way … [though] the shift in control from teacher to students is only recommendable if students is [sic] mature enough and have the motivation to take over the responsibility* (Nicolajsen, 2012: 552).

N.B. Dohn (✉)
Department of Design and Communication, University of Southern Denmark,
Kolding, Denmark
e-mail: nina@sdu.dk

© Springer International Publishing Switzerland 2016
T. Ryberg et al. (eds.), *Research, Boundaries, and Policy in Networked Learning*, Research in Networked Learning, DOI 10.1007/978-3-319-31130-2_9

- Quote 4: *The students do need to be self-motivated to do this [respond to each other] and synchronous communication does give extra impetus to this.* (Basquill, 2014: 344).
- Quote 5: *The peer rating system enables the participants to see what individual peers think about a response. The medals awarded to good responses act as "tokens of appreciation" and partake of a mechanism aimed at supporting motivation, engagement, and commitment to participation in the study group.* (Ponti, 2014: 234).
- Quote 6: *The peer support system needs to provide not only a communication and interaction structure, but needs to provide the affordances that motivate learners to use these to actively engage in interactions and actively promote sustainability of interactions* (Brouns & Hsiao, 2012: 23).

Other formulations stress the significance of community for 'engagement' and 'motivation', e.g.

- Quote 7: *[L]earners has [sic] to experience a sense of belonging, feel part of a community before engaging in interactions that come naturally in communities* (Brouns & Hsiao, 2012: 20).
- Quote 8: *The aim of using the JBT [an icebreaker tool] was to build a sense of community and thus increase engagement by providing a forum through which to foster the development of an online community. If this is looked at more closely, a sense of community develops when a common interest or environment is shared* (Carson, 2014: 54)

These quotes illustrate some variance in (implicit) understandings about motivation and engagement. Broadly speaking, the majority of the quotes appear inspired by individualist cognitivist motivation theory, in that they draw upon an understanding of motivation as a 'something' (an entity, state or process—its nature is not quite clear) which the individual 'has' 'inside' which drives him or her forward and which may be influenced—reinforced or weakened—by 'outside' stimulations. In some of the quotes, outside stimulations seem able to 'install' the 'something' in the individual by 'motivating' him or her. 'Engagement' similarly equivocates between something students have, show or do on the one hand and something we as educators do to them on the other. Or, alternatively, something we establish in them or make them do by 'motivating' them—there is some diversity in the views on the relationship between 'motivation' and 'engagement', too. The last two quotes on the other hand are more in line with socio-culturally inspired theories where engagement is treated as anchored in the social settings (community or cultural practices) in which the learner participates. This suggests—or at least opens the door to—another approach to motivation which centres less on what is 'inside' the individual and more on what is negotiated between people.

The variance in (implicit or explicit) understandings is found in the broader research literature, too. Compare, for instance, the following statements:

- Quote 9: *Facilitating discourse during the course is critical to maintaining the interest, motivation and engagement of students in active learning* (Anderson, Rourke, Garrison, & Archer, 2001: 7)

• Quote 10: *Communities' language use and ways of interacting have long been recognized as practices that bind people together across time and that serve as critical sources of group identity and coherence. As critical resources, they can be extremely influential in either inviting or excluding students in classroom interactions, providing key avenues for students' motivation to engage in learning activities* (Ares, 2008: 316).

However, as exemplified by contrasting Quotes 6 and 7, both from Brouns and Hsiao (2012), authors seem not always to be aware that there are divergent views at play here. The result is a vagueness and ambiguity of the terms which carry over to specific analyses of networked learning and recommendations for design of educational tasks. To illustrate with Brouns and Hsiao's specific case, there are thus different implications and presuppositions involved in speaking of engagement as something which can be motivated by a system's affordances (i.e. 'installed' in the individual) as opposed to being a trait which is inherently bound up with belonging to a community. The former calls for designing tasks and systems which utilize the right causal 'triggers' of 'inner' motivation. In line with this, the authors explicitly refer to social exchange theory which builds on the presupposition that "people weigh their benefits against the investment of participation" (23). Design principles would concern ways in which to maximize the benefits, cognitively and perhaps in terms of reputation and extrinsic rewards (ibid.).

Taking the communities perspective on engagement seriously would on the other hand imply making the issues of belonging and of learners' habituated practices the design starting point, not just a possible add-on to cognitive tasks. And it would imply doing so not only in terms of designing tasks which aim at establishing 'new common practices' for the given group of learners and help nurture a sense of belonging to the group. Depending on how large a part of the learners' life the course is meant to be, this kind of design considerations may certainly be relevant. Still, quite as important are considerations of the communities to which the learners already belong and the practices to which they are already habituated, because these are the 'critical resources' (cf. Quote 10) with which the learners come. And, according to the socio-culturalist, the 'critical resources' with which the learners come will have decisive influence on how they respond to the opportunities to learn presented in the course.

The paper by Brouns and Hsiao is in no way unique in apparently drawing on both the individualist cognitivist approach and the socio-cultural one. This very fact indicates that each of the approaches has insights which intuitively seem relevant to understanding and designing for networked learning, despite their theoretical incongruence. More specifically, the insights drawn from individualist cognitivist motivation theories are a) the significance of self-directedness and b) the distinction between intrinsic and extrinsic motivation. The insights coming from the socio-cultural theories concern c) that participation and engagement are anchored in social practice. Thus, there seems to be a need for developing a theoretical approach which makes possible the consistent integration of these insights and remedies the vagueness of the terms.

In this paper I sketch out such an approach and identify significant focus areas for the analysis of networked learning. In addition, I point out how questions typically posed within analysis and design of networked learning transform on this basis. My argument takes the following course: First, to clarify at the outset how the subsequent theoretical analysis relates to networked learning, I state my understanding of the field and foreshadow a few of the questions which my analyses will allow to pose or pose differently. Second, I briefly articulate the theoretical underpinnings of individualist cognitivist motivation theory and socio-culturally inspired theories of engagement and identity. Third, I challenge the theoretical underpinnings with examples of everyday situations which, for each approach, seem clear cases that they cannot account adequately for. Fourth, I draw on my concept of primary contexts developed in (Dohn, 2013, 2014) to argue for a practice-grounded intermediary position. I use this to further distinguish important questions in the analysis of networked learning at the level of discrimination between practices and at the level of participants' concrete actions. In conclusion, I briefly consider implications for the design of networked learning.

Initial Clarification of Theoretical Outset

My concern with networked learning in this paper is first and foremost with the type of learning processes which involve educational design at some point or at least ensue as the result of such design. That is, I am less taken up with completely informal learning networks e.g. in workplaces where meetings and learning exclusively happens 'as they go along' without any attempt at designing for learning, neither at the level of tasks and social relations nor at the level of work environment. I am, however, taken up with the way other settings than the one in focus in educational design affect and pose resources for sense-making within the setting in focus. So much so that I have suggested an amendment to the widespread definition of networked learning presented in (Goodyear, Banks, Hodgson, & McConnell, 2004) which precisely adds this dimension. My understanding of networked learning thus is:

> Networked learning is learning in which information and communications technology (ICT) is used to promote connections: between one learner and other learners; between learners and tutors; between a learning community and its learning resources; between the diverse contexts in which the learners participate. (Dohn, 2014: 30)

My point of departure for analysing networked learning is what I term a practice-grounded approach (Dohn, 2013, 2014). This approach is inspired by socio-cultural theories, in particular activity theory (Engeström, 1987; Säljö, 2000; Vygotsky, 1978) and situated learning (Greeno, 1997; Greeno & Middle School Mathematics Through Applications Project Group, 1998; Lave & Wenger, 1991; Wenger, 1998). Even more, it is inspired by the philosophers whose work lie at the root of the socio-cultural view (Packer & Goicoechea, 2000), i.e. Hegel, Marx, Heidegger, and Merleau-Ponty. Additional sources of inspiration are the later Wittgenstein and contemporary philosophical heirs to Wittgenstein and phenomenology such as

Hubert Dreyfus and Charles Taylor (Dreyfus, 1979, 2001, 2002; Taylor, 1985a, 1985b). A central claim is that we are always already in the world, coping with it as active embodied beings, before we start reflecting on it, and that when we do reflect, the words we use resonate with tacit meaning from our pre-reflective embodied doings. Of particular significance are our 'primary contexts', because they supply the principal anchorage points for meaning, though not the only ones. 'Primary contexts' I define as contexts which carry significance for the person in question, in which s/he involves him-/herself as a person and which s/he considers important for who s/he is.

When strangers at social gatherings ask us who we are, some or all of our primary contexts will usually be implicated in the answers we give. Family; profession; workplace; the specific department or professional group one works in; educational background (including perhaps the specific educational institution); social movement, religious community, or political party in which one participates actively; volunteer working context; and sports club are typical examples of contexts which are primary to us at least for a period of our lives. In a similar vein, Jarvis notes that when asked to complete the answer "I am (a)..." ten times in response to the question "Who am I?", most respondents place their occupation high on the list. He goes on to comment:

> The point is that we do identify with our work and the process of identification seems to move from performing a role to a sense of belonging to one of identifying with either the role or the organisation, or both. At the same time, since the respondents were able to put down several answers, if not all ten, indicates [sic] that there are a number of other social identities – indicating that they belonged to a number of communities of practice, some of which were more important than work, such as the nation, the ethnic people, the faith community and even leisure communities (Jarvis, 2007: 151–152).

My concept of 'primary contexts' is inspired by the way Jarvis here uses Wenger's term communities of practice to highlight, on the one hand that we all belong to several such communities, but that they on the other hand are not all equally important to us. I do wish to stress two differences between my view and Jarvis', though.

Firstly, I find the term 'social identity' too biased as the prime characteristic of what it is the 'primary contexts' supply us with. It seems to imply that social role—who we are or negotiate ourselves to be in relation to others in the practice—is what makes a primary context important to us. The domain of the primary context—the 'what' or content matter with which one engages in the practice—seems of less or no importance in itself. But if someone writes 'enthusiastic bird watcher' as one of the ten answers to who he or she is, the domain of birds, and ways of engaging with them, clearly is an essential part of what they are referring to. It is less clear that a social role is being described. In contrast to the terms 'communities of practice' and 'social identity' the term 'primary context' does not make any initial implicit presuppositions as to relative importance of a) the domain of the practice and b) the social relations of the people who engage in it.

Second, we do not necessarily identify with all of our primary contexts—we may also at points in our lives try to distance ourselves from them or even revolt against them. Examples would be the family (parents and siblings) for the young person who has just moved away from home, or a given religious faith for someone who has just converted to another faith. The struggle which a person may have in freeing him/herself from the influence of the home context or religion and 'finding him/herself' shows precisely how important those contexts are to him/her—even if negatively so. For the religious converters from, say, Danish Lutheran Christianity to Tibetan Buddhism, both of these religious practices will be 'primary contexts' for at least a period of time after the conversion. In contrast, their social identity (as described by Jarvis) will be determined only by the latter religious faith, because this was the only one they belonged to after the conversion.

Given my theoretical outset in the practice-grounded approach, individualist analyses of students' intrinsic or extrinsic motivation for participating in networked learning overlook questions such as i) how students' intrinsic motivation relate to their primary contexts (no straightforward causal connection or even a correlation need be presupposed as I shall show below); ii) how the tacit sense-making of the students' primary contexts are drawn upon in the learning tasks and iii) how the fact that they are/are not affects their motivational stance. To give one simple example, when analysing the contributions of students in a forum discussion, one has to ask, not only how different 'incentives' such as acquiring points-for-grades or social status through activity measures affect motivation. One must also analyse any deeper sense such incentives may have for the students from the practices in their primary contexts. This is important for understanding whether and how such a deeper sense may influence the way they will engage in the activities.

On the other hand, socio-cultural analyses of community participation tend to overlook the self-directedness with which some students choose to enrol in networked learning courses. Arguably, for very self-directed students such courses will be 'primary contexts' because of their content matter, even before they are participants in them. In consequence, socio-cultural analyses neglect questions about how self-directedness may influence the activity level of students, i.e. the amount of time and effort they put into getting 'a grip on' content matter (including the tacit aspects hereof). On my view, analysis of e.g. a forum debate should not only focus on issues such as positioning and opportunities to learn, but also on the influence of students' varying degrees of self-directed involvement.

Theoretical Underpinnings: Individualist, Cognitivist Theories

A standard educational psychology textbook definition of motivation, concurring well with most of the statements above, runs "Motivation is the process whereby goal-directed activity is instigated and sustained" (Schunk, Pintrich, & Meece, 2008: 4). This definition is individualist and cognitivist in that it focuses on goals which individuals are more or less conscious of pursuing and identifies motivation with that which 'persuades' them to enter and keep up the pursuit. The persuasive force may come from thoughts, beliefs or emotions (ibid.) but the important cognitivist point is that people are aware of the 'persuasion': They are aware, not only of the goals they have, but also of why they have them. At least to the level of being able to explicate the process that leads them to have the goals and thus to explain their actions as goal-directed activity. The definition does not actually say that the process of motivation is 'internal' to the individual, nor do the authors of the textbook explicitly state this. However, it is quite clear from the further treatment of the subject that motivation is seen as 'taking place' 'inside' the person. The very fact that this is not articulated as an assumption at all, but taken for granted, may testify to the fundamental status it has within the field of motivation.

A common point across different cognitivist approaches is a presupposition of agent self-directedness—agents choose for themselves which goals to pursue—as well as a lack of deeper inquiry into the background for why they choose goals as they do and have the motivations that they have: What decides whether a student will entertain a learning objective as a mastery or a performance goal (Ames, 1992)? How does it come about that a person becomes intrinsically motivated for pursuing precisely those activities or learning domains that s/he does (Ryan & Deci, 2000)? Even social cognitive theory which emphasises the role of social models for the individual's learning (Bandura, 1986, 1997) constrains focus to specific models in specific settings, rather than raising the background issue e.g. of why a teacher may come to be a model for one student and not for another. Research has been done for instance on how intrinsic motivation relates to certain intrapsychological needs (Ryan & Deci, 2000) and, in consequence, on what educators can do to support learners in developing intrinsic motivation for learning a given domain; yet the initial choice of goals, attitudes and models is taken to be something the individual just makes.

Another common point is that the concept of 'learning context' is often fully ignored. When it is taken into consideration, it is dominantly conceptualized through an implicit container metaphor of 'context' (Lave, 1993): The 'learning context' is for instance described as having 'boundaries', 'open' versus 'closed' 'spaces', with inventories and atmospheres. It is understood to be 'built' or 'established' on beforehand, independently of the specific learners who are to 'step into it' and 'move within its spaces'. The learners for their part are the self-contained beings that then interact within the boundaries given by the 'learning context' container. They will be constrained by its boundaries and inventory, may be influenced by its characteristics and may strive to change the form and content of it. But they do so as the self-directed, self-contained 'elements'/'particles' in the container, giving and receiving 'input'. They do not depend on the context as a significant medium for realizing their very being.

Theoretical Underpinnings: Sociocultural Theories

From quite another perspective, sociocultural theories, in particular situated learning theory, have theorized engagement as a matter of participation in social practices (Greeno & Gresalfi, 2008; Lave & Wenger, 1991; Packer & Goicoechea, 2000; Wenger, 1998). The term 'engagement' here is intended to cover simultaneously, inherently and constitutively, 'engagement in activities' and 'engagement with other people in the practice'. The basic premise is that "We are social beings" (Wenger, 1998: 4) who become who we are through mutual recognition between ourselves and others of our roles, possibilities, rights, and duties. This recognition, furthermore, is mediated through and anchored in the material practices we partake in together. Intellectual ancestry may be attributed to Hegel and Marx, the first stressing reciprocal recognition, the other materiality. The concept of self is the

> communal self [which] is always embedded in a co-constitutive self-other, self-societal dialectic... a self that is cut from the fabric of those sociocultural conventions and ways of life into which we are born as biophysical human beings... (Martin, 2007: 83).

Inherent to this view is therefore a very different understanding of 'context' to the one implicit in individualist theories: Individuals and contexts are woven together, each relying for their being—becoming what they are—through the co-constitutive interweaving. McDermott, citing Birdwhistell, provides an alternative metaphor for 'context' which is appropriate for this perspective, namely the rope. He stresses that a rope is made up of fibres which are discontinuous (no fibre goes through all of the rope), yet the rope looks and behaves as a continuous unity (McDermott, 1993). McDermott goes on to argue that, at the level of the rope, the fibres disappear as units of analysis, and that similarly for human practices, individuals disappear as units of analysis. Instead, they are ascribed traits on the basis of the organization of the whole:

> People mutually constitute contexts for each other by erasing themselves, by giving themselves over to a new level of organization, which, in turn, acquires them and keeps them informed of what they are doing together. (McDermott, 1993: 274).

McDermott uses this insight to argue that a certain child, Adam, who has been diagnosed with a learning disability (LD), is, in fact better understood as having been "acquired" by it:

> Adam is a fiber, which, when joined by other fibers, helps to make the rope, or in this case the category LD, into the unit of analysis. It is not so much that Adam is disabled as that he participates in a scene well organized for the institutional designation of someone as LD... [I]n this sense ... LD is a context that acquires children (274–275).

One important aspect of the rope metaphor is therefore the way context designates possible stances and actions of its participants—and the meaning which these stances and actions can have. The significance and place of each individual fibre is given to it through its interlocking with the others. However, the fact that fibres 'arrange themselves' to disappear because 'the scene is well organized' does not imply that the context's designation of stances and actions is deterministic. The process of 'self-arrangement' is quite as important. Each fibre has a part in the interlocking—does part of the arranging and interweaving. Therefore, though a fibre is enabled, constrained, and generally 'held in place' by the surrounding fibres, it and its significance and how it can interrelate is still partly negotiable. This focus on the role of the fibre-in-the-rope is somewhat lost in McDermott's description of how LD acquires Adam, but is a main point in the way I shall use the metaphor in the following. In contrast to McDermott (and many other socio-culturalists), I find that the metaphor of the rope makes it possible to uphold a double-sided unit of analysis, that of the 'person-in-context' (Järvelä, Volet, & Järvenoja, 2010; Nolen & Ward, 2008).

A fundamental point for sociocultural theories is that what we strive to know, and how we go about knowing it, is bound up with who we see ourselves to be. Packer and Goicoechea go so far as to say that "[K]nowing is not an end in itself, but a means to the ends of recognition and identity. The search for these ends is what leads people to "participate in communities in many different ways"" (Packer & Goicoechea, 2000: 235, for their part citing Greeno & Middle School Mathematics Through Applications Project Group, 1998: 10). Though not all situated learning theorists will accept this rather extreme formulation, still, the assumption of an intricate relationship between issues of identity and issues of cognition is inherent in central terms such as 'positioning' and 'participatory identity' (Greeno & Gresalfi, 2008; Greeno & van de Sande, 2007). 'Positioning' here refers to the degree of socio-cognitive status as a legitimate and knowledgeable contributor which is accorded in practice to a person in interaction with others—through the interaction itself—and to the corresponding opportunities for contributing to the interaction. 'Participatory identity', on the other hand refers to emerging patterns in the way participants take up such opportunities.

Given this interwovenness of issues of cognition and identity, engagement is viewed within situated learning as intrinsically related to belonging. Not just in the sense that a feeling of belonging to a community is conducive to the confidence with which a person ventures a contribution to it or promotes intrinsic motivation as Ryan and Deci would hold (Ryan & Deci, 2000). But in the stronger sense that within a community of practice, any participation in the form of negotiation of meaning of a resource, artefact, story or other of the community's "shared repertoire"(Wenger, 1998) will at the same time be a negotiation of one's status and identity in relation to the community, i.e. of one's way of belonging to it. And vice versa: any negotiation of one's identity in relation to the community will be a way of engaging with the people and resources in it. This goes, even when the participation takes on the form of non-participation (Wenger, 1998). Non-participation should here be differentiated from the situation where an issue of participation does not arise for the person in question. In the first instance, the person is formally and/or informally supposed to participate, but does not. Either because others in practice do not allow it (e.g. by ignoring a certain networked learner's posts) or because s/he chooses not to (e.g. by not contributing to an online discussion when supposed to do so). In the second instance, the person is not supposed to participate (a person not enrolled in a course is for example not supposed to post in the closed, online forum pertaining to the course).

The point here for situated learning theorists is that the very fact that non-participation is positioned for a person means that interrelated issues of engagement and belonging are involved. One recognizes here the sense of necessary relation between participation and belonging posited in Quote 7 by Brouns and Hsiao above. It should be noted, however, that the 'necessary relation' is largely one of definition, not of causal fact: Nothing will count as participation within situated learning, if there are not issues of belonging and identity at stake. To some extent, therefore, the seemingly provocative claims of situated learning are based on an ambiguity in the status of these claims as definitional versus empirical statements.

Within this approach, the questions raised in relation to individualist cognitivist motivation theories (such as where people's goals come from and what decides whether they pursue a learning objective as a mastery goal or a performance one) will be reformulated as questions concerning

- Who they seek to be
- How the positionings and identity negotiations of current and former communities of practices to which they belong(ed) allow them to take up opportunities for learning in the present situation
- How their prior engagement with the 'shared repertoires' of current and former communities of practice constitute affordances and constraints on their taking up of such learning opportunities.

Quote 10 from Ares above exemplifies a reformulation of the questions. To answer the reformulated questions, situated learning theorists have introduced the term 'trajectories of participation' (Dreier, 2008; Lave & Wenger, 1991; Wenger, 1998). In Wenger's words:

> As we go through a succession of forms of participation, our identities form trajectories, both within and across communities of practice… To me, the term trajectory suggests not a path that can be foreseen or charted but a continuous motion – one that has a momentum of its own in addition to a field of influences. It has a coherence through time that connects the past, the present, and the future. (Wenger, 1998: 154).

Examples of 'trajectory analyses' include Nielsen's research on music academy students (Nielsen, 1999), Østerlund's investigation of sales apprentices (Østerlund, 1997), Dreier's analysis of how people make psychotherapy matter in their everyday lives (Dreier, 2008), and Sfard's and Prusak's comparison of native and immigrant Israeli students' math practices (Sfard & Prusak, 2005). In all these cases, the authors investigate the different ways in which people project their futures and take up opportunities to learn, dependent on their participation, past and present, in different communities of practices and the negotiation of meaningful activity going on there. In individualist motivation theorist terms they thus investigate the construction and development of personal goals, on the presupposition that the construction and development is necessarily anchored in negotiation of social relations.

Challenging the Theoretical Approaches

As indicated by a few of the remarks above, for both individualist and sociocultural approaches there are important questions concerning motivation and engagement which cannot be posed as questions. The way issues are framed theoretically make them either invisible or answered on beforehand by definitional fiat. Thus, individualist theories take self-directedness for granted. Even if one were to ask "where the self-directed motivation came from", the question would be phrased in terms of an 'inner' process or state, identifiable as an entity in itself, which might perhaps be influenced by 'outer' stimuli from the 'context as container' or the other entities 'in' it. Sociocultural approaches, on the other hand, posit engagement as per definition an intertwined issue of pursuing identity and knowledge. Even if one were to ask "how come this person joined this particular networked learning course as opposed to others on the same domain", the answer to the question would be phrased in terms of the negotiation of meaning in the person's communities of practices, past and present, and its significance for the identity which the person projects for him/herself. Yet, from a low-level common sense point of view, there seem to be clear cases which challenge the presuppositions behind each of the positions.

To start with the sociocultural view: There are ample cases where children (and grown-ups) take up a hobby not promoted by their family and indeed perhaps not even negotiated as acceptable by their peers. Examples would be the amateur study of birds, the design of terrariums and aquariums, or the practice of Tai Chi. Of course, such hobbies do not exist in a void—the children will have been inspired by someone or someplace to take up the hobby. It is not *impossible* that issues of identity are involved. The choice of hobby may for instance be the result of negotiated positionings by child, family and peers of the child as 'different', 'in opposition' or 'in need of further challenges'. Or alternatively, of projections of the child, negotiated with the surroundings, to be like the Tai Chi master or a famous ornithologist. On the other hand, it may not. It seems highly problematic to postulate at the outset that such identity issues have to be involved, not just at the level of explaining that some non-promoted hobby is taken up, but at the level of explaining which one.

At some level of detail, the claim loses whatever credibility it may have at a general level: The only reason to say that identity issues definitely were at play in a child's hobby choice of coral reef aquariums over freshwater ones is a commitment to the thesis that questions of engagement are always intertwined with identity issues. Without this commitment, it seems much more plausible to explain the choice by reference to something in the domain (the object of the hobby) which attracted the child to it—say, the beauty of coral reefs as compared to freshwater plants. That is, it seems much more plausible to explain the choice with reference to individualist motivational concepts such as interest, intrinsic motivation or mastery goals.

Similarly, when analysing networked learning it seems reasonable to leave open for empirical investigation how interest and self-directed choice might influence which courses learners commit to and how. It appears biased to say the least to postulate at the outset that these issues must necessarily be understood on the basis of participation in certain communities of practice.

As for the individualist view: family, mandatory schooling, designated work units all constitute examples of settings into which one is more or less thrown, i.e. one does not come to be there by self-directed choice. One is forced to participate in these settings, i.e. non-participation is by the very fact that one is there at all a form of participation. One's mode of engagement is bound up with positionings and identity issues. To explain what goes on in these settings solely by reference to the participants' 'inner' states and processes fully neglects that the existence and value of these supposed states are themselves important issues of negotiation for the participants there. Several situated learning studies illustrate in detail how notions such as intrinsic/extrinsic motivation, self-efficacy and goal orientation, rather than being the *explanation* of interactions, are the *outcome* of them (e.g. Greeno & Gresalfi, 2008; Greeno & van de Sande, 2007). The implication for networked learning is that one should investigate how positioning and identity issues influence the way learners approach and take up opportunities to learn and interact with other learners.

The upshot of these considerations is that we need a reframing of the issues of motivation and engagement. This reframing should allow us to account both for situations in which agents approach new settings seemingly on their own self-directed accord and for ones in which they find themselves submerged and positioned whether they would self-directedly have chosen to or not. More importantly, it should allow us to investigate empirically how these different types of settings interplay—for individuals and for the people with whom they deal.

In terms of the different concepts of 'context' implicit in the individualist view and the socio-cultural one, respectively, the reframing should allow us to phrase questions which do not presuppose that we are always already co-constitutively involved (as fibres in the rope) in any context we partake in, nor that we are just elements in containers in existence independent of our being there. We need to be able to pose questions like "why do individuals approach some contexts with the intent of 'joining the rope'" (the self-directed case), "how is it that some persons act as if certain contexts were just containers to them?"(participation as non-participation), "how does a container become a rope for a person?", "how do different ropes interweave for a person? And how does it affect how they see new situations?"

In terms of design for networked learning, these questions transform into questions such as "should we design for courses that are containers or ropes for our participants?", "how can we design for containers to become ropes?", "how do we support people in interlocking as fibres in the rope, and how much space for negotiation of the interlocking process and result should we design?" and "how can we build on existing ropes in our designs?" These issues must be approached at two distinct levels (at least):

1. *The level of contexts*: we have to distinguish between contexts which are "ropes" or "becoming ropes" for people and those which are mere "containers". Quite as important we must acknowledge that there will be a continuum of context-states between the poles and that a given course may be a "rope" to some participants but a container to others.
2. *The level of activity*: in their actual doings, people weave in and out of contexts which have different kinds of import for them, some being more of a "rope" for them than others. Further, within any given context, they may care more about some tasks than others (in a range of different meanings of 'care about').

Articulating a Practice-Grounded Intermediary Position

In developing the required reframing of motivation and engagement, I build on the practice-grounded approach I introduced briefly above. This approach connects the concept of 'context' firmly to practices, understood as ways of going about the world and making sense of it on the background of our 'going-about'. According to it, a context is not delimited by its physical or virtual location, organizational affiliation or institutional realization, nor—in the first instance—by a particular set of people or social relations or by certain ways of describing or thinking about the world. Instead, it is delimited by what we do as embodied beings—by patterns and regularities in our dealings with the world.

These 'dealings with' may, of course, have physical, social, organizational, institutional etc. prerequisites, constituents, and consequences. However, the methodological point is that by taking the patterns and regularities of our 'dealings with' as outset we allow ourselves to investigate empirically what these prerequisites, constituents, and consequences *are*, rather than lay down their significance by decree. The practice-grounded approach accordingly points out the need to investigate the social mediation of practice, but leaves the form and degree of social mediation a question for empirical investigation. In consequence, it opens a different, intermediary way into the question of motivation and engagement than the individualist-cognitivist and the sociocultural approaches, respectively.

Thus, the practice-grounded position acknowledges—in agreement with the socio-cultural approach—that we are born into practices which form the practical outset for our understanding of the world, which shapes how we see ourselves, and where we come to be who we are, in mutual recognition with others. The practices we are born into are always among our primary contexts, at least during childhood and probably for all our lives. If not in the sense of positive identification with them then in the sense of contrastive differentiation from them. What makes these practices primary is, of course, in the first instance the social relations between child, caretaker and other 'significant others' participating in the practices, not what we do in terms of specific activities. However, since words take on meaning from actual doings, and in particular from doings in primary contexts, the way we go about the world in these early primary contexts will be an important anchorage point for our understanding and knowledge. Terms referring to eating will for example be deeply saturated with experiences of tackling knife, fork, and spoon for the Western child and of handling chopsticks for the Chinese.

Conversely—in concurrence with the individualist view—the position allows that sometimes it may be the actual doings themselves that make a specific practice primary for the person. That is, it allows that the explanation of for example a child's attraction to bird watching practices may be an intrinsic interest in birds which in some instances may not be in need of further explanation. It also allows that, especially as we grow up, some of the practices into which we are thrown, for example in education, do not take on a constitutive role for us. Instead, they start out and they stay containers to us (though they may be ropes to others around us). They are, that is, settings where we may have to spend some time, but which never become important to whom we are and where we only engage to the extent that we are—in the terms of the individualist—extrinsically motivated.

In contrast to both individualist and socio-cultural approaches, the position conjectures that in many instances, there will be an interweaving of social, domain-specific, activity-related, and identity-pursuit reasons for practices to become primary contexts for us. And, further, that this will increasingly be the case as we grow older and are allowed some choice of and within practices. Finally, diverging from both approaches, the position emphasizes the need for empirical investigations of these reasons: How are primary contexts of different kinds grounded in the pursuit of intrinsic interests, in social relations, in identity issues etc.? How do they come to be related to one another? What changes occur over the course of our lives in what constitutes primary contexts for us? In the terminology of rope and container: We need analyses of how the different ropes of our lives come to be, intertwine, entangle and come apart again. These accounts must take into account, firstly, that we at the outset meet some practices more as containers and some more as ropes, but that our attitude towards them may change over time (in either direction). And secondly, that traces of prior primary contexts may transform and be resituated in new ones because of their significance for our approach to and understanding of the world.

From the point of view of the practice-grounded position, neither of the terms 'motivation' and 'engagement' refer to any one type of state/process. Instead, both terms refer to a complex set of states and processes, anchored in the individual, but partly co-constituted through positioning and negotiation of interaction in social space. In this sense, they refer to phenomena located across the span of the so-called 'inner' and 'outer' realms. More specifically, this means the following: The practices we are born into delineate ways of sense-making and participation. At this very general level, motivation and engagement are therefore practice-dependent, understood as 'possible to envisage within the space of these practices'. But what it is possible to envisage is not determinable on beforehand, and neither is the degree of social mediation versus self-directedness of the envisaging. Restricting 'motivation' to the so-called 'inner realm' denounces the constitutive role which social practice has at the very general level and may have at more detailed ones, too. In effect, such a restriction renders 'the social' only a 'factor' delivering 'input' to 'influence' the individual, regarded as a pre-existing entity.

On the other hand, focusing only on the so-called 'outer realm', i.e. on the constitutive role of social practice, amounts to ignoring the self-directedness which obviously is at play at least at *some* level of detail in *some* of our choices of practices. It also makes it difficult to account for the phenomenological experience we have of first person agency and intentionality as well as of our motivation and engagement being lived by us.

The overall point is that we need to accept a continuum of possible states and processes, anchored in the individual, as 'motivational' or 'engaging'. This continuum will range from the very self-directed to the fully socially constituted. Accepting this amounts to taking the claim seriously that it is always an empirical question what 'sets us going' and how.

The implications of this view may be spelled out in the following way, addressing the abovementioned two levels in turn. First, at *the level of contexts*: Motivation and engagement are inherently related to contexts which are ropes to us (primary contexts), though not necessarily in any straightforward way. Some of our primary contexts are ones we have been thrown into without self-directed choice and others are ones we may fight to disengage from. Therefore, one cannot assume intrinsic motivation, as described by Ryan and Deci (2000) to drive the way people participate in their primary contexts: There is no reason to assume that people experience inherent satisfaction by participating in the activities of primary contexts which they would not self-directly have chosen. This is one reason why there need not be a correlation between people's primary contexts and their intrinsic motivation. One can, however, assume at least the form of engagement postulated by the socio-culturalist, where non-participation is one way of engaging, through negotiation of opposition and dismissal. One can also assume that persons care (positively or negatively or a complex of both) about their primary contexts and about phenomena, processes and ideas related to them. Finally, one can assume that the participants' epistemological take on the world is permeated with the tacit understandings of their primary contexts. By that fact alone, people's primary contexts are important anchorage points and important resources for sense-making, even when they distance themselves from some of them.

In contrast, practices which only take on the significance of container for us do not have the status of sense-making anchorage point, nor do they have an inherent relationship with motivation and engagement. This is not to say that a 'context as container' can have no motivational import. The degree to which it will have such import depends on whether the person in question approaches the practice as a container for self-directed reasons. Does s/he for example come out of interest for the domain, possibly with the intent of "joining the rope"? Or maybe with the intent of gaining a 'free space' away from the import of certain primary contexts? In analysing networked learning activities at this level, important questions include:

- To which degree do the activities constitute primary contexts for the participants—do they approach the networked learning practice as a rope or as a container?
- Are the participants there, in part or fully, for self-directed reasons, and how does this relate to their view of the practice as rope/container?
- How do their views on the practice as rope/container influence their participation in the networked learning activities—and vice versa?
- How does it affect interaction between participants if they differ in their view of the practice as rope/container?
- What other primary contexts do the participants have to draw on in sense-making and what is their motivational entanglement there?
- Do the networked learning activities require, support or hinder participants in making use of these other primary contexts in sense-making and how does this affect their view of and participation in the activities?

Second, *the concrete level of activity*: Within any given context, participants will like or care about some activities more than others. This goes for primary contexts, as well as for contexts of less or no importance to them, and it goes for contexts which they have self-directedly chosen at the general level as well as for ones they have been 'thrown' into. Taking out the garbage is a chore, whether done in the self-directedly chosen primary context of one's sports activities, in the primary context of the family one has been 'thrown into', or in the work group one has been assigned to. On the other hand, watching a funny movie may be entertaining in even the most 'container'-like of contexts such as a long-distance flight. This is another reason why there need not be a correlation between people's primary contexts and their intrinsic motivation: Some activities are simply not inherently satisfactory and others simply are, almost no matter which situation they take place in. Similarly, participants in networked learning may find some tasks more appealing than others, irrespective of the significance of the task for achieving a given learning outcome or complying with social expectations within a primary context. Engaging in the appealing ones 'for the fun of it' does not imply a commitment to the learning outcomes themselves or to the contexts they are pursued in.

These points, though banal in their everydayness, are often overlooked from both the individualist-cognitive and the sociocultural approaches. This is so, because of their focus on, respectively, the significance of cognitive rationalization (doing the task because one understands its importance for overall goals) and social relations (doing the task as a natural part of participating in the community of practice). From the practice-grounded position, though such factors may be influential, they need not be decisive: Learners' attitudes towards tasks are neither determined solely by the tasks' localization in a space of content-to-be-learned, nor by their localization in social space. And though a context such as an educational programme may be self-directedly chosen at a general level, the status of self-directed choice need not carry over to all—or any—of the specific activities to take place there.

Furthermore, any given task competes for learners' attention with a range of other things they might be doing: A characteristic of the networked world of today is that we can and often do participate in activities in more than one context at a time, e.g. taking part in a physical meeting, chatting with a friend on Facebook, checking emails, and browsing the internet. Thus, people do not necessarily stay in one context, primary or not, or stay focused on one task within the context, for a length of time. Instead, they may weave in and out of several contexts, some of them primary and some of them not. Their motivational entanglement, at both the general and the specific level, in other contexts may influence their engagement in the activities educators expect them to undertake. In analysing networked learning activities at this level, important questions include:

- Which activities do the participants care more about and which less—and why?
- Are explanations of 'care' given in terms of domain, procedures, social relations, etc.—and are they given at a general or specific level?
- How does the epistemological approach which they have from their (other) primary contexts influence their view of given specific activities?

- Do they accept tasks they do not care about — and how does their attitude affect their participation?
- How do their views of the activities at the general level (as 'rope' versus 'container') influence their attitude towards given specific tasks?
- How is their engagement in specific tasks influenced by cognitive rationalization and social relations?
- Which other factors are at play in deciding their attitude towards them?
- What other contexts do they partake in whilst participating in the networked learning activities? How do these other activities affect their participation in the latter, cognitively and motivationally?
- Do they resituate meaning from these other contexts or undertake activities in parallel without relating them?
- Do these other contexts constitute resources or distractions for the participants?
- Could these other contexts be used (better) as resources?

Concluding Remarks

This paper clarifies and challenges contemporary views of motivation and engagement as they appear within the networked learning literature. In particular, I suggest an approach which takes into account the insights of the prevailing individualist-cognitivist and socio-cultural views but accommodates better to seemingly well-known everyday cases. This approach, I argue, supplies a more adequate instrument for analysing networked learning activities. This is so because it highlights the complex interplay of the socially negotiated and the self-directedly chosen in the determination of a person's motivation and engagement. I point out that the individualist and the socio-culturalist approaches draw on metaphorical understandings of 'context' as 'container' and 'rope', respectively. I proposed that we need both metaphors to analyse how people approach different networked learning activities.

Further, on the basis of the concept of primary contexts I argue for a practice-grounded intermediary position. This position makes it possible to investigate empirically how different practices take on the significance of 'rope' or 'container' to people at different points in their lives. I identify the phenomena of motivation and engagement as a complex set of states and processes, anchored in the individual, but partly co-constituted through positioning and negotiation in social space. I illustrate how complexly these phenomena relate to practices regarded as 'ropes'/'containers'. Finally I discern important questions to investigate when analysing networked learning at the level of discrimination between practices and at the level of people's concrete actions.

By way of rounding off, a few comments on the implications for the design of networked learning are apposite. First, the metaphor of 'virtual classroom', widely used in design thinking, builds very directly on the view of context as 'container'. In contrast, the metaphor of 'community of practice', also in frequent use, leans on a 'rope' understanding of context. In designing for networked learning, it is important to explicitly consider one's expectations in this regard: Are participants viewed as independently existing elements to fill a pre-given educational container or as mutual co-constituents in an educational rope to be wrought? Have the learning tasks been designed in accordance with these expectations? Do one's expectations in this regard match those of the participants? If not, one needs to ensure at the very least that this fact—of different expectations—is brought to light.

Second, the designer should consider how the participants' epistemological approach from and motivational entanglement in their diverse primary contexts may influence their approach to the learning tasks. In addition, it is worth considering in each specific case, whether and how these primary contexts might be drawn on in resituated sense-making within the learning activities.

Finally, the designer should take into account that i) agreeability of task need not coincide with conduciveness for learning; ii) cognitive rationalization and social mediation may not be sufficient to bring learners to care for unpleasant tasks; and iii) engagement in pleasant tasks does not commit the learner to the wider objective of the task.

In sum, adequate design requires that one realizes the complex relationships between what learners care about, who they see themselves to be, how they make sense of new situations on the basis of their primary contexts, and how self-directedness and social mediation interplay in their views of given practices as 'ropes' or 'containers'. Quite as important, one has to acknowledge that some tasks may have to be carried out by the learners whether they like them or not. One *cannot* assume, as is often implicitly or explicitly done, that given the right cognitive and social design, any task may be made appealing to any learner. That would amount, in effect, to assuming that participants' motivation and engagement could be designed.

Acknowledgement Research for this article has been partly funded by a research grant from The Danish Council for Independent Research, Humanities, Grant No. DFF-4180-00062.

References

Ames, C. (1992). Classrooms: Goals, structures, and student motivation. *Journal of Educational Psychology, 84*(3), 261–271.

Anderson, T., Rourke, L., Garrison, D. R., & Archer, W. (2001). Assessing teaching presence in a computer conferencing context. *Journal of Asynchronous Learning Networks, 5*(2), 1–17.

Ares, N. (2008). Cultural practices in networked classroom learning environments. *International Journal of Computer-Supported Collaborative Learning, 3*(3), 301–326.

Bandura, A. (1986). *Social foundations of thought and action: A social cognitive theory.* Englewood Cliffs, NJ: Prentice Hall.

Bandura, A. (1997). *Self-efficacy: The exercise of control.* New York, NY: Freeman.

Basquill, J. (2014). Synchronous or asynchronous? That is the question: Are online classrooms the answer? In S. Bayne, C. Jones, M. de Laat, T. Ryberg, & C. Sinclair (Eds.), *Proceedings of the 9th International Conference on Networked Learning 2014* (pp. 343–346). Lancaster: Lancaster University.

Brouns, F., & Hsiao, A. (2012). Social learning in learning networks through peer support: Research findings and pitfalls. In V. Hodgson, C. Jones, M. de Laat, D. McConnell, T. Ryberg, & P. Sloep (Eds.), *Proceedings of the 8th International Conference on Networked Learning* (pp. 18–25). Lancaster: Lancaster University.

Carson, M. (2014). Promoting a community of practice online: How important is social presence? In S. Bayne, C. Jones, M. de Laat, T. Ryberg, & C. Sinclair (Eds.), *Proceedings of the 9th International Conference on Networked Learning 2014*. Lancaster: Lancaster University.

Dohn, N. B. (2013). "Viden i praksis" - Implikationer for it-baseret læring. *Res Cogitans, 1*, 94–128.

Dohn, N. B. (2014). Implications for networked learning of the 'practice' side of social practice theories - A tacit-knowledge perspective. In V. Hodgson, M. de Laat, D. McConnell, & T. Ryberg (Eds.), *The design, experience and practice of networked learning* (pp. 29–49). Dordrecht: Springer.

Dreier, O. (2008). *Psychotherapy in everyday life*. New York, NY: Cambridge University Press.

Dreyfus, H. (1979). *What computers still can't do*. New York, NY: Harper & Row.

Dreyfus, H. (2001). Phenomenological description versus rational reconstruction. *Revue Internationale de Philosophie, 55*(2), 181–196.

Dreyfus, H. (2002). Intelligence without representation–Merleau-Ponty's critique of mental representation the relevance of phenomenology to scientific explanation. *Phenomenology and the Cognitive Sciences, 1*(4), 367–383.

Engeström, Y. (1987). *Learning by expanding: An activity-theoretical approach to developmental research*. Helsinki: Orienta-Konsultit.

Goodyear, P., Banks, S., Hodgson, V., & McConnell, D. (Eds.). (2004). *Advances in research on networked learning*. Dordrecht: Kluwer.

Greeno, J. G. (1997). On claims that answer the wrong questions. *Educational Researcher, 26*(1), 5–17.

Greeno, J. G., & Gresalfi, M. S. (2008). Opportunities to learn in practice and identity. In P. A. Moss, D. C. Pullin, J. P. Gee, E. H. Haertel, & L. J. Young (Eds.), *Assessment, equity, and opportunity to learn* (pp. 170–199). New York, NY: Cambridge University Press.

Greeno, J. G., & Middle School Mathematics Through Applications Project Group. (1998). The situativity of knowing, learning, and research. *American Psychologist, 53*(1), 5–26.

Greeno, J. G., & van de Sande, C. (2007). Perspectival understanding of conceptions and conceptual growth in interaction. *Educational Psychologist, 42*(1), 9–23.

Järvelä, S., Volet, S., & Järvenoja, H. (2010). Research on motivation in collaborative learning: Moving beyond the cognitive–situative divide and combining individual and social processes. *Educational Psychologist, 45*(1), 15–27. doi:10.1080/00461520903433539.

Jarvis, P. (2007). *Globalization, lifelong learning and the learning society: Sociological perspectives*. London: Routledge.

Lave, J. (1993). The practice of learning. In J. Lave & S. Chaiklin (Eds.), *Understanding practice: Perspectives on activity and context* (pp. 3–32). New York, NY: Cambridge University Press.

Lave, J., & Wenger, E. (1991). *Situated learning - Legitimate peripheral participation*. New York, NY: Cambridge University Press.

Martin, J. (2007). The selves of educational psychology: Conceptions, contexts, and critical considerations. *Educational Psychologist, 42*(2), 79–89.

McDermott, R. (1993). The acquisition of a child by a learning disability. In J. Lave & S. Chaiklin (Eds.), *Understanding practice: Perspectives on activity and context* (pp. 269–305). New York, NY: Cambridge University Press.

Nicolajsen, H. W. (2012). Changing the rules of the game-experiences with Web 2.0 learning in higher education. In V. Hodgson, C. Jones, M. de Laat, D. McConnell, T. Ryberg, & P. Sloep (Eds.), *Proceedings of the 8th International Conference on Networked Learning* (pp. 551–558). Lancaster: Lancaster University.

Nielsen, K. (1999). *Musical apprenticeship: Learning at the academy of music as socially situated*. Ph.D. dissertation. Psykologisk Institut, Aarhus Univeristet, Aarhus.

Nolen, S. B., & Ward, C. J. (2008). Sociocultural and situative approaches to studying motivation. In M. Maehr, S. Karabenick, & T. Urdan (Eds.), *Social psychological perspectives on motivation and achievement. Advances in motivation and achievement* (Vol. 15, pp. 428–460). London: Esmerald Group.

Østerlund, C. (1997). Sales apprentices on the move. A multi-contextual perspective on situated learning. *Nordisk Pedagogik, 17*(3), 169–177.

Packer, M. J., & Goicoechea, J. (2000). Sociocultural and constructivist theories of learning: Ontology, not just epistemology. *Educational Psychologist, 35*(4), 227–241.

Ponti, M. (2014). "Remember to hand out medals": Value and peer rating in an online open study group. In S. Bayne, C. Jones, M. de Laat, T. Ryberg, & C. Sinclair (Eds.), *Proceedings of the 9th International Conference on Networked Learning 2014* (pp. 228–235). Lancaster: Lancaster University.

Ryan, R. M., & Deci, E. L. (2000). Intrinsic and extrinsic motivations: Classic definitions and new directions. *Contemporary Educational Psychology, 25*(1), 54–67.

Säljö, R. (2000). *Læring i praksis - Et sociokulturelt perspektiv*. København: Hans Reitzels Forlag.

Salmon, G. (2003). *E-moderating: The key to teaching and learning online* (2nd ed.). London: Routledge.

Salmon, G. (2013). *E-tivities* (2nd ed.). New York, NY: Taylor & Francis.

Schunk, D. H., Pintrich, P. R., & Meece, J. L. (2008). *Motivation in education: Theory, research, and applications*. Upper Saddle River, NJ: Pearson Prentice Hall.

Sfard, A., & Prusak, A. (2005). Telling identities: In search of an analytic tool for investigating learning as a culturally shaped activity. *Educational Researcher, 34*(4), 14–22.

Taylor, C. (1985a). *Philosophical papers: Volume 1, Human agency and language* (Vol. 1). Cambridge: Cambridge University Press.

Taylor, C. (1985b). *Philosophical papers: Volume 2, Philosophy and the human sciences*. Cambridge: Cambridge University Press.

Vygotsky, L. S. (1978). *Mind in society: The development of higher psychological processes*. Cambridge, MA: Harvard University Press.

Wenger, E. (1998). *Communities of practice*. New York, NY: Cambridge University Press.

Chapter 10
The Methodological Challenge of Networked Learning: (Post)disciplinarity and Critical Emancipation

Petar Jandrić

Introduction

According to a well-known definition, networked learning is "learning in which information and communication technology is used to promote connections: between one learner and other learners, between learners and tutors; between a learning community and its learning resources" (Goodyear, Banks, Hodgson, & McConnell, 2004: 1). The basic elements of this definition—people, technologies, and connections (material and intellectual)—have always been present in the academic disciplines of the industrial era, though arguably manifested differently through each discipline. At the same time, there have also been political aspects to these elements and their interrelationships; theoretical accounts of networked learning have been closely related to critical theory and radical approaches to education (Jandrić, 2015). This chapter explores how networked learning has its origins in the disciplines, how it is partially breaking away from disciplinary boundaries, and considers its political aspirations towards a more just society through its theoretical and practical inquiries into knowledge creation and learning.

The role of the disciplines has been a theme of previous books and conferences in this Research in Networked Learning series. Conole 2010: 6) has spoken about "birth disciplines" of networked learning researchers and the impact that these may or may not have on epistemological stances. In the preface to The Design, Experience and Practice of Networked Learning, the editors analyse key achievements in the field and recognize that the "wide range of theoretical positions and different aims for conducting Networked Learning research is followed by a set of different methodological approaches" (Hodgson, De Laat, McConnell, & Ryberg, 2014: 18).

P. Jandrić (✉)
University of Applied Sciences, Zagreb, Croatia
e-mail: pjandric@tvz.hr

© Springer International Publishing Switzerland 2016
T. Ryberg et al. (eds.), *Research, Boundaries, and Policy in Networked Learning*, Research in Networked Learning, DOI 10.1007/978-3-319-31130-2_10

While this might result in multidisciplinary perspectives, and interdisciplinary dialogues, moving away from the disciplines (or being "postdisciplinary") may take other forms. At the 2012 Networked Learning Conference in Maastricht, Parchoma organised a dedicated symposium "Transdisciplinary research in technology enhanced/networked learning practices" (Parchoma, 2012), providing some themes for the current chapter.

The need to recognise people, technology and the connections between them in a postdisciplinary way can be seen in practice in related initiatives such as the European Union STELLAR project (Sustaining Technology Enhanced Learning at a LARge scale—http://www.stellarnet.eu/). A quote from their project report offers the metaphors of bridging and silos, the latter being a common pejorative word associated with academic disciplines.

> Breakthroughs in Technology Enhanced Learning research are more likely to occur when people come together across the different people-centred and technical-centred disciplines, working as interdisciplinary research teams. This involves bridging the two 'silos' within TEL research: on the one hand a more technical-centred silo and on the other hand a more people-centred silo.

> (Sutherland, Eagle, & Joubert, 2012: 4)

This seems to speak to some of the elements of the definition of networked learning identified above, if we allow 'bridging' to stand for making material and intellectual connections. Yet, bridging silos does not feel as though it will get rid of them. Furthermore, the combination of a technical-centred silo and a people-centred silo identified in the above quote does not draw a full picture of networked learning. According to Sterne, "a discipline encompasses intellectual, institutional, and political dimensions. Disciplines are not neutral, and in analysing them we must consider their relations to other disciplines, to their purported objects, and their internal relations as well" (Sterne, 2005: 250). To fully exploit the methodological diversity of postdisciplinary perspectives, therefore, the technical-centred silo and the people-centred silo need to be complemented by a third silo related to political dimensions of networked learning. In Habermas's theory of knowledge, the third silo corresponds to emancipation and critical theory (Habermas, 1987)—a connection that has been made within both scientific disciplines and social science disciplines (Jandrić & Boras, 2012). This connection justifies the need for emancipatory interest and helps us establish the research approach within the wider framework of critical theory. However, Habermas's three spheres of human interest (technical, practical, and emancipatory) (Habermas, 1987) do not quite fit our starting definition of three main elements of networked learning (people, technologies, and connections) (Goodyear et al., 2004: 1), and should not be used interchangeably.

This chapter explores the rise of disciplinarity through the lens of emancipatory interest and critical theory, and shows that research methods in contemporary networked learning are a hybrid between traditional disciplinarity and postdisciplinarity. It explores the relationships between disciplinarity and technique, and links them to education and class. It shows that the postdisciplinary nature of networked learning escapes the logic of technoscientific determinism, and defines the question of disciplinarity as a battlefield between various values and ideologies. On that basis, it concludes that networked learning practitioners should dismiss inert postmodern approaches to research methodologies and use active neo-Marxist approaches in the struggle to transcend the limitations of technoscience. The chapter places disciplinarity into the context of the network society, and shows that the inner contradictions between traditional disciplinarity and postdisciplinarity have firmly remained in place. Finally, it explores emancipatory potentials of various postdisciplinary approaches, and calls for an appropriate balance between complex and often contradictory forces which constitute networked learning as we know it.

The Rise and Fall of Disciplinarity

According to Goodyear and Carvalho, networked learning is the phenomenon which "predates the computer age, takes on a particular character and salience in the period from about 1980 to 2020, and becomes normal and invisible thereafter" (2014: 444–445). In order to understand the relationships between networked learning and disciplinarity, therefore, we need to start our analysis from its roots in the cradles of Western civilisation: ancient Greece and Rome.

In times of peace, Archimedes of Syracuse investigated the quadrature of the parabola, explored the ways to efficiently elevate water up the hill, counted the grains of sand that will fit inside the universe… In times of trouble, he developed war machines (Pickover, 2008). In his day, Archimedes was hardly an exception. Ancient philosophers did not maintain rigid borders between disciplines. Instead, they studied anything they found important and challenging. Certainly, this does not imply that everybody did everything: 'Archimedes the Engineer' is best known for his war machines, while 'Aristotle the Natural Philosopher' is mostly remembered as one of the founding fathers of Western thought. Ancient Greek city-states had carpenters, doctors, soldiers and peasants. However, distinctions between various occupations had been practical rather than theoretical: strictly speaking, ancient Greeks had never developed the concept of narrowing people's expertise into firm disciplinary frameworks (Stiegler, 1998). Perhaps, they simply did not need distinct disciplines: humankind was young, and its knowledge was still manageable within a single lifetime. Unsurprisingly, such views of human knowledge had direct implications for education.

In 'De Oratore', Cicero lists typical subjects taught in Roman schools: "in music, numbers, sounds, and measures; in geometry, lines, figures, spaces, magnitudes; in astronomy, the revolution of the heavens, the rising, setting, and other motions of the stars; in grammar, the peculiar tone of pronunciation, and, finally, in this very art of oratory, invention, arrangement, memory, delivery" (2001). In this list Cicero clearly outlines the later concept of 'liberal arts', which acquired its more or less final form sometime during the seventh century. There are seven liberal arts, which are divided in two main disciplines: 'the Trivium' and 'the Quadrivium'.

The Trivium consists of grammar, rhetoric and logic, while the Quadrivium consists of arithmetic, geometry, music and astronomy (ibid). These seven liberal arts are still reflected in organisational structures and curricula of contemporary schools and universities. In this ways, Cicero's views on education have literally shaped the contemporary world.

Insightful engagement in diverse interests requires high levels of skill and motivation. Therefore, human specialisation is a dialectical mix of ability and preference. The most famous example of a polymath—a person whose expertise spans over various fields of arts and science—is perhaps Leonardo da Vinci. His success in diverse activities including, but not limited to painting, anatomy, music, science, architecture and writing, have served as on-going inspiration for centuries (Bambach, Stern, & Manges, 2003). However, some obstacles cannot be overcome even by the most extraordinary talent. Since the Renaissance, human understanding of the world has significantly grown and it has become increasingly difficult to simultaneously achieve high levels of proficiency in sciences and arts. Using another concept attributed to Cicero, da Vinci is therefore a mere 'exception that proves the rule' that the inevitable logic of scientific progress had slowly but surely transformed 'the Renaissance man' into 'the Specialist'. However, 'sauce for the goose is often not the same as sauce for the gander'. According to Parker's text written in late nineteenth century, in ancient Greece and Rome

> the epithet liberalis denoted that which was proper for a free man in contradistinction to that which was suitable for a slave; but it had acquired most of those secondary meanings which are retained in our word 'liberal' now when there are no slaves. A liberal education is a gentleman's education, and the liberales artes were the gentlemanly arts (1890: 417).

During notoriously anti-intellectual Middle Ages feudal masters could do basic reading and calculus, while their vassals could see letters only during church processions and tax collections. During the Industrial Revolution, the bourgeois studied science, engineering and economics while the proletariat did petty accounting and basic mechanics. During the nineteenth century, arts suitable for a gentleman have been dubbed 'Really Useful Knowledge' while arts suitable for a slave have been dubbed 'Useful Knowledge' (Johnson, 1988). Deep into the twentieth century, arts suitable for a gentleman have been reflected in classic liberal education consisting of "all-round development of a person morally, intellectually and spiritually" while arts suitable for a slave have been reflected in vocational training (Peters, 1972: 9). Educational specialisation has always been for the poor, while only the rich could afford to freely cross disciplinary boarders. Since the dawn of Western civilisation, disciplinarity has always been dialectically intertwined with education and class.

At the end of the twentieth century, the age-old disciplinary structure of human knowledge has started to dissipate. With the rise of the network society, traditional disciplinary approaches have been challenged in almost all areas of human activity (Castells, 2001; Nicolescu, 2008; Van Dijk, 1999). Consequently, contemporary networked learning is far from hegemonic disciplinary discourse painted in the above analysis. Actually, researchers in networked learning and the more generalist fields such as technology enhanced learning have reached a wide consensus about postdisciplinary nature of the relationships between human learning and information and communication technologies (Nicolescu, 2008; Parchoma, 2012; Parchoma & Keefer, 2012; Sutherland et al., 2012, etc.). However, this general consensus does not bring an end to methodological challenges facing networked learning. As we shall argue throughout this chapter, the transition from traditional disciplinarity to new postdisciplinarity is closely linked to emancipation and social change.

In the case study of disciplinarity in international doctoral supervision, Parchoma and Keefer have shown that:

> As the TEL/NL field remains primarily interdisciplinary, marked by multiple hegemonic discourses contributing discrete pieces to overarching initiatives (Klein, 2006; Lotrecchiano, 2010), epistemological and methodological boundary-crossings may be challenged by different "disciplinary domains," definitions of "truth" claims, and "original work".

> (Parchoma & Keefer, 2012: 504)

Similar combinations of disciplinarity and postdisciplinarity can be found in more general studies of digital media (Sterne, 2005), and in Nicolescu's pioneering work in transdisciplinarity (Nicolescu, 2008). This is hardly a surprise, as science of today firmly stands on the shoulders of its past. Following historical development from ancient non-disciplinary science, through development of traditional disciplines, and then back to postdisciplinarity, it is impossible to conceive of a 'pure' postdisciplinary research methodology without reference to traditional disciplinarity. This dialectic reaches all the way to terminology, as the concept of postdisciplinarity arrives into being only in reference to disciplinarity.

The transition from disciplinarity towards postdisciplinarity does not imply a clear-cut replacement of one distinct approach with another. As networked learning embraces its postdisciplinary nature, its research methods are still haunted by their disciplinary origins. Therefore, research methodologies in networked learning are always a hybrid between disciplinary and postdisciplinary approaches. Through the legacy of traditional disciplinary approaches, the ancient correlation between disciplinarity, education, and class still retains some of its power. Yet, the over-reaching consensus about postdisciplinary nature of networked learning introduces novel opportunies for challenging these hegemonic relationships. With one foot in traditional disciplinarity and the other foot in various postdisciplinary approaches, networked learning turns methodological choices into an arena of political struggle. In order to explore this struggle further, we shall situate the dialectic between disciplinarity and networked learning in relation to technique.

Disciplinarity and Technique

In one of core textbooks of 'the Frankfurt School of Social Science', Horkheimer and Adorno clearly link disciplinarity with the Enlightenment.

> The Enlightenment discerned the old powers in the Platonic and Aristotelian heritage of metaphysics and suppressed the universal categories' claims to truth as superstition. In the authority of universal concepts the Enlightenment detected a fear of the demons through whose effigies human beings had tried to influence nature in magic rituals. (2002: 3)

In its iconoclastic quest towards modernity, the Enlightenment introduces calculation as the measure of all things. "For the Enlightenment, anything which cannot be resolved into numbers, and ultimately into one, is illusion; modern positivism consigns it to poetry" (ibid: 4–5).

Based on a similar argument, Herbert Marcuse shows that technology becomes ideological through appropriating values and ideas into own way of functioning. According to Marcuse,

> the historical achievement of science and technology has rendered possible the translation of values into technical tasks – the materialization of values. (…) Consequently, what is at stake is the redefinition of values in technical terms, as elements in the technological process. The new ends, as technical ends, would then operate in the project and in the construction of the machinery, and not only in its utilization. Moreover, the new ends might assert themselves even in the construction of scientific hypotheses – in pure scientific theory. From the quantification of secondary qualities, science would proceed to the quantification of values. (1964: 239)

After entering the field of ideology, technique must necessarily pass beyond the historical stage of neutrality and enter the realm of active politics. Therefore, quantification and calculation of epistêmê are the main reasons which lead to "one of the most vexing aspects of advanced industrial civilisation: the rational character of its irrationality" (ibid: 9).

In the famous 'Only a God can save us' interview, Heidegger succinctly sums up much of the previous argument:

> The fields of sciences lie far apart. The manner of handling their objects is essentially different. This disintegrated multiplicity of disciplines is held together today only through the technical organization of universities and faculties, and through the practical direction of the disciplines according to a single orientation. At the same time, the rooting of the sciences in their essential ground has become dead. (1981)

More recently, in his introduction to 'Technics and Time, 1: The Fault of Epimetheus', Stiegler starts the discussion with pre-Homeric distinction between technê and epistêmê, technique and knowledge, arts/crafts and philosophy (1998: 1). Although ancient understanding of those terms cannot be directly translated into the contemporary context, this distinction clearly denotes the existence of two worlds: the world of ideas and the world of practice. According to Stiegler, the conflict between these worlds is the essence of technics. Since the dawn of civilisation, people have always been surrounded by technical entities such as stone carved knives, bow and arrow. However, human development has brought technics into all aspects of the society such as work and social organisation. Therefore, the battlefield between technê and epistêmê is the site of transformation of 'the Renaissance man' into 'the Specialist'. During this struggle, scientific thought has been technicised by a technique of calculation. However, describing the world in elegant mathematical formulae and manipulating them by logical reasoning has taken its toll: epistêmê has lost its identification with love for knowledge. "Technicization through calculation drives Western knowledge down to a path that leads to a forgetting of its origin, which is also forgetting of its truth. This is the 'crisis of European sciences'" (ibid: 3). A few years after, Steigler concludes that

Science is then no longer that in which industry invests, but what is financed by industry to open new possibilities of investments and profits. Because to invest is to anticipate; in such a situation, reality belongs already to the past. The conjugation of technology, of science and of the mobility of capital, orders the opening of a future explored systematically by experimentation. This science become technoscience is less what describes reality than what it destabilizes radically. Technical science no longer says what is the case (the 'law' of life): it creates a new reality. It is a science of becoming – and, as Ilya Prigogine and Isabelle Stengers showed, of the irreversible. (2007: 32)

Looking into the rich tradition of 'the Frankfurt School of Social Science', it becomes clear that the rise of technoscience is dialectically intertwined with the rise of disciplinarity. As a postdisciplinary field with elements of traditional disciplinarity, networked learning simultaneously contains some characteristics of epistêmê (such as the belief in universal categories and values), some characteristics of technê (such as attempts to quantify these categories and values), and some characteristics of the battle between the two (or technoscience). Disciplinary aspects of networked learning lead towards technoscience which, in turn, paves the way towards the crisis of European sciences. However, postdisciplinary features of networked learning lead against technoscience, against the crisis of European sciences, and towards opportunities for creating new social arrangements. Thus, hybrid research methodologies of networked learning transcend the logic of technoscientific determinism, and become a battlefield between opposing values and ideologies. As a science of becoming, networked learning leads towards an uncharted terrain—and it is up to researchers and practitioners to direct its further development.

What are the opportunities for directing that development? During the past few decades, 'the Frankfurt School' has branched in diverse directions from permissive postmodernist readings to revolutionary critical pedagogy. According to McLaren and Farahmandpur, postmodern approaches "often blunt an understanding of contemporary society and unwittingly agitate for a re-enactment of the fate of society that constitutes the object of its critique" (McLaren & Farahmandpur, 2005: 20). By passive acceptance of the relationships between networked learning and technoscience, which are inherent to disciplinarity, researchers and scientists are creating a self-fulfilling prophecy which perpetuates the crisis of European sciences. In order to provide educators with a more active role in social change, postmodern approaches that were fairly popular during 1980s and 1990s (i.e. Giroux, 1991; McLaren, 1995) are slowly but surely returning to their Marxist roots, which treat "discourses not as sanctuaries of difference barricaded against the forces of history but as always an interpretation naturalized by the libidinal circuits of desire wired into the culture of commerce and historically and socially produced within the crucible of class antagonisms" (ibid: 21). In the context of neo-Marxism, practitioners of networked learning should actively struggle to transcend its methodological roots in technoscience, and firmly embrace its postdisciplinary nature. Certainly, this is not an either-or choice between disciplinarity and postdisciplinarity, as both methodological approaches are inherent to the field of networked learning. In order to provide more nuanced guidance, therefore, the following analysis explores the question of disciplinarity in the context of contemporary digital networks.

Disciplinarity and the Network

Disciplinarity had always been the poor man's fate—although, admittedly, experts in narrow fields such as watch-making and alchemy have always been highly praised. Following the exponential rise in complexity of our tools, however, disciplinarity has entered all social strata from surgery to commerce. For example, according to Varma, "the term 'geek' is slang for a person who has encyclopaedic knowledge of computing and is obsessively fascinated by it, but is socially inept, exhibits odd personality traits, excludes normal social and human interests, and spends free time being 'social' on a computer" (2007: 360). Traditionally, narrow specialisation contained in this definition held negative perceptions. However, "the terms geek, hacker, and nerd have negative connotations though recently they have become less pejorative, mostly because they denote competence in technology. Their culture has been described as the 'third culture'; a pop culture based in technology" (ibid). In this way, popular digital culture has legitimised disciplinarity in all strata of the society.

Traditional science has undergone major changes in two opposing directions. Nominally, 'blue-skies research' is more praised than ever. However, advancing human understanding of the world is a rare privilege. Social sciences and humanities are slowly but surely being replaced by immediately profitable technological research; explanatory research has been almost completely wiped out by applied research. As a consequence, shows Braben, "new scientific fields are not being created. Today's technologies are short-lived variations on seminal discoveries made decades ago. Intellectual capital is therefore being consumed faster than it is being replaced" (2002: 770). Linking research with economy, he concludes that "if the portfolio of intellectual capital is not expanded, preferably with generic technology, the New Economy brings diminishing returns and puts us on a fast track to global economic stagnation" (ibid: 771). Braben's Promethean belief that science can solve or at least significantly postpone the world's problems could easily be challenged by Illich's Epithemean insistence on balance between human beings and our environment (1973). However, his analyses clearly describe bitter consequences of the recent changes in structures of scientific research.

In the network society, traditional science has experienced a strong polarisation between blue-skies research and applied research with the strong tendency towards the latter. Science and research has always gone in hand with education. Unsurprisingly, the world of education is also profoundly divided: there is on one side "a 'teaching aristocracy' that does not consider itself as workers and on the other a pauperised teaching labour force" (McLaren & Kumar, 2009). As of recently, the number of the first has clearly been lowered at the expense of the latter. Such trends, described as "reproletarianisation" of teachers (McLaren & Kumar, 2009), have already poured from scientific discourse to fiction. Novels such as Alex Kudera's 'Fight for Your Long Day' (2010) and Lee Ryan Miller's 'Teaching Amidst the Neon Palm Trees' (2004) reveal first-hand insights into the depressing mechanisms of the creation and perpetuation of an intellectual under-class. Day by day, fresh cohorts of teachers and scientists fall into the rabbit hole of Guy Standing's 'new dangerous class'—the precariat—whose existence alternates between sporadic episodes of low-paid adjunct positions and the dole (2011, 2014). These people's specialised knowledge does not mean much without social and economic capital. Actually, as many members of the precariat can witness, high levels of (educational) specialisation often work directly against their economic interest (Goral, 2014; Maynard & Joseph, 2008).

The past few decades have caused turmoil at the intersection between disciplinarity, research, education and class. However, the described changes have merely reinforced the existing power relationships and caused further social stratification. There is nothing new under the sun: disciplinarity is still for the poor, and intellectual width is still for the rich. However, the stakes have skyrocketed beyond limits. In many aspects of contemporary life, disciplinarity has created and/or reinforced theoretical and practical dead-ends which may endanger the whole of humankind. Physics may develop amazing new nuclear power plants, but we need all sorts of expertise (medical, engineering, biochemical) in order to deal with consequences of disaster in Fukushima. Medicine may prolong our lives for a few more decades, but economy must supply pensions and medical care for the long-lived. When computers sneeze, world economy and natural environment catch serious colds: 'butterfly effects' indiscriminately jump across continents, disciplines and systems of reasoning. Newly created fields such as environmental science or networked learning have no other choice but to draw methods and theories from more than one system of reasoning. Even the most traditional fields, such as philosophy and history, must step down from the 'ivory towers' of their disciplinary methodologies and acknowledge the logic of the network. In the words of Castells, "the Internet is the fabric of our lives" (2001: 1)—and its logic, in the sense of Jacques Ellul's 'technique' (1964), is literally everywhere. The nature of the contemporary network society is directly opposed to the concept of a strict scientific discipline—and this reflects clearly in the field of networked learning (Nicolescu, 2008; Parchoma, 2012; Parchoma & Keefer, 2012; Sutherland et al., 2012, etc.).

However, just like in Stiegler's description of ancient Greece (Stiegler, 1998), theoretical rejection of disciplinarity is not directly related to organization of daily matters. At worldwide universities, divisions between academic and non-academic positions have never been sharper (Goral, 2014; Maynard & Joseph, 2008; McLaren & Kumar, 2009; Standing, 2011, 2014). Furthermore, hybrid nature of research methodologies in networked learning implies that the majority of practitioners still make their living in disciplinary trades such as web design, management or teaching. In the complex environments of networked learning, it is highly unlikely to expect the birth of the new 'homo universalis'. Actually, as Illich clearly argues in 'Tools for Conviviality', the very structure of contemporary technologies makes the birth of a contemporary Leonardo da Vinci literally impossible (1973). However, hybrid nature of research methodologies in networked learning causes tectonic movement in the century-old logic of traditional epistemology. At the one hand, traditional disciplinary approaches offer 'safe' research methods with clearly defined causes and consequences—they might perpetuate inequality, but at least we understand how they work. At the other hand, however, "the term "postdisciplinarity" evokes an intellectual universe in which we inhabit the ruins of outmoded disciplinary structures, mediating between our nostalgia for this lost unity and our excitement at the intellectual freedom its demise can offer us" (Buckler, 2004). The STELLAR project and similar initiatives show that postdisciplinarity also bears significant practical consequences, as it "explicitly recognises that it is out of the tensions and conflicts between different disciplinary perspectives that innovative approaches and solutions to problems arise" (Sutherland et al., 2012: 1).

Conceptually, the Internet has not significantly altered the hybrid nature of research methodologies in networked learning. Instead, following a general trend experienced by various social phenomena during their transformation towards the network society (Van Dijk, 1999), the complex dynamic between disciplinarity and postdisciplinarity has been radically intensified. Networked learning firmly remains disciplinary and postdisciplinary, technê and epistêmê, technoscientific and scientific, postmodern and neo-Marxist—and the schism between these polarities is as deep as ever. In the age of the network, human learning cannot be saved from disciplinarity, because disciplinarity is deeply engraved in our understanding of the world. Yet, socially conscious networked learning cannot remain confined within the disciplinary research universe, and needs to move towards postdisciplinarity. In order to balance these opposing forces, the following paragraph explores emancipatory potentials of various postdisciplinary approaches to networked learning.

The Postdisciplinary Challenge

Postdisciplinary approaches are usually divided into four main groups: multidisciplinarity, interdisciplinarity, transdisciplinarity, and antidisciplinarity. By and large, these concepts are still in flux, as their development is far from complete. For instance, this chapter follows Nicolescu and uses 'postdisciplinarity' as a generic term for all research approaches that reach beyond disciplinarity (2008), while Parchoma and Keefer (2012: 502) use the same term for a more specific approach which Nicolescu calls antidisciplinarity. In order to avoid terminological misunderstandings, the following paragraphs will first briefly outline the main postdisciplinary approaches, and then explore their potentials for emancipation in the context of networked learning.

"Multidisciplinarity concerns studying a research topic not in just one discipline but in several at the same time" (Nicolescu, 2008: 2). For instance, computers can be studied within the fields of engineering, urban planning, social science, environment, human health, and education. Multidisciplinary approach deepens our understanding of computers, and enriches our usage and development of computers. However, its goals are always contained within the realm of a single home discipline. In the field of engineering, studies of computers in educational settings may be conducted in order to improve computer screens. In the field of education, studies of computers and education may be conducted to develop school strategies that deal with health consequences of prolonged exposure to computer screens. At the policy level, studies of computers and education may lead to recognition that some students have access to better computer screens, or that parents of some students are unaware of problems pertaining to exposure to computer screens. On that basis, they might propose a local awareness-raising project, or an improved approach to healthcare, or new legislation for minimum quality of computer screens.

Such multidisciplinary studies of computers and education may improve computer screens, or school practice, or healthcare, or national technical standards, or the ways we deal with poverty. However, multidisciplinary research is always oriented to a particular disciplinary area: producers of computer screens typically have little interest in classroom pedagogies, and community workers typically have little to do with technical legislation. Such fragmentation, which is fairly typical for corporations and government bodies, is useful in solving isolated practical problems. However, as it structurally divorces issues pertaining to knowledge from those pertaining to education or class, multidisciplinarity still retains problems characteristic for traditional disciplinary approaches.

In interdisciplinary research, "an issue is approached from a range of disciplinary perspectives integrated to provide a systemic outcome" (Lawrence & Després, 2004: 400). Based on analyses of various generic definitions, Ralston identifies four main aims of an interdisciplinary research:

> (1) to bridge between academic disciplines, subdisciplines or schools of thought; (2) to recruit a wide range of teachers, students, researchers, professionals and even technologies in order to gain a more complete perspective; (3) to assemble tools or approaches from multiple disciplines in order to resolve an especially challenging problem; and (4) to cross traditional academic boundaries for the purpose of improved research or teaching. (2011: 309)

Interdisciplinarity provides maximum level of integration of scientific disciplines that can be reached without disturbing the traditional epistemic structure. In this context, networked learning may use knowledge from diverse fields such as psychology and computer science in order to improve teaching and learning. Now, technology producers work together with educators, psychologists, and community workers to produce an educationally useful, healthy, sturdy, and affordable computer screens for a certain group of people. A very successful case in the point is the 'One Laptop Per Child Initiative', which has achieved tremendous worldwide success with its $100 laptop (2015). However, an interdisciplinary research project still uses "primarily multiple hegemonic discourses contributing discrete pieces to an overarching initiative", and it may only sporadically "involve temporal epistemological boundary-crossings" (Parchoma & Keefer, 2012: 502). Disciplinary borders are crossed, but they remain firmly in place; traditional disciplines are cross-fertilised, but they always 'know' their roots; research methodology may transcend disciplinary borders, but interpretation of results always remains subject to criteria of each integrated discipline. In spite of sporadic breaking of epistemic borders, therefore, interdisciplinary networked learning is still dominated by its traditional disciplinary identity.

Transdisciplinarity takes a radically different approach. Here, "the focus is on the organisation of knowledge around complex heterogeneous domains rather than the disciplines and subjects into which knowledge is commonly organised" (Lawrence & Després, 2004: 400). Disciplinary borders are erased and cannot be defined in a traditional sense; no-one has the exclusive right to research methodologies and interpretation of results. Transdisciplinary research is "necessary when knowledge about a societally relevant problem field is uncertain, when the concrete nature of problems is disputed, and when there is a great deal at stake for those concerned by the problems and involved in investigating them" (Hirsch Hadorn et al., 2008: 37). On such basis, Novy asserts that transdisciplinary knowledge

> is context-sensitive and grasps complexity, integrates multiple perspectives and opposing interests. In such settings, transdisciplinarity takes an ethical position in favour of rationality and democracy and creates places of dialogue, based on an educational approach that questions assumed certainties. As action and reflection are dialectically related, the identification of socially relevant problems is crucial for social action. (2012: 138–139)

Transdisciplinary knowledge, or "mode 2 knowledge" (Becher & Trowler, 2001; Parchoma & Keefer, 2012: 502) significantly differs from multidisciplinary and interdisciplinary knowledge. In this context, the relationships between computers and education are explored using "methodological pluralism developed in response to the research context", and present a "collaborative research effort to resolve a complex real world problem" through "interaction between theory and application" (Parchoma & Keefer, 2012: 502). Disciplinary knowledge is transformed, and transdisciplinarity "prompts teachers and students to raise new questions and develop models of analysis outside the officially sanctioned boundaries of knowledge and the established disciplines that control them" thus enabling critical educators to become true "border crossers" (Giroux, 1992; Giroux & Searls Giroux, 2004: 102). In this way transdisciplinarity opens new epistemological and practical challenges, questions the existing systems of knowledge and domination, and acquires genuine potentials for emancipation and social change.

Finally, antidisciplinarity "provides the grounds for a critique of the limits on knowledge production in other disciplines" (Kristensen & Claycomb, 2010: 6). In this context, "every question may be asked and every change may be considered" (Giroux & Karmis, 2012). Parchoma and Keefer (who, as mentioned earlier, use the term postdisciplinarity), say that it "is noted for encompassing ontological stances where organising structures of disciplines and their methodologies do not hold, symmetry across intellectual and social practices is acknowledged, and multiple independent voices are equally valued" (Parchoma & Keefer, 2012: 502–503). As opposed to interdisciplinary and transdisciplinary approaches, antidisciplinarity does not try to recombine or transcend disciplinary knowledge in order to produce a new quality. Instead, it fundamentally resists all disciplinarity. As it gives voice to all strata of the society, and provides all voices with exactly equal amount of power, antidisciplinarity is even more empowering than transdisciplinarity. Giroux's transdisciplinary educators are "border crossers" (1992), while antidisciplinary educators operate in a universe without borders. As traditional links between disciplinary knowledge, education, and class, disappear, antidisciplinary networked learning thus becomes genuine emancipatory praxis. However, studies of antidisciplinarity are still in their infancy, and its epistemological and practical consequences are still far from clear.

Multidisciplinarity and interdisciplinarity still retain many features of traditional disciplinarity: they are closely linked to education and class, perpetuate existing social orders, and work within the realm of technoscience. Interdisciplinarity and transdisciplinarity break traditional links between education, disciplinarity, technoscience, and class, and offer opportunity for critical networked learning and social change. The multidisciplinary nature of networked learning is widely recognised: computers are simultaneously studied in schools of computing, sociology and education, while education is simultaneously studied in schools of education, philosophy and computing. Interdisciplinarity is accepted widely, but not universally: some researchers naturally transfer knowledge and methods between disciplines, while others still insist on traditional methodological approaches. During the past few years, transdisciplinarity is in the strong rise, and the associated epistemological and practical challenges attract increasing interest from networked learning research community (Hirsch Hadorn et al., 2008; Jandrić & Boras, 2012; Novy, 2012; Parchoma, 2012; Parchoma & Keefer, 2012). Finally, the elusive field of antidisciplinarity is completely 'off the known charts'—for now, can be interpreted merely as 'food for thought'.

Conclusion

This chapter shows that research methodologies in networked learning have a hybrid identity—researchers unanimously agree about the need for postdisciplinarity, yet historical legacy and everyday praxis retain many characteristics of traditional disciplinarity. The question of research method is not merely epistemological and/or practical. Analysing the historical rise and fall of disciplinarity, the relationships between technologies and human beings, and the human condition in the network society, this chapter shows that research methods in networked learning are inherently linked to politics and emancipation. On that basis, the chapter explores emancipatory potentials of various (post)disciplinary approaches to networked learning.

Traditional disciplinarity is closely linked to education and class. Its epistemological borders are closely followed by class borders between various strata of the society, and its rise is dialectically linked to technoscience. In this way, disciplinary methodologies and practices sustain and reinforce traditional social inequalities. Multidisciplinarity and interdisciplinarity are clearly more efficient than traditional disciplinarity, as they provide more nuanced solutions to contemporary challenges. They are closely linked to technoscience, and they creatively re-arrange traditional disciplinary knowledge without disturbing its core epistemological assumptions and hegemonic discourses. As they reproduce the traditional epistemological and social orders, however, multidisciplinarity and interdisciplinarity offer little opportunity for emancipation—in this respect, they are very close to traditional disciplinarity. Transdisciplinarity challenges hegemonic discourses, rejects their links to technoscience, and enables genuine critical social action. It turns critical educators into practical and epistemological "border crossers" (Giroux, 1992), and opens various paths towards critical emancipation. Finally, antidisciplinarity rejects all disciplinary borders, and creates an egalitarian social and research universe.

Certainly, the found conclusions do not imply that disciplinary, multidisciplinary, or interdisciplinary networked learning is necessarily hegemonic. On the contrary, the networked learning community is proud—and rightfully so—of its theoretical grounding in critical theory and active emancipatory praxis (Hodgson, McConnell, & Dirckinck-Holmfeld, 2012: 292). Often, a successful disciplinary project focused to a certain community may emancipate more people that the most elaborate anti-disciplinary effort. However, theoretical opportunities for such emancipation are limited—and this chapter seeks to expand opportunities for emancipation offered by transdisciplinarity and antidisciplinarity by revealing political agendas built into networked learning research methods. Unsurprisingly, the identified opportunities arrive at a high price. To most people, multidisciplinarity and interdisciplinarity arrive naturally because it does not seem to significantly intervene into the existing structure of our understanding of the world. Moving towards transdisciplinarity and antidisciplinarity, however, networked learning reaches further and further from the 'safe zone' of traditional science and encounters more and more unanswered questions.

Disciplinarity, multidisciplinarity, and interdisciplinarity are imbued within the existing social and technoscientific orders. In spite of significant epistemological and practical achievements, therefore, these methodological approaches are structurally unable to provide radical social change. Transdisciplinarity and antidisciplinarity are better suited for critical networked learning, as their position outside of dominant disciplinary power relationships provides genuine potentials for emancipation and social transformation. In this way, the seemingly innocent field of research methodologies has become a battlefield between values, worldviews, and ideologies. Yet, sides in this battlefield are not marked particularly clearly. In theory and practice, research methods in networked learning are a hybrid between disciplinary and postdisciplinary approaches. From early days of Western civilisation until the age of the network, traditional disciplines can be found even in the most advanced postdisciplinary approaches. Vice versa, in the contemporary network society, even the strictest disciplinary approaches to human learning will break at least some traditional disciplinary borders. As practitioners of networked learning, therefore, we cannot escape from the hybrid nature of research methodologies in our field. For the time being, we can only embrace this nature and seek an appropriate balance between its constituting forces. However, this does not imply passive acceptance of the current state of affairs. Our current research methods may be grounded in traditional disciplinarity, but our eyes should be directed high into the blue skies of a critical, emancipatory research framework for networked learning—and this implies concentrating our research efforts towards transdisciplinarity and antidisciplinarity.

Acknowledgements   I want to thank Christine Sinclair, Sarah Hayes, Constantine D. Skordoulis, Sian Bayne, Thomas Ryberg, Maarten de Laat, and anonymous reviewers, for their valuable criticisms and suggestions.

References

Bambach, C., Stern, R., & Manges, A. (2003). *Leonardo da Vinci, master draftsman*. New York, NY: Metropolitan Museum of Art New York.

Becher, T., & Trowler, P. R. (2001). *Academic tribes and territories: Intellectual inquiry and the culture of disciplines*. Buckingham: Society for Research into Higher Education & Open University Press.

Braben, D. W. (2002). Blue Skies Research and the global economy. *Physica A: Statistical Mechanics and its Applications, 314*, 768–773.

Buckler, J. A. (2004). *Towards a new model of general education at Harvard College*. Retrieved April 14, 2013, from http://isites.harvard.edu/fs/docs/icb.topic733185.files/Buckler.pdf.

Castells, M. (2001). *The Internet galaxy: Reflections on the internet, business, and society*. Oxford: Oxford University Press.

Cicero, M. T. (2001). *Cicero on the ideal orator (De Oratore)*. Oxford: Oxford University Press.

Conole, G. (2010). Theory and methodology in networked learning. Paper presented at the Networked Learning Conference Hotseat. Available online at http://cloudworks.ac.uk/cloud/view/2881. Accessed 11 Aug 2015.

Ellul, J. (1964). *The technological society*. New York, NY: Vintage Books.

Giroux, H. A. (Ed.). (1991). *Postmodernism, feminism and cultural politics: Rethinking educational boundaries*. New York, NY: State University of New York Press.

Giroux, H. A. (1992). *Border crossings*. New York, NY: Routledge.

Giroux, D., & Karmis, D. (2012). Call for papers: Cahiers de l'idiotie No 6 – Université/University. Ottawa: Cahiers de l'idiotie. Retrieved April 14, 2013, from http://www.cahiers-idiotie.org/.

Giroux, H. A., & Searls Giroux, S. (2004). *Take back higher education: Race, youth and the crisis of democracy in the post-civil rights era*. New York, NY: Palgrave Macmillan.

Goodyear, P., Banks, S., Hodgson, V., & McConnell, D. (Eds.). (2004). *Advances in research on networked learning*. Dordrecht: Kluwer.

Goodyear, P., & Carvalho, L. (2014). Introduction. In L. Carvalho & P. Goodyear (Eds.), *The architecture of productive learning networks*. Boca Raton, FL: Taylor and Francis. Kindle Edition.

Goral, T. (2014). Unintended consequences: The rise-and fall-of adjuncts in higher education. *University Business, 17(3)*.

Habermas, J. (1987). *Knowledge and human interest*. Cambridge: Polity Press.

Heidegger, M. (1981). "Only a God Can Save Us": The Spiegel interview. In T. Sheehan (Ed.), *Heidegger: The man and the thinker* (pp. 45–67). Chicago, IL: Precedent Press.

Hirsch Hadorn, G., Biber-Klemm, S., Grossenbacher-Mansuy, W., Joye, D., Pohl, C., Wiesmann, U., & Zemp, E. (2008). The emergence of transdisciplinarity as a form of research. In G. Hirsch Hadorn, H. Hoffmann-Riem, S. Biber-Klemm, W. Grossenbacher-Mansuy, D. Joye, C. Pohl, U. Wiesmann, & E. Zemp (Eds.), Handbook of transdisciplinary research. Berlin: Springer, 19–42.

Hodgson, V., De Laat, M., McConnell, D., & Ryberg, T. (Eds.). (2014). *The design, experience and practice of networked learning*. New York, NY: Springer.

Hodgson, V., McConnell, D., & Dirckinck-Holmfeld, L. (2012). The theory, practice and pedagogy of networked learning. In L. Dirckinck-Holmfeld, V. Hodgson, & D. McConnell (Eds.), *Exploring the theory, pedagogy and practice of networked learning* (pp. 291–307). New York, NY: Springer.

Horkheimer, M., & Adorno, T. W. (2002). *Dialectic of enlightenment: Philosophical fragments*. Stanford, CA: Stanford University Press.

Illich, I. (1973). *Tools for conviviality*. London: Marion Boyars Publishers Ltd.

Jandrić, P. & Boras, D. (Eds.). (2015). Critical learning in digital networks. New York, NY: Springer.

Jandrić, P., & Boras, D. (2012). *Critical e-learning: Struggle for power and meaning in the network society*. Zagreb: FF Press & The Polytechnic of Zagreb.

Johnson, R. (1988). "Really useful knowledge" 1790–1850: Memories for education in the 1980s. In T. Lovett (Ed.), *Radical approaches to adult education: A reader* (pp. 3–34). London: Routledge.

Klein, J.T. (2006). Resources for interdisciplinary studies. *Change, 38*(2): 50.

Kristensen, R. G., & Claycomb, R. M. (Eds.). (2010). *Writing against the curriculum: Anti-disciplinarity in the writing and cultural studies classroom*. Plymouth: Rowman & Littlefield Publishers, Ltd.

Kudera, A. (2010). *Fight for your long day*. Washington, DC: Atticus Books.

Lawrence, R. J., & Després, C. (2004). Futures of transdisciplinarity. *Futures, 36*(4), 397–405.

Lotrecchiano, G.R. (2010). Complexity leadership in transdisciplinary (TD) learning environments: A knowledge feedback loop. *International Journal of Transdisciplinary Research, 5*(1), 29–63.

Marcuse, H. (1964). *One-dimensional man*. Herbert Marcuse Archive.

Maynard, D. C., & Joseph, T. A. (2008). Are all part-time faculty underemployed? The influence of faculty status preference on satisfaction and commitment. *Higher Education, 55*(2), 139–154.

McLaren, P. (Ed.). (1995). *Postmodernism, post-colonialism and pedagogy*. Albert Park, VIC: James Nicholas Publishers.

McLaren, P., & Farahmandpur, R. (2005). *Teaching against global capitalism and the new imperialism*. Oxford: Rowman & Littlefield Publishers, Inc.

McLaren, P. & Kumar, R. (2009). Peter McLaren in an interview with Ravi Kumar: Being, Becoming and Breaking-Free: Peter McLaren and the Pedagogy of Liberation. Radical Notes, February 19. Retrieved April 14, 2013, from http://radicalnotes.com/2009/02/19/being-becoming-and-breaking-free-peter-mclaren-and-the-pedagogy-of-liberation/.

Miller, L. R. (2004). *Teaching amidst the neon palm trees*. Miami, FL: 1st Book Library.

Nicolescu, B. (2008). In vitro and in vivo knowledge – Methodology of transdisciplinarity. In B. Nicolescu (Ed.), *Transdisciplinarity – Theory and practice* (pp. 1–22). New York, NY: Hampton Press.

Novy, A. (2012). "Unequal diversity" as a knowledge alliance: An encounter of Paulo Freire's dialogical approach and transdisciplinarity. *Multicultural Education and Technology, 6*(3), 137–148.

One laptop per child initiative. (2015). Mission. Retrieved May 14, 2015, from http://one.laptop.org/about/mission.

Parchoma, G. (2012). Transdisciplinary research in technology enhanced/networked learning practices. In V. Hodgson, C. Jones, M. De Laat, D. McConnell, T. Ryberg, & P. Sloep (Eds.), *Proceedings of the 8th International Conference on Networked Learning* (pp. 496–497). Maastricht: Maastricht School of Management.

Parchoma, G., & Keefer, J. M. (2012). Contested disciplinarity in international doctoral supervision. In V. Hodgson, C. Jones, M. De Laat, D. McConnell, T. Ryberg, & P. Sloep (Eds.), *Proceedings of the 8th International Conference on Networked Learning* (pp. 498–505). Maastricht: Maastricht School of Management.

Parker, H. (1890). The seven liberal arts. *The English Historical Review, 5*(19), 417–461.

Peters, R. S. (1972). Education and the educated man. In R. F. Dearden, P. H. Hirst, & R. S. Peters (Eds.), *Education and the development of reason* (pp. 3–19). London: Routledge and Kegan Paul.

Pickover, C. A. (2008). *Archimedes to hawking: Laws of science and the great minds behind them*. Oxford: Oxford University Press.

Ralston, S. J. (2011). Interdisciplinarity: Some lessons from John Dewey. *American Dialectic, 1*(2), 309–321.

Standing, G. (2011). *The precariat: The new dangerous class*. London: Bloomsbury Academic.

Standing, G. (2014). *A precariat charter: From denizens to citizens*. London: Bloomsbury.

Sterne, J. (2005). Digital media and disciplinarity. *The Information Society, 21*, 249–256.

Stiegler, B. (1998). *Technics and time, 1: The fault of epimetheus*. Stanford, CA: Stanford University Press.

Stiegler, B. (2007). Technoscience and Reproduction. *Parallax, 13*(4), 29–45.

Sutherland, R., Eagle, S., & Joubert, M. (2012). *A vision and strategy for technology enhanced learning: Report from the STELLAR Network of Excellence*. Bristol: University of Bristol.

Van Dijk, J. (1999). *The network society: Social aspects of new media*. Thousand Oaks, CA: Sage.

Varma, R. (2007). Women in computing: The role of geek culture. *Science as Culture, 16*(4), 359–376.

Author Index

© Springer International Publishing Switzerland 2016
T. Ryberg et al. (eds.), *Research, Boundaries, and Policy in Networked Learning*, Research in Networked Learning, DOI 10.1007/978-3-319-31130-2

Subject Index

© Springer International Publishing Switzerland 2016
T. Ryberg et al. (eds.), *Research, Boundaries, and Policy in Networked Learning*, Research in Networked Learning, DOI 10.1007/978-3-319-31130-2

Lightning Source UK Ltd.
Milton Keynes UK
UKOW06n0815181116

287913UK00001B/38/P